# ENGLISH COURT LIFE

*By the same author*

Land of France (*with Lord Holden*)
The English Country House
The English Garden
The English Interior
Wessex
The Age of Wren
London Homes
Normandy and Brittany
The Victorian Home
The Châteaux of France

1   Charles I dining in public

*Reproduced by gracious permission of Her Majesty The Queen. From a detail of a painting attributed to Gerard Houckgeest*

# ENGLISH
# COURT LIFE

## FROM HENRY VII
## TO GEORGE II

·

*Ralph Dutton*

B. T. BATSFORD LTD
LONDON

*First Published* 1963


© Ralph Dutton 1963

MADE AND PRINTED IN GREAT BRITAIN BY WILLIAM CLOWES AND SONS, LTD.
LONDON AND BECCLES FOR THE PUBLISHERS
B. T. BATSFORD LTD
4 FITZHARDINGE STREET, PORTMAN SQUARE, LONDON, W.I

# Contents

# Acknowledgment

Figures 1, 3, 13, and 16 are reproduced by gracious permission of Her Majesty The Queen.

The author and publishers wish to thank the following for permission to reproduce the other illustrations appearing in this book:

The Ashmolean Museum, for fig. 5, and for fig. 29 (from the Sutherland Collection).

The Trustees of the British Museum, for figs. 10, 19, 22, 33, 35, and 36.

The Trustees of the Chatsworth Settlement, for figs. 14 and 15.

The College of Arms, for fig. 4.

The Syndics of the Fitzwilliam Museum, Cambridge, for fig. 11.

The Guildhall Library, Corporation of London, for fig. 25.

The Mansell Collection, for figs. 2, 20, 24, and 26.

The National Portrait Gallery, for figs. 6 and 30.

The Duke of Portland and Essex Record Office, for fig. 7 (from *Elizabethan Essex*).

Radio Times Hulton Picture Library, for figs. 23, 32, and 34.

The Duke of Roxburghe, for fig. 17.

The Royal Academy of Arts, for figs. 8 and 17.

Simon Wingfield Digby, Esq. for fig. 8.

# List of Illustrations

9

LIST OF ILLUSTRATIONS

# INTRODUCTION

It may be as well at the outset to indicate the modest aims of the following pages. Although the time that is covered is long, the subject is severely restricted. My purpose is to show the influence of the reigning monarch on the way of life carried on at his court, and also how and where he lived. It is a purely social narrative, and there is no attempt to describe the monarchs and their reigns from a political aspect, nor indeed to touch on anything but the lighter and more personal side of history.

A convenient point of departure for a story of manners or of taste is the accession of Henry VII, when the Middle Ages finally closed with the self-destruction of the English nobility during the Wars of the Roses, and the rise of new families which were to dominate English history for centuries to come. It makes a neat beginning to start at the opening of a dynasty, but it was perhaps the second Tudor king whose reign marked the more decided turning-point in English life: for it was Henry VIII who introduced the first breath of the Renaissance into England and with it the beginnings of a more cultured and, it may be added, more comfortable way of life.

Where to end is more difficult to decide, but 300 years are a long enough span to cover; and this reaches approximately to the death of George II in 1760. On reflection this seems an appropriate place to plant the final full stop. The sixty years of George III's reign, bridging the transition from the eighteenth to the nineteenth century, marked changes in the social structure of which this good but poor-witted monarch was probably unaware. The shattering world-events of his reign must have impressed themselves on him even when his brain was clouded—the revolt of the American colonies, the French Revolution, the menace and eventual defeat of Napoleon, with the glory of Rodney and Wolfe dimming before the greater brilliance of Nelson and Wellington; there were enough sensational events here to fill a century. But the more gradual and subtle social changes were probably not fully apparent even to intelligent observers of the social scene until they had taken place.

When George III came to the throne the era of privilege enjoyed by the powerful families was at its height: the great landowners were more important people in the country than the representative of the House of Hanover, who was supposed to be their master. The King received the traditional obeisances from the nobility, but there their deference ended. During the later decades of the eighteenth century the position began slowly to alter, and the unquestioned advantages which had been so agreeably enjoyed by patricians for so long were no longer dumbly accepted by the people of the country. Moreover, a rich middle class was rising and beginning to encroach on the closely guarded preserves of those whose distinguished pedigrees made them consider themselves as belonging to the only class of importance in the country. There were distressing examples of men with little to recommend them, except their money and their political importance, being given seats in the House of Lords. There were Bubb Dodington, whose inelegant name was concealed beneath the more graceful appellation of Lord Melcombe, and Sampson Gideon, whose Jewish extraction was hidden by the English-sounding title of Lord Eardley. It must be owned that as seen in perspective from the 1960's the reduction in the lustre of privilege was no more than relative, but a parallel can perhaps be found between the social changes which took place during George III's long reign and George V's shorter tenure of the throne.

These would seem good reasons for ending the story of Court life with the death of George II, when, in spite of *bourgeois* monarchs, the social structure still appeared as impervious to change as it had been for decades past. Furthermore, the Court of the first two Georges, in its courtiers rather than in its king, belonged more to the Stuart era than to the respectable, middle-class reign which followed. The raffish courtiers and corrupt politicians who surrounded these two bewildered kings were little different from those who had harassed the lives of William III and Anne. Alone above the sea of intrigue stood out the massive figure of Sir Robert Walpole: to all appearances no more than a bluff, hard-drinking Norfolk squire, but in fact endowed with a mind of such political subtlety that he was able to keep on a fairly even keel the often rocking boat of the Hanoverian dynasty.

The three centuries which the following pages cover show the gradual decline of the Court as the principal centre and patron of the arts in the country. Henry VIII, in spite of the coarse and brutal side of his character which predominated during the latter part of his reign, had a genuine interest in the arts—principally music—and was fully conscious that it behoved him to be the leader of his countrymen in stimulating an interest in this direction, as well as advancing the prestige of England in the political balance of Europe. Indeed, he doubtless realised that the second could not be achieved without the first, and that the great Continental countries were disinclined to regard as an equal a backward nation to which the arts of the Renaissance had not yet penetrated.

It was a difficult task for the King to overcome the extreme insularity of his countrymen, but it was one in which Henry showed a constancy which was singularly lacking in other directions. On the other hand, when a courtier such as Wolsey indulged in patronage of the arts so lavishly that the King's leadership was rivalled, disaster ensued.

Elizabeth I nobly maintained her father's tradition and, although her naturally parsimonious nature restricted her encouragement of the visual arts, at least so far as architecture was concerned, her brilliant intelligence made her Court a true centre for the most gifted men in the country. Her reign marked the zenith of the importance of the Court in the cultural life of England: from the time of her death there was a slow decline. Charles I was by nature a generous and enthusiastic patron of the arts, and his collection of pictures, had his reign run to its normal span, would have become one of the finest in Europe; while the great palace envisaged at Whitehall before calamity overtook him, if carried out, would have housed the Kings of England with a dignity and splendour which would have been the envy of every other crowned head.

The Stuarts were aware that patronage of the arts was one of the duties of a king, and Charles II, although no aesthetic character, had a gift for attracting brilliant people to his Court and for encouraging them in pursuit of their arts—though the evanescent art of conversation was the one which probably had for him the greatest appeal—while even their last representative on the throne, Queen Anne, in a fumbling way made tentative efforts to carry on the tradition. But for many years the Court had been losing its position as the principal cultural centre of the country, and the torch had passed to the great landowners who patronized generously artists and craftsmen in the building and decoration of their country houses, in which they then gathered outstanding writers, musicians, and wits. This decentralisation was an inevitable process, but it was hastened by Queen Anne's lethargy and the absolute disinterest in the arts, and suspicion of clever men, which distinguished the first two Hanoverian kings.

The attitude of a ruler to the arts is only one aspect of Court life, and one on which much has been written. In the following pages I have dwelt rather on the lives of kings and queens in a more domestic direction, and have endeavoured to show how their characters, and their relations with each other, affected the atmosphere of the Court; and at the same time to provide a few glimpses of the human side of their lives—a side which was usually submerged beneath the ritual of royal protocol.

# Tudor

## Court Life

# Chapter 1

# HENRY VII

The light of history has been cast so brightly and so constantly on the Kings of England that their personal merits have been fairly accurately assessed, and the qualities and defects of their characters have been weighed with some measure of general agreement. But two figures in this long line who remain highly enigmatic are the last of the Plantagenets and the first of the Tudors—Richard III and Henry VII—those monarchs whose reigns may be said to mark respectively the close of the Middle Ages and the opening of modern history.

Richard's reign was short and turbulent, and he had no years of prosperity and peace which might have made it impossible for Shakespeare to represent him as uniformly sinister, however intent he might have been on purveying Tudor propaganda. But Henry spent twenty-four years on the throne, and thus was exposed for almost a quarter of a century to the searching criticism of historians. And yet his true character remains elusive. Of his courage and his sagacity there can be no two opinions; but was he cruel or clement, was he parsimonious or prodigal? To these questions there seems to be no certain answer.

A psycho-analyst would note in the rather curious circumstances of his birth and upbringing factors which might have had a strange influence on the mind of a child. When Henry was born on 28th January 1457 in Pembroke Castle his father, Edmund Tudor, Earl of Richmond, had already been dead for two months, while his mother had not yet completed her fourteenth year. This early maternity seems to have affected the mother's physical development, for she remained very small in stature. Pembroke Castle was the property of Henry's uncle, Jasper Tudor, Earl of Pembroke, who took charge of the child; but in 1461 Pembroke was attainted, and Henry passed into the care of the ardent Yorkist William Herbert, who later obtained the earldom of Pembroke from Edward IV when he first seized the throne from Henry VI. Henry Tudor remained more or less a prisoner until 1470, when Henry VI was restored to the throne, and the boy came once again into the care of his uncle.

These strange vicissitudes cannot have failed to influence the character of an intelligent youth, who must early have learnt the advantages of subterfuge and deception. It is very natural that in maturity he generally concealed his feelings and his emotions, so that his true personality remains obscured beneath a protective cover of deception.

The question which is of interest here is whether his reputation for parsimony was fully deserved, for on this characteristic depended the train of Court life, and the degree of glamour which surrounded the monarch and his queen. Just as Richard for centuries bore a reputation for unredeemed wickedness, so Henry's outstanding characteristic was generally accepted as black avarice; and as evidence of this is put forward the treasure in gold and silver worth £1,800,000, and the jewels valued at over £100,000, which he left at his death, while the royal coffers at the opening of his reign had been singularly ill-furnished.

Contemporary accounts, however, present a different picture, and there are many references to feasts, pageantry, tournaments, and general display which one has come to connect more closely with the Middle Ages, or with royal festivities during the following reign. Henry may not willingly have incurred the great expenditure entailed by these jollifications, but he early realised that with the Crown he had taken on a tradition of ostentation. The people expected their king to live in splendour, and he prudently, if reluctantly, fell in with the popular desire. But he early realised that this could be achieved without unduly straining the national resources. His ingenious scheme was to impose heavy fines in place of imprisonment on the richer transgressors; and by this means his treasury benefited and he himself gained a reputation for clemency.

It is said by Francis Bacon, though probably incorrectly, that when he came to London after his victory on Bosworth field, Henry drove to Archbishop Bourchier's palace at Lambeth in a closed chariot, greatly to the disappointment of the populace, who had expected their new ruler to appear as a triumphant figure on horseback followed by a brilliant retinue. This initial error, if indeed it occurred, was quickly rectified when a few days later he left Lambeth and passed through the City to take up his residence in the Tower. On this occasion the people of London had a full view of the young man of twenty-eight, who was their king by conquest rather than by descent, and was followed on horseback by a crowd of lords spiritual and temporal anxious to show their loyalty to their *de facto* ruler. Three days later, on 30th October 1485, the Archbishop, who only two years earlier had placed the crown on Richard III's cunning head, anointed and crowned the no less scheming cranium of young Henry Tudor.

It was generally assumed that Henry's marriage to Elizabeth of York,

18

who, as the eldest daughter of Edward IV, was regarded by many as the true heiress to the throne, would take place immediately. But it was not until January in the following year, after some very plain speaking on the part of the dutiful Commons, that the ceremony took place. Here, then, was a suitable occasion for display, and Henry gave a feast at Westminster on a scale which none of his predecessors could have excelled. The list of more than fifty dishes divided into two courses has survived, and inevitably includes such ornamental but indigestible birds as peacock and swan, with a host of smaller fry such as larks, quail, pheasants and partridges, cooked apparently with the lavish use of the sweet herbs which were at that period so highly favoured.

Thus the representatives of the red and the white roses could legitimately share a bed, but they did not as yet share the Crown. According to Francis Bacon, Henry was "no indulgent husband", and he suggests that the King's aversion to the House of York remained so strong that throughout the marriage his attitude to the Queen was cold and distant. Undoubtedly Henry was highly unwilling to acknowledge that his best legal claim to the throne was in right of his wife, and probably for this reason he delayed Elizabeth of York's coronation until he felt that the crown was firmly settled on his own head.

However, eventually, on 25th November 1487, Henry allowed his wife to be crowned with great pomp at Westminster. Here once again was an appropriate opportunity for the King to show that he could successfully emulate the pageantry of the Plantagenets; and frugality was thrown to the winds in order to provide a display sufficiently magnificent to rouse the populace to enthusiasm, though at least part of the expense was defrayed from other sources than the royal coffers. It had been made abundantly clear to the rich merchants of the City of London that handsome contributions to the expenses would be a welcome, and prudent, gesture.

On the 23rd of the month the Queen, splendidly dressed in robes of royalty and accompanied by the Countess of Richmond, her mother-in-law, and a retinue of peers and peeresses, left Greenwich in the royal barge for the Tower. Following the Queen came a crowd of boats belonging to the City companies, all emblazoned with their respective coats of arms and decorated with banners and streamers, while the oarsmen wore the liveries of their various crafts. Music added to the festive nature of the occasion, and a Red Dragon of Wales, mounted on one of the barges, spouted flames into the water with brilliant effect in the soft winter light. At the Tower, Elizabeth was welcomed by the King with every sign of conjugal affection, which was happily noted by the crowds.

On the following day the Queen, seated in a litter beneath a canopy

19

borne by knights of the body, was conveyed to the Palace of Westminster through streets hung with tapestry, cloth of gold, and velvets and silks. In every window were spectators, and at various points the piping voices of children, dressed as angels, sang the praises of the Queen. The greatest splendour was reserved for the coronation ceremony itself on the morning of the 25th in Westminster Abbey. The Queen, dressed in purple velvet with adornments of ermine and pearls, and with a gold and jewelled band in her hair, walked in procession from Westminster Hall to the Abbey, where in the presence of fifteen bishops, seventeen abbots, and the greatest nobles of the country the ceremony took place with all the traditional pomp. The King took no part in the proceedings, but watched from a latticed stage which had been erected close to the high altar. Feasts and dancing followed in Westminster Hall, and two days later the Queen returned to Greenwich.

Henry had thus fulfilled his obligations, and made the representative of the House of York both his wife and his crowned queen; but after this brief and brilliant interlude Elizabeth passed into the dim background of the King's life, except for moments of prominence when she gave birth to a child. These events were conducted with great ceremony, and in the Regulations of the Household very exact instructions were laid down for the "deliverance of a queen". The walls and ceiling of the chamber were to be hung with "rich arras" and the floor carpeted; the bed was to be "arrayed with sheets of fine lawne or fine raynes, great pillows with a head sheete . . . a pane of ermines embroidered with rich cloth of gould". There were many further instructions designed to ensure that the infant prince or princess made its entry into the world in surroundings of suitable splendour.

Seven times the Queen endured the elaborate ritual, but there seems to have been no particular royal residence which was preferred for these occasions. The first child, for example, Prince Arthur, was born at Winchester in 1486; Margaret two years later seemingly at Sheen; Henry in 1491 at Greenwich; and Katherine, the last child, at the Tower. Of the three sons and four daughters who were born to Henry and Elizabeth, only one son and two daughters lived to produce children: Henry VIII; Margaret, who married James IV of Scotland and so became the progenitor of all English monarchs after Queen Elizabeth I; and Mary, who was briefly Queen of France and later Duchess of Suffolk, marrying her second husband, to the dismay of the French court, a month after the death of her first.

Elizabeth survived the birth of her fourth daughter by only nine days, and on 11th February 1503 she died in the Tower at the age of thirty-nine. The King appears to have been unexpectedly affected by her death, and

2   Henry VIII and Francis I meeting at the Field of the Cloth of Gold

*From a contemporary illuminated manuscript*

3   Henry VIII with Queen Catherine (Parr) and his son, Prince Edward (later Edward VI). To left and right are Princesses Mary (Mary I) and Elizabeth (Elizabeth I)

*From a painting of the school of Hans Holbein the Younger*
*Reproduced by gracious permission of Her Majesty The Queen*

4   Henry VIII jousting before Catherine of Aragon

*From the Westminster Tournament Roll*

5   Hampton Court Palace in 1538

*Detail of a drawing by Anthonis Wyngaerde*

ordered her burial to take place with all the pomp that had been seen at her coronation fifteen years earlier. While 636 masses were being said in London, her body was embalmed and placed in a lead coffin, which was enclosed in another of wood covered in white and black velvet. Ten days later the coffin was placed on a chariot with sable trappings and drawn by six horses, while behind was borne an effigy of the Queen dressed in royal robes and with a sceptre in her hand. A long retinue of officials and nobles, prelates and abbots, followed the coffin to Westminster Abbey, where it rested till the following day when the funeral was conducted with appropriate ceremony, and the coffin was lowered into the grave prepared for it.

The descriptions of these various ceremonies which appear in Leland's *Collectanea* make it clear that Henry did not allow a spirit of frugality to reduce the magnificence of the parade on the occasions when he thought it desirable; but one senses that it was not personal pleasure in these displays but rather a determination to show that in spite of his lack of royal blood he could, if he wished, outshine the splendour of the Plantagenet kings. His was not a personality which stirred the enthusiasm or affection of the populace, though there must have been gratitude for the peace which his rule brought to the country; but the sporadic displays which he staged on suitable occasions maintained the good humour of the common people, while from time to time he entertained the upper classes with feasts conceived on an unexpectedly lavish scale.

The Venetian diplomat who wrote *A Relation of the Island of England* about 1497 was greatly impressed by the "sumptuous table" which he found at the English Court, and mentions that on two occasions he was present when "there might be 600 to 700 persons at dinner". And he adds that "his people say that his Majesty spends upon his table £14,000 sterling annually" and so maintains "the ancient usages of England", although he noted that he was "frugal to excess in his own person". Indeed on banquets he must have exceeded the expenditure of the majority of his predecessors on the throne.

In addition to the abundance of the King's table, the observant Venetian described with enthusiasm the rich display of silver plate which was to be seen in London, and he suggested that there were more silver vessels in the goldsmiths' shops in the Strand than "in all the shops in Milan, Rome, Venice, and Florence put together". No doubt the King's tables were loaded with "salt cellars, drinking cups, and basins to hold water for the hands" with even greater profusion than those of his subjects, and it is remarkable that in this art at least this backward island could outshine the High Renaissance of Italy.

There was another direction in which this thrifty monarch indulged in

23

great outlay, and that was in building. It is true that his undertakings were confined to two, but both were of the greatest nobility, and they represented the finest examples of ecclesiastical and domestic architecture constructed at that period. The Henry VII Chapel at Westminster still stands unaltered in the full beauty of its soaring and delicate tracery—it is perhaps the finest flower of Perpendicular Gothic—but of Richmond Palace there are now only drawings and a few sparse remains from which the splendour of this royal residence can be assessed.

In the year 1502 the Chapels of the Virgin Mary and of St. Erasmus at the east end of Westminster Abbey were demolished, and on their site the new building arose, the first stone being laid by the Abbot, John Islip. The King's primary intention was to provide a suitable setting for the body of Henry VI, which had originally been buried at Chertsey, but which was removed to St. George's Chapel at Windsor by Richard III. It seems that the remains of this saintly king were in fact interred in this splendid chantry, but no monument marks the place, and it is the less pious bones of the builder and his neglected spouse which now have the place of honour beneath Torrigiano's exquisite tomb.

The original royal residence of Sheen, as it was known until Henry changed its name to Richmond in honour of his own earldom of Richmond in Yorkshire, was a fairly small building. It had been largely rebuilt by Henry V, more as a fortress than a palace, and was surrounded by a moat fed by the waters of the Thames, on the banks of which it stood. From early in his reign, Henry VII made it a place of frequent residence, but he appears to have made no more than minor alterations to the fabric. In December 1499, while the King was staying in the palace, a fire broke out and almost the whole of the ancient building was destroyed. Two years later a new palace of great size had risen on the site. It was a spreading, three-storied building with long, mullioned windows and high cupola-crowned towers rising above the level of the battlements amidst a forest of elaborate chimney-stacks. Richmond thus became by far the most magnificent of all the royal residences which were strung along the Thames—Windsor, Westminster, the Tower, Greenwich: none of these boasted such grandeur combined with so high a degree of domestic comfort as was to be found in the newly built and newly named Richmond.

Bacon no doubt wrote justly of Henry that he was "magnificent in his building, sparing in his rewards". And from the same source one gains a picture of the King playing the part of regal splendour so as to fulfil the expectations of his subjects, but taking little personal pleasure in the role. He was in reality "sad, serious and thoughtful", and "in Triumphs and Jousts, and Tourneys, and Balls and Masks . . . he was rather a Princely and Gentle Spectator than seeming much to be excited". He may have derived far greater pleasure from augmenting and preserving his personal treasure than on spending money on empty but unavoidable pageantry. But the construction of his chapel at Westminster would seem to have been an enterprise on which he embarked with unreserved enthusiasm, and there—to quote Bacon once again—"He dwelleth more richly Dead in the monument of his Tomb, than he did alive in Richmond, or in any of his Palaces."

# Chapter 2

# HENRY VIII

Few monarchs can have ascended a throne under such brilliant auspices as the young Henry VIII. Providence had apparently lavished on his circumstances and on his person every benefit which could contribute to the success and happiness of his reign and life. Where good fortune is so abundantly provided, some essential gift is usually withheld; but the gloomiest prophet in the spring of 1509 could not have expected that the factor which was destined to warp the career of this vigorous young man was his inability to sire a healthy male heir. It was his passionate desire to perpetuate his own line rather than his amorous proclivities, though these were not negligible, which underlay nearly all the events which make his reign one of the most vital in the history of England.

Henry was born on 28th June 1491, and so was a few weeks under eighteen years of age on his father's death on 23rd April 1509. The throne to which he succeeded was firmly established; indeed it had never been very seriously threatened during the twenty-four years since his father had seized it. Not only had Henry VII achieved this almost miraculous security, in spite of there being many with better claims to the Crown than himself, but he had also in a measure created a new impression of royalty—an impression peculiar to the Tudor dynasty, which was distinct from that of the Plantagenets. Though so unspectacular, so unglamorous a figure, Henry VII had shrewdly instilled the theory of Tudor majesty into the English people; and it was thus that Henry VIII, who exemplified the concept of majesty so much more fully than his father, ascended the throne with confidence.

Had it been his elder brother, Arthur—the delicate, studious youth—who had succeeded in his place, it is probable that the popular enthusiasm would have been more tempered, or at least would have been less long sustained. But Henry was endowed with every grace of body as well as with an intellect which was far above the average. The defects in his character seemed insignificant, and merely those to be expected in a youth so richly favoured by Fortune. He was certainly, and excusably, vain; he was mentally indolent—but mental and physical energy are seldom

26

companions, and of the latter he had no lack; he was all his life intensely self-indulgent in eating and drinking, and this largely led to the early deterioration in his physique. But these seemed superficial faults.

It is curious that no portraits exist of Henry as a young man. We know well the unattractive picture he presented in middle life, and it is inevitably thus that we think of him. But for the beauty of his appearance during the first years of his reign one must rely on contemporary descriptions —on those and also on the suit of armour preserved in the Tower of London which shows his admirable proportions. He was six feet two inches tall, with a waist of thirty-five inches and a chest of forty-two inches. In figure he must have resembled his Plantagenet grandfather, Edward IV, who was probably the most handsome of his line. Henry's hair was auburn and, though this seems difficult to credit from later portraits, his face was said to have had an almost feminine delicacy. His pale skin, which is evident from his portraits and is a not unusual accompaniment of auburn hair, probably led to this impression. His least attractive feature was his nose, which was high-bridged and massive. It was no doubt to disguise this unbecoming protuberance that he was almost invariably portrayed full-face.

The high quality of Henry's intelligence was early recognised, and both Erasmus and Sir Thomas More regarded the young Prince as a brilliant boy. Henry's education was of the intensive variety considered beneficial to the offspring of royalty, and he had the advantage of being brought up in a Court frequented by the most cultured men of the age, that age when the teaching of the Renaissance was first beginning to affect English life. Thus Henry was the earliest English monarch to be educated under the influence of Humanism. The names of several of the young Prince's teachers are known. Giles D'Ewes taught him the French language, and either he or André trained his handwriting into that curious compromise between the clear Italian script and the cramped Gothic writing which was usual at that period. But his most famous master was John Skelton, Henry VII's Poet Laureate, whose own singular mingling of poetic feeling and coarseness would seem to have impressed itself on his young pupil's receptive mind.

An early meeting with Erasmus and More took place in 1499 when Henry was eight or nine years old. The former was staying with Lord Mountjoy near Greenwich, when More came to take him for a walk to a neighbouring village. This must have been Eltham, where the royal children spent much of their youth. More presented to Henry an ode which gave the boy great pleasure, and he sent a note to Erasmus while they were at dinner asking for something from his pen also. On returning home the man of letters composed a poem, "finished ... within three days", which praised Henry VII and his children, and commended the youthful Prince's devotion to learning. This precocious love of letters was barely maintained, for though Henry developed into a theologian, he was far from being an intellectual. Nevertheless as King, Henry encouraged the arts and made his Court the cultural centre of the country to an even greater degree than that of his father, but for none of the arts, except for music, does his interest seem to have been very deep or abiding. His intense love of music survived even into those latter years of his life when his body was tortured by pain and his mind was darkened by suspicion and cruelty. He was said to be an accomplished performer on the organ, lute, harpsichord, and flute, and an inventory made in 1542 of the goods in the Palace of Westminster mentions over forty musical instruments.

For many years there was no dwindling of his physical energy. In hunting, in jousts, in many different games he showed a prowess which was equalled by very few of his subjects. The Venetian Ambassador Giustiniani, whose despatches throw a dispassionate light on the early years of Henry's reign, was highly impressed by the young King's outstanding athleticism. In 1515 he wrote: "He draws the bow with greater strength than any other man in England, and jousts marvellously. ... He is very fond indeed of hunting, and never takes this diversion without tiring eight or ten horses." The same writer had also watched the King playing tennis and, though the Ambassador may have been baffled by the rules of the game, he was enthusiastic about the beauty of the spectacle. "It is the prettiest thing in the world to see him play," he wrote, "his fair skin glowing through a shirt of the finest texture."

With these attainments, it was not surprising that the young King found physical amusements, in which he excelled, more attractive than the dry business of directing affairs of state, where in any case his immature judgement was controlled by older men. But when some state occasion demanded that he should appear in the pageantry of majesty, he would throw himself into the role with great pleasure and with admirable grace. His physical vanity was flattered, and he would deck his splendid body with the utmost richness, and organise his retinue so that he presented the ideal of regal splendour. This was to him an occupation even more enthralling than hunting or tennis.

The invaluable Giustiniani describes just such an occasion when he presented his credentials on his appointment as Ambassador in April 1515. The King was at Richmond, a palace in which he seldom stayed in later years, and Giustiniani made a ceremonious journey thither along the Thames in a royal barge. The King spared no pains to impress the newly appointed representative of this friendly and important state, and all the glamour of the Tudor Court was marshalled for this purpose. The Venetians, accompanied by a large retinue which had been sent to conduct them, entered the hall of the palace where they were served with a collation consisting only of bread and wine according to English custom. They were then escorted through a suite of rooms hung with splendid tapestries between the ranks of the King's guard of 300 halberdiers, "all as big as giants", till they reached the presence chamber, at the end of which the King was standing before a throne gleaming with gold brocade and with a canopy of golden velvet above it. On a cushion covered in cloth of gold lay the long Sword of State. The King's dress was in no way inferior to the splendour of his surroundings, and was a somewhat embellished version of the robes of the Garter. He wore a satin doublet striped in white and crimson, with scarlet hose slashed from the knee upwards. From his shoulders hung a mantle of violet velvet with a long train lined with white satin, on his head was a jewelled cap of crimson velvet, and round his neck a chain studded with precious stones from which hung the jewelled pendant of St. George. His fingers were loaded with rings, and at his waist was a pouch of cloth of gold containing a dagger.

On the right of the King stood eight Knights of the Garter, and on the left a group of distinguished prelates in full pontificals, while heralds and attendants lent further distinction to the scene. The Ambassador then addressed the King for half an hour in Latin, and received a reply in the King's name from a "Doctor of the Parliament". This tedious but necessary performance being at an end, the deputation attended mass, and was then entertained by the King to a magnificent and cheerful banquet.

These gorgeous ceremonies were no doubt infinitely agreeable to Henry's personal vanity, but there was a purpose in them beyond this— one which the King, with his astute mind, fully perceived. The credit of England in the eyes of the Continental powers was not particularly high. The Plantagenet dynasty had ended in a sombre turmoil of murder and internecine strife; the brilliant light of earlier reigns had been largely extinguished; the usurper Henry Tudor had been accepted with extreme reservation. If England was to regain its importance in Europe, it was essential for the young King to show that he was firmly established on the throne, that the royal treasury was full to overflowing, and that the English Court was as cultured and richly equipped as any in the world.

In achieving this objective, the elaborate displays staged by the King were highly successful; but they had one, or perhaps two drawbacks. A ceremony such as Giustiniani described could not be quickly staged. The Court did not normally live in such a state of pomp. The knights,

29

the prelates, even the halberdiers had to be gathered together and arrayed in their magnificent uniforms; and this took several weeks to organise, so that foreign envoys had sometimes to wait impatiently for a month or so for an audience. But the King maintained his principle till late in his life, when he can no longer have presented a very glamorous appearance as the focal point of elaborate ceremonial.

The second drawback was financial: the displays were a severe drain on the treasury. Henry VII's prudent manipulations had provided his son with a very handsome fortune, a fortune which probably seemed inexhaustible to the young King, but which before very long was to prove so depleted in the good cause of creating *una bella figura* as to lead to grave difficulties. Indeed the desire for heirs and the quest for money became two dominant factors in Henry's reign.

But more than a decade of kingship was to pass before either became a major anxiety, and meanwhile there were ample and rewarding opportunities for the pageantry which was so invaluable in building up the theory of majesty both in the eyes of foreigners and of the populace of England. The young Henry stirred far greater enthusiasm by his handsome appearance and dashing style than did his father by his intense industry and concentration on the affairs of the country. How natural, then, it must have seemed to Henry to leave the dull routine in the capable hands of his Chancellor, Warham, Archbishop of Canterbury, and of his Lord Privy Seal, Fox, Bishop of Winchester, rather than to attend to these burdensome matters himself; and no doubt these two able prelates were more than content that the impetuous young King should expend his energies on physical amusements rather than on interfering in the direction of the country.

These two men were the paramount influence in Henry's early life. Bishop Fox had baptised the infant Prince, and fifteen years later had, with Warham, strongly advocated Henry's marriage with Catherine of Aragon. The advice of the bishops and the exhortations of his dying father can have left Henry little option in the matter of his marriage, and there is indeed no evidence that he embarked on it with the least reluctance. Thus on 11th June 1509, seven weeks after his father's death, Henry was married in private at Greenwich to his brother's widow.

That these sagacious men of the world should have supposed that the marriage would bring lasting happiness to the participants seems improbable, but no doubt they were of the opinion that the immediate benefits to be gained more than counterbalanced the uncertainties of the future. Catherine's substantial dowry, over which there had been constant wrangling since Prince Arthur's death, would be secured; the alliance between Spain and England would be strengthened; and there seemed no reason to suppose that Catherine would not give birth to a number of male children. The fact that Henry was six years younger than his bride mattered little for the present, but it must have seemed probable that in ten or fifteen years, however fertile Catherine might have been, the marriage would end in difficulties.

In the event Catherine found child-bearing singularly difficult, and the next decade was punctuated with miscarriages, stillbirths, or infants which survived their birth only a few days. There was great national rejoicing when the Queen produced a son on New Year's Day, 1511, but jubilation turned to mourning when the infant died seven weeks later. The little corpse was buried with great pomp in Westminster Abbey at a cost, it is said, of more than £10,000. At Catherine's sixth birth, on 18th February 1516, the child survived and was christened Mary. In November 1518 Catherine had another stillborn child, and this was her last pregnancy. Even Henry's vow to lead a crusade against the Turks in person if he should be granted a male heir apparently left the Deity unmoved. For several years he continued to hope that the miracle might occur, but by 1525, when the Queen was forty years old, it was clear that his hopes were in vain, and estrangement between the royal couple, which had been growing for some years, became almost complete.

But before this disappointment came to cloud the King's life there were several years of brilliant happiness. Henry, little troubled by affairs of state, was able to indulge to the utmost his passion for every form of sport, particularly perhaps for the jousts and tournaments, amidst the pageantry of which he was able to appear before enthusiastic crowds as one of the most accomplished performers—a noble and princely figure, who contrasted so gratifyingly with his ageing brother-in-law, Louis XII, King of France.

It was by no means only the privileged who had the pleasure of watching the entertainments staged by the King and his courtiers: the public was also freely admitted. Thus a close link was formed between the King and his subjects, and it was a link which both Henry VIII and Queen Elizabeth valued and fostered. Probably no English monarch, till this century, had a closer human contact with his subjects than these two. Without the sympathy which was thus formed between the King and his people, Henry might well have encountered far greater opposition to the arbitrary manner in which in later life he governed the country. His attitude to England was that of a landowner to his estate: it was his to do with as he pleased, and it is remarkable how rare were the hostile reactions to this despotic attitude.

There were other more sentimental amusements to vary the vigorous round of jousts and hunting: there was, for example, a traditional performance which took place on May morning in the woods near Green-wich. Of this, once again, the best description has been left by the Venetian Ambassador, to whom these more or less annual junketings seemed inexpressibly romantic and beautiful. At Greenwich, he says, he joined the Queen, who was dressed in Spanish costume and was mounted on a white horse. Then, accompanied by her sixteen ladies, they rode upwards of a mile into the country where in a glade they found a triumphal car drawn by griffins with human faces (and no doubt human bodies as well) which was filled with singers and musicians. Having passed this hazard, they came upon 300 of the King's Guard bearing bows and arrows, and "all dressed in green, in the German fashion". The fact that they represented Robin Hood's merry men was lost on the Ambassador. Eventually the King came into sight mounted on a bay Frieslander and dressed from head to foot in green velvet. So brilliant and splendid a figure did he appear on his curvetting horse that the dazzled Ambassador wrote, "I fancied myself looking at Mars."

Within the woods arbours had been built with boughs, and here the company, suitably graded according to rank, were served by the pretended outlaws with outlaws' food—venison and wine—"to their great contentacion" as the historian Hall wrote in his description of the same scene. When the feast was over the whole company returned to Greenwich to the accompaniment of the music of trumpets and drums.

Here, indeed, seems the essence of "Merrie England", which Henry was preserving, probably unconsciously, during the early years of his reign, and of which he was the personification until frustration and illness turned him from the glamorous monarch into the soured tyrant.

The masques and banquets which were also a favourite feature of Court life seem less redolent of "Merrie England", since they continued into future reigns when merriment was no longer a supposed feature of national life. The masques often included elaborate sets which must have required careful preparation, but in spite of their complication they seem to have borne the ingenuous style of amateur theatricals. A description has survived of a "grand masque" held on Twelfth Night, 1515, in the Great Hall at Eltham Palace, the splendid building which had been raised during the reign of Edward IV, and which still survives in its full magnificence. After a performance of *Troilus and Pandarus* performed by choirboys—the sort of ordeal to which every century has grown accustomed—the principal entertainment of the evening took place, which was played by the lords and ladies of the Court. A mock castle had been erected across one end of the hall; this was attacked by a bevy of knights, but after a graceful skirmish the onslaught was beaten back. The ladies then emerged from the castle and joined both the victorious and the vanquished knights in a ceremonial dance. The masque was followed by a banquet of 200 dishes.

Here then there was a robust entertainment giving opportunity for frolic and dancing, but without any of the intellectual quality which illuminated the masques of the following century when, with words written by Ben Jonson, Samuel Daniel or others, and with settings and clothes designed by Inigo Jones, the performances became works of art rather than high-spirited romps.

Henry and Catherine on their marriage found themselves in possession of a fair number of royal residences in the close neighbourhood of London. Within the boundaries of the City stood the Tower, with its stout walls, gateways, and battlements the proud emblem of monarchy. But though the ancient fortress had been considerably domesticised during previous reigns, a process which Henry continued, it remained a residence merely for state occasions rather than a dwelling for long and agreeable visits; while the fact that it combined the functions of both palace and prison can hardly have been conducive to a very festive atmosphere. It was from the Tower that two of Henry's queens set out on triumphant journeys for their coronations at Westminster; it was to the Tower that two of them were brought never again to emerge.

The Thames provided a more convenient and a safer highway than the narrow, crowded streets of the City, or the rough roads in its vicinity: it was on the banks of the river, therefore, that the royal houses were built, with the single exception of Eltham which stood on a slight elevation at some distance from the water. Far upstream was the great castle of Windsor, but this had too much of the formidable quality of the Tower to make it a very congenial residence; also, its distance from London lessened its convenience. In close proximity to London, then, were Westminster, Richmond, Greenwich, and Eltham—an adequate collection, it might have been supposed, but there were to be important additions during Henry's reign.

The constant movement of the Court from one house to another, and thence to one of the royal residences in the distant country-side, was the order of life throughout Henry's reign, even to the last years when transport of his bloated body from place to place must have put a heavy strain on his stamina. These perpetual changes suggest a restlessness of temperament on the part of the King, and this may well have been the case, but in addition there were practical reasons for leaving a palace after a few weeks' residence.

These reasons were those of hygiene. Erasmus's well-known description of the condition of the rush-covered floors he found in some English houses raises a picture of almost inconceivable insalubrity. The general

33

custom, when a floor became too disgusting, was to add a covering of fresh rushes. Indeed the system was that of a present-day deep-litter house for chickens. In view of these insanitary principles it is not surprising that outbursts of sweating-sickness and plague were a fairly regular hazard of life.

In the royal residences the conditions were far better, at least in the principal rooms; and there is no suggestion to be found, for example, in the Venetian Ambassador's descriptions of the Court, that the handsome galleries with their tapestry-hung walls and cloth of gold draperies, in which he had his audiences with the King, were in anything but immaculate condition. This was largely due to Henry's own insistence on a high degree of hygiene, about which he drew up very rigorous rules:

> "The haute-pace to be cleane kept, soe that noe ale, water, broken meate, or other thing conveyed out of the King's chamber, be cast or remaine there, to the annoyance and filthynesse of the same."

But the back regions, where these rules were not enforced, must have been very different, and after some weeks in one palace it was prudent to move on to another. Indeed the term "to sweeten" in a fresh residence is an expression often found in contemporary writings.

Henry was probably more inclined to this constant change of residence than his subjects, though those who were able followed the same routine, for the King—so courageous in most directions—was well known to be unusually nervous of being exposed to the contagion of plague. On this subject the French Ambassador, Marillac, wrote to François I: "He is the most timid person in the world in such cases", and his rules of hygiene were designed to eliminate danger of infection.

The most commodious and convenient of the royal houses which Henry inherited from his father was Richmond Palace which, having been built with a domestic and not a defensive purpose in view, must have provided far more cheerful accommodation than a grim building such as the Tower. During the early years of his reign, Henry was much at Richmond, but later his visits both there and to Eltham became rare, and one senses that those buildings, where his father's spirit was strongest, tended to become uncongenial to him. Perhaps this sentiment increased as the Treasury, which his father had so astutely and carefully filled, gradually emptied under his own extravagance. In any case, even when Hampton Court, Nonsuch, Whitehall, and St. James's had been added to the collection, it was Greenwich, and always Greenwich, which Henry favoured above all others.

The original Palace of Westminster was largely abandoned as a residence early in his reign, and little residential use was made of various buildings belonging to the Crown which stood on the north bank of the

Thames amongst the chain of fine houses in private hands which joined the City to Westminster. The ancient Palace of the Savoy, with its long royal connection, had been reduced to ruins during Wat Tyler's insurrection. Henry VII began the building of a hospital on the site which was completed during the reign of his son. The foundation soon deviated, however, from its charitable intention and became the abode of criminals and vagabonds, for it possessed the privilege of providing sanctuary for debtors. And the adjacent building of Baynard's Castle with its tall towers rising direct from the waters of the Thames was seldom inhabited by Henry VIII.

The King, thus, had no agreeable palace in the immediate neighbourhood of the City and Westminster, those twin centres of metropolitan life, until he gained possession of York Place, Cardinal Wolsey's sumptuous palace, in 1529. This splendid building, together with the great wealth which was seized by the King from his discredited Minister who in any case died in the following year, was a highly useful acquisition. Under its new name of Whitehall—a name adopted it seems on account of the whiteness of the stone in which it was built—it became the principal palace of London, and such it remained until its destruction by fire in 1698. In 1536 Henry increased the size of the already spacious building by the addition of a number of "distinct, beautiful, costly, and pleasant lodgings". He also enclosed with a wall of brick and stone a park extending from the Sanctuary at Westminster almost to Charing Cross, and built in it, on a site close to the Palace, a tennis court and cockpit. The whole motley collection of structures was generally referred to by the old name of Palace of Westminster.

Several years earlier than this, Henry had gained possession of the Cardinal's splendid new house of Hampton Court. Wolsey had selected the site for the great house he proposed to build with infinite care. A panel of eminent physicians had been invited to advise on the most suitable place within twenty miles of London, and Hampton had been unanimously recommended for its "extraordinary salubrity". In 1515 the foundations of the spreading structure in brick and stone were begun; and a gracious building gradually arose which, in spite of its traditional towers, battlements, and moat, was designed to provide the domestic advantages of sunlight, warmth, and convenience to a degree unthought of in the average contemporary great house. In addition to this, Italian craftsmen had been called in to add embellishments in the taste of the Renaissance to the sober brick walls. This great enterprise took nearly eight years to complete, and surpassed any of the existing royal houses in the beauty of its design and the richness of its decoration. To anyone less blinded by his own power than the Cardinal, it must have been

35

evident that this rival palace would excite extreme jealousy in the King. And this indeed occurred to such an intense degree, that Wolsey had no option but to present his newly finished house to his royal master.

The danger of too great a display of wealth was a hazard which ministers too frequently disregarded: in the following century the fall of Fouquet and the seizure of his magnificent domain by Louis XIV followed much the same lines as the tragedy of Wolsey. Indeed there were obvious advantages to a monarch in having a rapacious minister whose wealth could be confiscated with every evidence of righteousness; thus the royal treasury would greatly benefit without loss of prestige.

With the acquisition of Hampton Court, Henry abandoned Richmond as a residence. At first Wolsey, as some compensation for being dispossessed of the house on which he had spent so much time, care, and money, was allowed to live there; but when he fell from grace, he was compelled to move out of the palace into a lodge in the park. It was an agreeable building apparently, for Cavendish, Wolsey's secretary and biographer, wrote of it as " . . . a very pretty house, and a neat, lacking no necessary rooms that to so small a house were convenient and necessary". From Richmond, Wolsey retired to York—the first occasion on which he had visited his see—whence he never came further south again than the Abbey of Leicester, where he died in November 1530 on his tragic journey back to London under arrest.

A happier inhabitant of Richmond Palace was Anne of Cleves who was granted it as a residence after the annulment of her marriage in 1540. Here she lived in great contentment, spending a large part of her annuity of £4,000 on adorning with elaborate clothes her far from beautiful person. And here Henry visited her on a number of occasions and, conjugal obligations being fortunately at an end, was charmed and soothed by her amiability and good humour.

But this was many years ahead, when Henry had lost the glamour and handsomeness of youth, and his character had become embittered by personal reverses. The highest point of those early flamboyant years of his reign was reached in 1520 at his meeting with François I on the Field of the Cloth of Gold at Guines. This spectacular encounter was the last flourish of the age of chivalry, and perhaps the first occasion on which Henry realised that the wealth accumulated by his father was not inexhaustible. The expenditure incurred by the rival monarchs was immense, and must have been as crippling to the French Treasury as it was to the English. The two Kings were rivals not only in the magnificence of their display but also physically—in their youth, in their strength, and in their good looks—for only three years separated them in age: Henry was twenty-nine and François twenty-six.

It was an occasion fully after Henry's own heart—an occasion for splendour of setting and of costume, an occasion for presenting a heroic figure in tournaments and jousts, an occasion for exhibiting a warm geniality towards the French King for whom he had in reality a deep jealousy and distrust. The concrete results from this picturesque and extravagant festivity were negligible, and Henry returned to England with little achieved in return for the immense expense.

The following years were to contain sobering periods for the young monarch, who until now had experienced nothing but undiluted popularity: he was to find that the search for money and the suggested imposition of new taxes to remedy his impoverished condition were to induce so dark a mood in Parliament and people that it was necessary to devise other methods of refilling the exchequer.

An essential measure for the restoration of the King's finances was to restrict the waste, extravagance, and pilfering which were rife in the royal household, and to this end in 1526 Wolsey drew up the "Statutes of Eltham" which were contrived "for the establishment of good order, and reformation of sundry errours and mis-uses in the most honourable Household and Chamber". The seventy-nine paragraphs of this draconian document covered a wide variety of details of domestic life in whatever house the King should be in residence. A number are addressed to the cooks and those in charge of the complex offices connected with the stupendous business of providing food for a populous court, such as the Acatry, Confectionaries and Loafery, Larder, Spicery, Sea-Fishery, Poultrey, and a host of others.

Many of the rules are highly revealing in that they indicate the abuses which were presumably general practice. For example the Master Cooks were given an allowance of twenty marks each to provide clothing for the scullions so that "they shall not go naked or in garments of such vileness as they now doe, nor lie in the nights and dayes in the kitchens or ground by the fire-side". Here again was an effort on the King's part to introduce more sanitary conditions in his palaces. Perhaps with the same intent, it was forbidden to keep dogs in the precincts of the Court, though an exception was made for "some few small spaniells for ladyes or others".

We learn that until this time "sundry noblemen, gentlemen, and others doe much delight and use to dyne in corners and secret places". This cosy practice the Cardinal, in the King's name, resolutely forbade, and from thence forward all noblemen, both spiritual and temporal, were required to eat their principal meals in the halls provided for this purpose.

The longest paragraph of all is devoted to the behaviour of the royal retinue when the King passed a few days in the country-house of a nobleman. It had been usual when the visit ended for the servants to purloin such useful objects as "lockes of doores, tables, formes, cup-boards, tressells and other ymplements of household". The results, indeed, must have been very similar to the occupation of a house by the Services during the past war. It is observed that these predatory habits bring dishonour to the King and displeasure to the unfortunate owner of the house. To remedy this situation ushers and harbingers are to be appointed, who must not only keep a sharp eye on the fittings of the house, but also ensure that the host is not robbed of "deer, connies, fish, fruit, corn, grass" and so forth.

In all it is clear that Wolsey's Statutes were admirably devised to inculcate a more economic and seemly way of life in the motley crowd of men and women who circulated in the royal orbit, and whose principal interest was to secure every possible perquisite for themselves. Whether the King himself took much interest in this attempt to bring order into his household must be doubtful, with the exception of those rules directed towards hygiene, nor does it seem that they were particularly effective in restoring the parlous condition of the royal finances; but their intention was most praiseworthy.

This period of financial stress marked the beginning of the transition of the carefree playboy, airborne on the enthusiasm of his people, into the crafty monarch who realised that he must resort to devious means to achieve his ends. The two diverse sides of Henry's character, which make his personality so puzzling, developed rapidly. On the one hand there was the impetuous, short-tempered tyrant, who consigned his closest asso-ciates and friends to the block without apparently a vestige of pity or re-morse, while on the other there was the subtle schemer who was prepared to exercise patience and charm in order to have his way. On the proposal for new taxes he found it prudent to give in : on the question of the annulment of his marriage to Catherine of Aragon, which also brought him great unpopularity, he stood firm. Upwards of a decade passed from the time that Henry had conceived the idea of divorce till he eventually found himself, by the annulment pronounced by Cranmer, Archbishop of Canterbury, once again legally a bachelor. His marriage to Anne Boleyn, however, had already taken place in secret towards the end of January 1533, the King then being forty-one and his bride twenty-five.

Henry's love for Anne was not long sustained after marriage, but it had burnt brightly during the thwarting years when he was still hoping for a papal annulment of his first marriage. Some of his letters to Anne have survived and indicate his amorous feelings. In the summer of 1528 he wrote: "Wishing myself (specially an evening) in my sweetheart's arms, whose pretty dubbys I trust shortly to cusse". And the brilliance of Anne's coronation showed the pride and pleasure he felt in his new bride —a pleasure which was not universally shared by his subjects, many of whom felt much sympathy for the discarded Queen Catherine.

However, the King was in no way deterred from staging one of the greatest pageants of his reign, and he knew the national character well enough to be sure that a magnificent display would always be popular, even if its purpose did not have general support. The programme followed very closely the lines of the coronation of Henry's mother, Elizabeth of York, forty-six years earlier, but how different in station was the principal performer in each of the pageants! In the first the Queen was the rightful heir to the throne of England, in the second she was a girl of fairly modest origin.

On the last day of May 1533 the King and his bride embarked in the royal barge at Greenwich; and, accompanied by a great concourse of decorated vessels containing all the dignitaries of the City of London and a vast fleet of smaller craft filled with citizens, they moved majestically upstream to the Tower. From the boats rose a tumult of music and singing, and as the royal party reached the ancient fortress bursts of artillery fire crashed out from the battlements—so loudly, indeed, that all the windows in the vicinity were shattered.

The following morning the King left for Westminster by water, and shortly afterwards Anne emerged from the Tower carried in an open litter hung with cloth of gold and escorted by a company of cavalry. She was dressed in a robe of crimson brocade with a necklace of huge pearls round her neck, and on her head was a jewelled chaplet. Arches and decorations in the streets were designed to make this a triumphant procession, but, as an eye-witness recorded, "there were not, I think, ten people who greeted her with 'God save you'".

From Westminster Hall, Anne passed to the high altar in the Abbey and the gorgeous ceremony proceeded in the presence of the nobility of England, all obedient to the will of their tyrannical sovereign; but the majority doubtless with hatred of the upstart queen in their hearts. They had less than three years to wait for their revenge.

Whether Anne Boleyn was guilty of all the charges made against her will always remain in some doubt, and, since the records of her trial were destroyed, historians can support whatever opinion they wish. They can believe with Agnes Strickland that it was a question of "a fickle tyrant" crushing "a royal victim", and that the false accusations were due to the fact that Henry's affections had passed to Jane Seymour; or one may prefer to believe the contemporary record of the unknown Spaniard who professed to know all the details of Anne's infidelity with Mark Smeaton, and also how this was accomplished in spite of the little privacy she enjoyed in the crowded life of the Court.

The Spaniard was naturally a violent partisan of Queen Catherine's, and was all too ready to lend an attentive ear to gossip derogatory to her supplanter. His "Chronicle" portrays a version of the scene of Joseph and Potiphar's wife, though without the triumph of virtue. During the King's absence at Windsor, an elderly lady-in-waiting, who slept in a room adjacent to that of the Queen, concealed the young man, an accomplished performer on the virginals, in a cupboard. When the other ladies had retired to bed, she brought Mark naked into the Queen's room where he hid bashfully behind the bed curtains. As soon as the old lady retired, "Anne went to the back of the bed and grasped the youth's arm, who was all trembling, and made him get into bed. He soon lost his bashfulness and remained that night and many others." Anne's other admirers were presumably introduced by the same obliging *entrepreneur*.

This may have been a fanciful picture, but would seem to be nearer the truth than Miss Strickland's determined advocacy might suggest. The King apparently believed in Anne's infidelity, and it seems to have been a severe blow to a man of such intense physical vanity. For in spite of the fact that he was unbecomingly stout, and was probably almost completely bald, for he was never portrayed without his head being covered with a velvet cap, he must have still seen himself as the brilliant and attractive figure that he had been in his twenties.

Whether he ever again inspired physical love in any of the women he subsequently married is rather doubtful, but that he was deeply in love with Jane Seymour is abundantly clear. Her evident reluctance to marry him would seem to show that her feelings were cooler than had been those of Catherine, or probably those of Anne, though the latter's were closely entangled with personal ambition.

In any case Jane's gentle opposition had no chance of prevailing against the domineering character of her royal lover, and on 30th May 1536, when Anne's decapitated body had been only eleven days in its coffin, the marriage took place privately "in the Queen's closet at York Place". The sixteen months which the marriage lasted were a period of complete conjugal happiness for Henry, and his grief when Jane died on 24th October 1537, twelve days after giving birth to Prince Edward, was profound. Jane was buried in St. George's Chapel, Windsor, with a royal pomp, perhaps in posthumous compensation for the fact that she had never had the privilege of coronation; and also in gratitude that she had provided the male heir for which, during the past quarter of a century, he had so passionately wished, and which had been so distractingly withheld.

6   Henry VIII with his father, Henry VII

*From the cartoon attributed to Hans Holbein the Younger*

7   Elizabeth I
*From the painting by Marcus Gheeraerts the Younger*

Henry's character was not one to remain indefinitely darkened by sorrow, and within eighteen months the French Ambassador was reporting that the King's spirits had revived. "He now gives himself up to amusement", he wrote, "going to play every night upon the Thames, with harps, chanters, and all kinds of music and pastime. He evidently delights now in painting and embroidery, having sent men to France, Flanders, Italy and elsewhere for masters of this art."

This extract illuminates the most agreeable aspect of the King's complex character—his interest in the promotion of the arts. He must have been aware that England, of which his Court was the cultural centre, fell behind France in its artistic development. François I, always his rival, had founded the schools of Amboise and Fontainebleau for the study of painting, sculpture, and architecture; he had even persuaded the illustrious Leonardo da Vinci to come to the former, and there spend his last years.

Henry, by the force of his own personality, had gathered the cultural, as well as the spiritual, leadership of the country into his own hands, and it was a condition which was never exactly to recur in the history of this country. The King had no prejudice against foreigners or foreign ideas, and in this direction he was unlike many of his subjects. Visitors from the Continent were made welcome at Court, and the King was sympathetically inclined towards their tastes and fashions. It was thus through the medium of the Crown that the arts of the Renaissance were made familiar to the English nobility; but even with the royal example in view, the Renaissance made only a slow advance against the rigid and insular ideas held by the majority of the literate people in the country.

It was difficult to persuade the great Continental masters to come to this backward island, but Henry was not altogether unsuccessful. Early in his reign Torrigiano, the Florentine sculptor, had modelled the splendid monument to his father which still adorns the Henry VII Chapel at Westminster, but perhaps even more important in the history of English art was the arrival of Hans Holbein, the younger, on these shores. This genius, who was both painter and architect, was instrumental in introducing the arts of the Renaissance, and it is to him that we owe our knowledge of Henry's appearance from middle age onwards. The full-scale cartoon, now in the National Portrait Gallery, for the fresco in Whitehall Palace is an admirable example of Holbein's twin arts: in front straddles the massive figure of the King, while his father—a posthumous portrait—stands on a step behind him. The background consists of a sumptuous niche flanked by pilasters supporting a deep frieze, and the whole is decorated in the richest Renaissance taste.

This drawing dates from 1537, the year after Holbein had been appointed court painter to Henry VIII; and from this time forward till his death six years later he was industrious in drawing the likenesses of the important figures who thronged, like fascinated moths, round the dangerous flame of royal favour. Holbein's pencil brings reality to many who would otherwise be no more than names, and names remembered principally for the tragedy of their violent deaths.

In the year following the death of Jane Seymour, and perhaps as a distraction to his genuine if short-lived sorrow, Henry began the building of the fabulous palace of Nonsuch. It might have been supposed that there were already a sufficient number of royal residences in the neighbourhood of London; but these all lay either on the banks or in the valley of the Thames, and perhaps, during the twenty-three years since Cardinal Wolsey had been directed to Hampton for its salubrity, Henry had found that an elevated site was more propitious to his no longer very healthy body. There may have been a further reason: none of the existing palaces was designed in a style which could credibly be called that of the Renaissance. There was nothing which could compare to François I's vast *château* of Chambord.

Thus on rising ground twelve miles south of Westminster, Henry began his great new palace, a true emblem of Tudor pride and the ostentatious product of a new and vigorous dynasty. The village of Cuddington was demolished, and in place of the humble peasant dwellings there arose a singular version of a building in the Renaissance style, a building which the architects of Italy would barely have recognised as being inspired by the classical structures of their country. The main body of the Palace indeed, with its circular corner towers, was a hybrid between the vernacular English style and the manner of the *châteaux* standing in the valley of the Loire; but the plaster decoration which enlivened the timber-framed upper part of the house was created by Italian craftsmen in the full exuberance of the Renaissance spirit.

Perhaps Henry hoped to entertain his next bride in this glamorous palace, but in the event the structure was still unfinished at the time of his death, and there is little record of the Court spending much time in the incomplete building. Thus the Palace had not reached a condition to play any part in the humiliating fiasco of the arrival of the unfortunate Anne of Cleves.

Stimulated by the glowing reports of the poor lady's looks provided by Thomas Cromwell, which were supported by a miniature specially painted by Holbein, a magnificent reception had been prepared for this paragon of beauty. On 27th December 1539 the Princess landed at Deal, and, escorted by an ever-growing train of nobles and high church dignitaries, she proceeded slowly through Kent to Rochester, where she arrived on the last day of the year and was lodged in the palace of the Bishop.

Henry, who was awaiting his bride impatiently twenty miles away at Greenwich, decided to forestall the arranged programme and to call privately on Anne on New Year's Day in order, as he said to Cromwell, "to nourish love". What should have been a romantic and passionate meeting was a disaster. The King recoiled from this mature woman with her homely, heavy-featured face and clumsy figure, which was in no way helped by the elaborate and unfashionable clothes in which she was decked. Lord Russell, who was present, said "he never saw his highness so marvellously astonished and abashed". Anne's reactions to the King have not been recorded, nor indeed were they a matter of any moment; but it is probable that the appearance of this stout, ill-tempered man was as different from what she had been led to expect as was hers in the eyes of her future husband.

Never before in the course of his life had this singularly headstrong man been so violently thwarted; but his desperate efforts to find some legal means to avoid the marriage were in vain, and the whole magnificent performance of Anne's reception at Greenwich, which Henry had planned on the most sumptuous lines with troupes of nobles and horsemen in brilliant array, had to be carried through. In the presence of this great concourse, Henry felt obliged to play up to his public and to greet his consort with an appearance of pleasure; and at least he must, as always, have derived great pride from being the central and most vivid figure, in his velvets, satins, and jewels, in the glamorous pageant he had devised. His physical aversion to Anne, however, persisted; six months after the wedding means were found of annulling the marriage; and a week or two later—as a rather well-worn bridegroom—he was united to Catherine Howard.

The empty parade which had been staged at vast expense to welcome "the Flanders Mare" marked the end of the pageantry which had been so spectacular a feature of Court life since the beginning of Henry's reign. The spirit of showmanship, which was one of the King's predominant characteristics during the greater part of his life and had gained him great popularity with the people, was becoming extinguished before the increasing irascibility of his temper. Also, self-deceiving though he was, Henry must have realised that with his swollen and unwieldy body he no longer presented a very heroic or romantic figure amidst the glamour of tournaments and processions.

However, the restless round from one royal residence to another continued and was destined to continue till the end of the King's life. From Whitehall to Greenwich, and thence to Eltham, Hampton Court,

8 The Tower of London, c. 1543

From a drawing by Anthony van Wyngaerde

Oatlands, or Windsor, with occasional excursions further afield to Winchester, Pontefract, or York, the royal train with all the impedimenta of life lumbered about England. But the Court had lost its gaiety and glamour, and in place of the tournaments and jousts the public had to depend for its amusement on the public executions of great nobles. For the King it was a cheaper method of providing entertainment, and probably it was equally acceptable to the populace.

The King's marriage to Catherine Howard, who was then aged about twenty and the most attractive of his wives, must have led the Court to expect some return of the sunshine of earlier years. But for poor Catherine there were few festivities. The marriage took place in private at Oatlands, probably on 22nd July 1540, and there was no coronation. It would almost seem as if Henry, in spite of his infatuation, was not anticipating a very durable alliance. However, although forty-nine and far from healthy, he still hoped for further progeny; and perhaps if Catherine had been fortunate enough to give birth to a child he would have been less ready to consign her to the block after only eighteen months of marriage. As it was, on 13th February 1542, as much on account of the indiscretions of her past as of her present, Catherine was executed on the same spot on which Anne Boleyn had suffered less than six years before, and her body joined the bones of Anne beneath the flagstones of St. Peter ad Vincula.

The failure of this injudicious matrimonial venture combined with increasing pain from ulcers on his legs, which had troubled him intermittently for a number of years, cast Henry into a sombre mood, and the French Ambassador reported that he was "sad, and disinclined to feasting and ladies". All trace of "Merrie England" had indeed faded from Court life. Nevertheless on 12th July 1543 he married Catherine Parr, not presumably still with the hope of children, for his new wife had had none by either of her two previous marriages, but rather as a woman on whose virtue and kindness he could depend. Exercising the self-delusion which had supported him so conveniently through life, Henry considered this only his second marriage, the first being to Jane Seymour: the remainder having been annulled, at least according to his own conscience, were non-existent. Thus, with complacency, he rendered both his daughters illegitimate.

The three and a half years which the marriage lasted till the King's death on 28th January 1547 must have been far from agreeable for Catherine. The King's body became increasingly stout and his ulcerated legs were constantly painful: he was often so immobile that he had to be carried in a chair from room to room, and his temper became even more violent and unpredictable. It might have been supposed that the position of a wife so attentive and patient as Catherine would have been unassailable. But on the contrary it was rumoured that Lord Chancellor Wriothesley had endeavoured to persuade the King to commit her to the Tower on a charge of heresy. It seems remarkable that Henry, to whom the imprisonment of his wives came so easily, should have refused.

The restless journeyings continued, and in November 1546 the King was at Windsor, then at Hampton Court, and in the following month he stayed at Oatlands. At the beginning of the new year, however, he returned to Whitehall, and this was his last journey, for at 2 a.m. on 28th January he died aged fifty-five years and seven months.

# Chapter 3

# EDWARD VI

In the long line of English monarchs, Henry VIII stands out as one of the great figures, and this is due more to the vigour of his personality than to his success as a ruler. He certainly achieved the first of his conscious objectives, to enhance the position of England in international affairs; but in internal matters he was far less successful, and the thirty-eight years of his reign brought little prosperity to his country. Indeed on his death England was in a state of religious and financial chaos. The church was menaced by a rising wave of protestantism, while the treasury had never fully recovered from the thoughtless extravagance of his early years. Moreover, his heir was only ten years old, and his accession stirred little of that united enthusiasm amongst the people that had shone so brilliantly after the death of Henry VII.

In the event, the six rather tragic years of Edward VI's reign were dominated by the struggle for power between the Dukes of Somerset and Northumberland, with the final victory for the latter; and it was against a complex background of intrigue and deceit that the young King's character had to develop. At an age when a boy in normal circumstances would have had no cares, Edward was brought in contact with any number of problems and difficulties culminating in the trial and execution of his uncle Somerset. The latter event, however, seems to have left him strangely unmoved, and in his journal he merely noted the loss of his near relative and guardian without adding a single word of sorrow. The definite personality which was emerging in the youth is shown in Hester Chapman's study of *The Last Tudor King*; but at a time when his characteristics were becoming more marked, he entered into that period of alternating illness and partial recovery, which after several months ended in his painful death on 6th July 1553 at the age of sixteen.

In spite of this early death, Edward had already shown two marked traits which were directly inherited from his father—his love of pageantry and a will of unusual determination in one so young. Whether, if he had lived, the self-will and craftiness of the Tudor strain, or the rashness and arrogance which led to the rise and fall of the Seymour family, would have predominated must remain an interesting speculation.

It is clear that during the last year or two of his life he was becoming restive under the opposition which he often met in private from his advisers, and which contrasted so markedly with the exaggerated ceremony with which he was treated in public. The latter was no doubt expressly insisted on by Northumberland in order to maintain the prestige of the Crown, although it was set on so young a head. To the English, accustomed to the Tudor tradition, the formality of Court life appeared natural, but to foreigners it seemed incredible, indeed humiliating, that even the greatest noble should drop on to his knee each time he was addressed by the boy King.

The Florentine Ambassador, Ubaldini, was positively shocked at the inequality of status which existed between the royal Princesses, Mary and Elizabeth, and their brother when they dined at the royal table. The Princesses were not allowed chairs, but only benches, and these had to be carefully set so far from the head of the table that they were not beneath the canopy which covered the King. Furthermore they had to make constant obeisance before they took up their humble positions. "I have seen the Princess Elizabeth drop on one knee five times before her brother ere she took her place", wrote the Ambassador, no doubt mentally contrasting this excessive ceremonial with the more straightforward manners to be found at the courts of the great monarchs of Europe.

However, this elaborate etiquette was not of Edward's creating, and death came too soon for him to have imprinted his personality on his surroundings, his advisers, and his friends, so that Court life as embraced in this survey did not properly exist, and one must pass on to the austere régime of his successor.

# Chapter 4

# MARY I

Few royal children can have had a more bewildering upbringing than the two daughters of Henry VIII. At one moment they would be treated as royal princesses, and be afforded all the ceremony of high rank; at another their stock would slump disastrously on the social scale, and they would be looked on as no more than inconvenient royal bastards. Their father's affection likewise was singularly vacillating, while the attitude of their diverse stepmothers varied from intense hostility to a very genuine love. Furthermore, sometimes one would be in favour, sometimes the other: quite often both lay beneath a dark cloud of hostility, and occasionally both would emerge simultaneously into the golden sunshine of their proper status.

In spite of their difference in age—Mary was born on 18th February 1516, Elizabeth not until seventeen and a half years later—it might have been expected that these violent vicissitudes of fortune would have forged a close link between them; but this was never so, and they remained throughout Mary's life of an oil-and-water incompatibility. Mary never overcame the hatred and contempt she had felt for Anne Boleyn who had supplanted her royal mother in the matrimonial bed, while Elizabeth was always aware of the superiority of her mental equipment to that of her rather dull-witted sister. Both had inherited a full measure of their father's personal pride and self-will.

Mary's birth at Greenwich had of course been acclaimed with popular enthusiasm, and her christening, which took place at the church of the Grey Friars at Greenwich three days later, was solemnised with a pomp suitable for the first surviving child of Henry and Catherine. The silver font generally used for royal baptisms was hastily brought from Canterbury Cathedral, while amongst the royal and noble godparents was the plebeian but highly influential figure of Cardinal Wolsey. The infant Princess's life was given a brilliant opening.

Mary grew into a girl of agreeable appearance. She was slight in stature, had pleasant features, and she had inherited the pale skin which had been so highly rated in her father when he was a young man. One of her notable features was her long blond hair which her father greatly admired, and to which with paternal pride he would draw attention. A Venetian diplomat wrote that on one occasion the King took off the little Princess's cap in order to show her "profusion of silver tresses as beautiful as ever seen on human head". While she was young there was little sign of that tight-lipped, bigoted look which clouded her face after she ascended the throne. In temperament she was reasonably cheerful and gay; she possessed her father's love of music in full measure, and was an accomplished performer. In addition she was unexpectedly fond of jewellery and fine clothes.

Thus, in all, Mary was a princess of average attraction, and as the daughter of an important monarch was a desirable candidate in the marriage market. She did not lack suitors. Don Luiz of Portugal, and the Margrave of Brandenburg—the first a Catholic, the second a Protestant —had been proposed as possible husbands; and to a marriage with Don Luiz Mary had consented. But the negotiations petered out largely owing to the uncertainty of Mary's value as a political counter. A later potential suitor was the ambitious Thomas Seymour, the brother of the Protector. The Dowager Queen Catherine Parr, whom he had married within a few months of Henry VIII's death, died in childbirth in 1548, and Seymour then conceived the idea of raising his career to the highest summit by securing the hand of one of the Princesses. His preference was naturally for Elizabeth, then an attractive girl of fifteen, but his boisterous advances had not been rewarded, and he turned his attentions to Mary who had the advantage of being the immediate heir apparent to the throne. He tactfully chose music as a suitable channel of approach, and suggested that since the Princess had been deprived of her favourite pastime while staying with her brother at St. James's Palace, where no music was allowed, she might welcome the services of his own musician, Walter Earle, to give her lessons in playing the virginals. When Seymour was arrested soon after making this graceful overture, Earle was closely examined as to whether he had not been instructed to combine his lessons with subtle praise of his master.

The accession of her brother to the throne did little to improve Mary's position, and her personal security as well as her prospects remained as uncertain as during her father's reign. When Edward's health began to fail and the likelihood of his reaching maturity and begetting an heir became doubtful, she may well have suspected that Northumberland, in spite of his veneer of goodwill, was devising a scheme to deprive her of her right to the throne under Henry VIII's will. Her friends warned her to suspect Northumberland's cordiality, and to give small credence to his encouraging reports about the King's health.

On 4th July 1553, she received a summons to come to Greenwich to see her brother, but when she reached Hoddesdon two days later she was given a secret message that Edward was dead. Northumberland had hoped to keep the King's death secret, and had Mary continued her journey unwarned there is little doubt what her fate would have been.

Fully aware of her danger, Mary at once turned eastward and travelled swiftly to her house at Kenninghall in Norfolk, whence she moved a few days later for greater security to the strongly fortified castle of Framlingham. Then opened one of the periods in Mary's life—there was to be another a few months later—which showed the remarkable reserve of fortitude that lay within her repressed personality. The unhappy and subjugated life which she had led can have provided little training for action, and yet at this moment of extreme crisis in her life she not only overcame extraordinary difficulties and dangers with prudence and courage, but was also able to promote enthusiasm for her person and her cause.

Whatever may have been her fears during her brother's lifetime, the double shock of hearing of his death, which she had not been led to expect, and also that he had bequeathed the crown to Lady Jane Grey, brought to the surface qualities which otherwise might have remained latent. After burning brightly for a short while, this noble spirit was to be quenched by the sorrows and bigotry of the greater part of her short reign.

The anxiety felt by Mary during her first days at Framlingham must have been intense. The Catholics of Norfolk had flocked at once to her support, but these alone could have done little against Northumberland backed by the authority of the Council. However, good fortune was at hand. Six ships had been sent to Yarmouth to intercept Mary had she attempted flight to the Continent, but the captains and crews came over to her side, and their example was soon followed by the towns of Norwich, Yarmouth, and Colchester.

From East Anglia enthusiasm for Mary swept westwards across England to London; and Northumberland, who had reached Cambridge with a large body of troops, found himself bereft of support and was presently arrested. On the last day of July, Mary left Framlingham for London, and on 3rd August entered the City on her way to the Tower accompanied by a procession of 700 gentlemen in suits of velvet riding before her, and with Princess Elizabeth and her ladies, and a troop of a thousand horsemen with spears and guns following behind. Thus in triumph she reached the palace-fortress where her young rival and her husband were already imprisoned.

The national enthusiasm for Mary was said to have exceeded even that shown for her father on his accession. Henry was a glamorous youth and also an adept at sustaining the devotion of the people; but Mary, a woman of thirty-seven and in poor health, had neither the qualities nor the strength to present herself as a popular idol once the first burst of joy was past. Nevertheless she had inherited enough of her father's spirit of showmanship to know that a splendid coronation was called for, and that this would add greatly to the security of her position; it would also raise her credit with the Continental states. There was, however, an unfortunate difficulty in carrying out this desirable scheme: no money was available. It was a condition which was to inhibit Mary's activities throughout her reign; but on this occasion the deficiency was remedied by a loan of £20,000 from the merchants of the City.

Fortified by this substantial contribution, preparations for the ceremony went forward. There had been many splendid coronations in the past; but tradition provided no exact precedent for this occasion, for Mary was the first queen regnant in English history to be crowned. The only other queens by right since the Conquest, Matilda and Elizabeth of York, had not been accepted as regnant. However, the plans followed as far as possible the customary lines.

Leaving St. James's Palace for Whitehall on 28th September she entered the royal barge at Whitehall steps and, accompanied by Elizabeth and a retinue of ladies, was rowed slowly downstream to the Tower. As was usual on such occasions, a great procession of decorated boats followed the Queen, conveying the important functionaries of the Court and the City, while barges containing the public provided a cacophony of music and singing. Her entry into the precincts of the Tower was signalised by the inevitable ear-splitting cannonade from within the walls. These crude sounds of rejoicing must have been bitter hearing for Jane Grey in her prison room.

Two days later, on 30th September 1553, Mary set forth in grand procession through the streets of the City for her coronation at Westminster, following the same route as her enemy, Anne Boleyn, just twenty years earlier. Mary's parade was, if possible the more spectacular. She drove in a chariot drawn by six horses with trappings of red velvet and was attended by 70 ladies and 500 gentlemen, including the foreign Ambassadors, on horseback. Triumphal arches spanned the streets. The conduits at Cornhill and Cheapside ran with wine, and perhaps stimulated the bursts of song which greeted her at several points along the route.

The two occasions, with two such divergent principal actors, had an unexpected feature in common. While all the prepared display of rejoicing was there, with banners and decorated houses, singing children and music, there was a marked lack of warmth in the popular acclaim of both Queens. Anne may have anticipated jealousy and hostility; but to Mary, whose entry into London less than two months earlier had been greeted with delirious enthusiasm, this fickle change of heart must have seemed inexplicable and sadly chilling.

But the dissensions which were to continue throughout the five years of her reign had already begun. The Catholics despised her clemency to the supporters of Jane Grey, while those who had escaped the axe felt no gratitude for their lives but only a sense of grievance for the heavy fines which the Queen, in pursuance of her grandfather's prudent purse-filling plan, had imposed. The populace might have felt warmer loyalty for the Queen if a large number of public executions had been provided for their amusement.

However, the coronation ceremony passed off with the traditional splendour and without any untoward incident. The chancel of Westminster Abbey was hung with tapestry and the floor was strewn with rushes. Across these, on a boarded pathway, the Queen in a crimson robe, and followed by Princess Elizabeth and Anne of Cleves, here making one of her rare *sorties* from her comfortable retirement, accompanied by a retinue of ladies, walked in procession to her seat on a dais covered with cloth of gold. The splendid ceremony was conducted with its usual magnificence in the presence of a throng of bishops and noblemen, and the Queen received the orb and two sceptres as both King and Queen, while in her capacity of the former she was girt with a sword and had golden spurs bound to her heels. Amidst this brilliant crowd, however, several important figures were noticeably absent: the Archbishop of Canterbury and a number of other prominent bishops had been lodged in prison.

The absence of these eminent ecclesiastics must have cast a slight chill on the proceeding, and have drawn attention to the dissension which the whole of the congregation knew to be seething below the veneer of loyal pageantry; and yet to the many who rated the pleasures of life higher than religious convictions, the advent of a new monarch gave promise of new gaiety and entertainment. The Court of King Edward had been conducted on lines of austere, almost puritanical simplicity; but Mary, in the sudden radiance of her new position, gave way to the love of finery and splendour which was such a surprising feature of her character. For all her adult life it had been suppressed: after a brief flowering it was to wither in the chill wind of trouble and ill-health.

The sombre colours, the subdued tones of the boy King's court were cast away, and Mary and her ladies appeared in dresses of the brightest shades. This predilection was observed by the Spanish Ambassador, who tactfully suggested to his Queen that she should send Mary gifts of "ribbands, collars, sleeves and other fal-lals, since she takes more pleasure in clothes than almost any woman alive". The halls of St. James's Palace, the royal residence which she frequented by preference, rang with the music of which she was so passionately fond, and for a few months life was imbued with a high-spirited and innocent gaiety. For the Queen, partly as a result of the restricted life she had led, had a simple, almost childish mentality. Her knowledge of the ways of the world was very slight, and her understanding of broad language so vague that she had to be reproved by one of her ladies for repeating a word she had heard used by the Lord Chamberlain, as being entirely unsuited to the lips of a queen.

Had her grasp of political affairs been a little more extended, her comprehension of public sentiment more developed, she would perhaps have eschewed the Spanish marriage which was to have such a baneful effect on her reign and on her character. In spite of her thirty-seven years, Mary's thought on her accession turned at once to matrimony. At last she was in a position to choose a husband for herself, a man who would bring comfort to her bleak life and enable her, as she optimistically hoped, to bear a Catholic heir. That Philip was her own choice, she was simple enough to suppose; but in fact Charles V's Ambassador had introduced his master's project into the Queen's mind so subtly that she believed the idea to be her own. Once she learnt that Philip showed no reluctance, the strongest opposition would not turn her from the marriage.

And opposition there indeed was. As soon as rumours of the proposed alliance began to circulate, it became clear that both the Council and Parliament viewed it with intense disfavour; only the merchants, who foresaw an increase in profitable trade in the close union with the Low Countries that the marriage would promote, showed approval. The people of the country shared the views of Parliament: the Queen's husband would be King, England would be ruled by a Spaniard, and would become no more than a dependency of Spain—a parallel to Burgundy or Flanders—and if Mary and Philip produced a son the political complications might well become almost insoluble.

But the Queen was not deflected by any thoughts of these difficulties. A Catholic suitor, the most eligible match in Europe, had come into her loveless life, and was offering her his hand with apparent enthusiasm. It would have required a strength of mind far beyond what she possessed to reject this brilliant chance of happiness. The fact that Philip was eleven years her junior and, before the marriage was mooted, had addressed her as "my beloved aunt", and furthermore that they had never seen each other, seems to have caused her no anxiety. She was determined on the project, and that obstinate expression which was soon to settle on her features must have been constantly at this time to the fore. All her English advisers discouraged the plan, and even her trusted cousin Cardinal Pole recommended her to remain single—perhaps bearing in mind that he had once been looked on by some as a suitable husband for the Queen. Since he had never taken the vows of priesthood there would have been no legal bar to the marriage. However, the letters of Charles V extolling the charms of his son and the benefits of marriage gave her comfort and support, while Simon Renard, Charles's Ambassador, was always at hand to give her encouragement in overcoming every hindrance.

The opposition felt throughout the country took an active form in the simultaneous outbreak of no less than four insurrections, but of these only that in Kent under the leadership of Sir Thomas Wyatt assumed proportions dangerous to the Queen. Wyatt and his troops reached the outskirts of London; but Mary, with the same fortitude she had shown at the time of her brother's death, refused to seek safety in the country, and instead rode into the City and delivered a rousing speech, in the presence of the Lord Mayor and Aldermen, to a great crowd of citizens begging for their support against the rebels. She then returned to Whitehall and prepared for the siege she anticipated.

This did not materialise for several days, for her timely oratory had brought the City to her support, and Wyatt found London Bridge barred against him. He therefore moved upstream, crossed at Kingston, and advanced on London from the west. Along Knightsbridge he came with his troops, on to the slopes above St. James's Palace, and so on to Charing Cross. Meanwhile within Whitehall Palace there was considerable confusion. The Queen remained calm, but her ladies, as well as many of the courtiers, were in a state of panic. A vivid account of the scene has been left by that engaging figure, Edward Underhill, known as the Hot Gospeller, who in spite of his Protestantism was one of the Queen's Gentlemen Pensioners. He believed that he was in greater safety while he remained at Court than if he left it, and his reasoning seems to have been sound. Thus on 7th February he found himself in his armour at Whitehall Palace amongst the Papists, ready to defend the building against Wyatt and his troops. The Queen remained "in the Gallery by the Gatehouse", while her supporters, who had been stationed outside the Palace, rushed hastily within the security of the walls, and the gates were closed and barred behind them, "whereat the rebels shot many arrows".

After an interval, during which the varied and ill-organised garrison seem to have given way to terror and despair, some of the bolder spirits decided that mere passive resistance against a small band of archers was a rather ineffective course of action, and they obtained the Queen's permission to open the gates. The garrison, with such show of courage as they could muster, then sallied out, and finding that the rebels had disappeared, marched bravely up and down outside the Palace walls till a message was brought that Wyatt had been captured. The Queen expressed great gratitude to her Gentlemen Pensioners for their valour, and allowed each one to kiss her hand. In addition she made "large promises how good she would be to us: but few or none of us got anything". The Queen, indeed, was in no financial position to distribute largesse very freely.

It transpired that an engagement at Charing Cross had ended the rebellion. Wyatt and his weary men were no match for the Queen's troops under Pembroke, and Wyatt with the other leaders were captured and lodged in the Tower, while his men melted away. The insurrection was over. Had it succeeded, Mary would probably have changed places with Jane Grey and her husband, and the English crown would perhaps have descended in a different line. As it was, the rebellion ensured the execution of Jane, and set Mary firmly on the throne.

Henceforward there was no question but that the Spanish marriage would take place, and an embassy of suitable distinction was sent out to Spain to escort Philip to England. On 12th July 1554 he embarked at Corunna on the *Espiritu Santo*, a Biscayan merchantman, and on the following day with all flags flying sailed for England, and his second venture in matrimony. Mary of Portugal, whom he had married when he was sixteen, had died three years later leaving him with one son. Accompanying the *Espiritu Santo* were the combined fleets of England and Spain.

After a voyage of a week, the ships arrived in the Solent, and on Friday, 20th July, Philip disembarked at Southampton. He was rowed ashore in a magnificent royal barge manned by twenty oarsmen dressed in the Queen's green and white livery, and the barge itself was lined with tapestry and brocade. He was greeted on the jetty by a deputation of nobles, and on the orders of the Queen he was immediately invested by the Earl of Arundel with the Order of the Garter.

During the week-end Philip remained in Southampton, attending Mass on each day, and exchanging gifts with Mary who awaited him at Winchester. Arriving from the torrid heat of Spain, Philip may have anticipated finding in England at least a tepid, northern sunshine. If so, he was disappointed, for throughout his stay in Southampton deluges of rain descended, and on the Monday morning the splendid cavalcade set out for Winchester, ten miles away, to the accompaniment of a "cruel wind and down-pouring rain". Philip must indeed have felt that his filial duty was being excessively tried in undertaking this depressing journey—with an ageing bride at the end of it.

Between six and seven in the evening the drenched *cortège* arrived at the gates of Winchester, where it was met by the Mayor and local dignitaries; thence, to the deafening sound of the prescribed cannonade, the Prince was escorted to the Deanery, where he was lodged. At ten o'clock that evening, dressed in nether-stocks of white and silver, and a superb black velvet robe bordered with diamonds, he made his way on foot across the Deanery garden to the adjacent bishop's palace of Wolvesey, where he had his first interview with the Queen.

Mary and Philip are said to have conversed pleasantly for half an hour, though the Queen spoke little Spanish and the Prince no English; but their true sentiments at this anxious encounter were never disclosed. Neither can have seen any physical beauty in the other. The Queen's poor health was already showing in her appearance, and the freshness of youth had long since vanished, while Philip was meagre in stature with a large, oddly shaped head, thinly covered with sandy hair; his face was pale, and his small eyes were blue and weak. He was in no way a heroic figure, even in his sumptuous clothes. But he was heir to the greatest kingdom in Europe, and Mary was in no state to be captious or disappointed.

Two days later, on the festival of St. James, the patron saint of Spain, the wedding took place in the Cathedral. Before the ceremony began it was announced that Charles V had handed over the Kingdom of Naples to his son, so that Philip and Mary could be married on terms of equality as a king and a queen. The four-hour service proceeded with full ceremony and splendour, and was conducted by Stephen Gardiner, the bishop of the diocese. It was an occasion on which the Queen's love of fine clothes could be indulged with every justification, and nothing seemingly could have been more splendid than her wedding gown. That it was a matter of putting rather old wine into a new bottle in no way daunted her. Her robe was richly brocaded on a gold ground, and the long train was sewn with pearls and diamonds; beneath this she wore a dress of white satin embroidered with silver, and on her head was a coif bordered with diamonds; her shoes and *brodequins* were scarlet. On her breast she wore the exquisite diamond which had been sent to her by Philip on their betrothal.

After the wedding had been solemnised Mary and Philip, with a brilliant company of bishops and courtiers, repaired to Wolvesey, where in the great hall, which was hung with arras for the occasion, a magnificent banquet was set out. Every possible attempt was made to impress the young bridegroom with the opulence of the country into which he was marrying. Gold plate both for use and for ornament gleamed on the tables, musicians discoursed gentle music from the gallery, and during an interval in the repast heralds proclaimed a Latin oration in praise of matrimony.

Behind this display of splendour and gaiety, the discord, which persisted throughout Mary's reign, was growing even in close proximity to the royal couple. Edward Underhill, who had not abandoned his post in the Queen's entourage and had come to Winchester for the festivities, was exchanging sharp words with Master Norreys, the Catholic usher, in the Chamber of Presence at Wolvesey. After almost coming to blows, Norreys vowed he would get the Queen to dismiss this heretic from his post, but in the event the threat did not materialise and Underhill remained, and was able to benefit by a custom usual on a happy occasion such as this:

> "The second course at the marriage of a King is given unto the bearers; I mean the meat, but not the dishes, for they were of gold. It was my chance to carry a great pasty of a red deer in a great charger, very delicately baked. . . . The which pasty I sent unto London, to my wife and her brother."

In the brief happiness of the first months of her marriage, perhaps the first true happiness Mary had ever known, she was able to forget the dissension which continued to distract her country. At last she was able to share the responsibility of ruling an obstinate people, a task which during the past twelve months she had found an intolerable burden. She modelled her way of life to some degree on the lines of her father's Court, and at first adopted his restless habit of moving constantly from one residence to another. A day or two after the marriage, the royal couple went from Winchester to Basing House in the north of the same county, and thence to Windsor, Richmond, Southwark, Whitehall, and so to Hampton Court, where Mary and Philip remained quietly in retirement for a time as a mark of respect for the death of the Duke of Norfolk. The gates of the Palace were closed, and no longer was the populace able to walk freely into the courtyard. This gave great offence, and was naturally attributed to the influence of the Spanish Prince.

When the Court mourning, which had so happily prolonged the honeymoon, was over, Mary and Philip returned to Whitehall, and here in November a great tournament was arranged, the last to be held in England—except the Eglinton Tournament, that frustrated attempt to re-create in 1839 the Age of Chivalry in an age of mackintoshes and umbrellas. The purpose of the festivities of November 1554 was to celebrate the return of Cardinal Pole to England, and it also gave the English and Spanish courtiers an opportunity to unite in the friendly rivalry of jousts.

Philip's presence brought a new life to Mary's Court. The restricted English atmosphere gave way to a sophisticated international style introduced by the notable figures from the diverse countries which made up the Spanish dominions. There was the Duke of Alva, who was later to exercise his latent cruelty on the Protestants of the Low Countries, with his Duchess; there were the romantic and handsome figures, Count Egmont and Count Horn, who were to be the victims of Philip and Alva on account of their Protestant faith; there was Ruy Gomez, afterwards the celebrated Prime Minister of Spain; and there were many others of the same quality who for a short while brought a sudden glamour to the quiet English Court.

During the early months of 1555, the Queen's happiness was greatly increased by her conviction that the near-miracle had occurred and that she was to bear a child. In April she retired to Hampton Court to await the event to which she so intensely looked forward. The most elaborate domestic arrangements were made, and a bevy of ladies and midwives was constantly in attendance. A cradle "very sumptuously and gorgeously trimmed" stood ready in the Queen's bedchamber to receive its precious occupant, and women were at hand to nurse the child and to rock it in its handsome little bed.

Meanwhile Parliament petitioned Philip to agree to become regent until the child came of age in the event of the Queen dying in childbirth: to this he graciously consented. For two months the whole of England remained in a state of intense expectation, and there seemed to be only a few who questioned the likelihood of a middle-aged woman in poor health giving birth to a living child. The Queen was not amongst those who doubted, but the French Ambassador, Noailles, was, and his opinion brought comfort to his master, Henri II, who dreaded the strengthening of the Anglo-Spanish alliance, which would have been brought about by the birth of an heir.

On the morning of the last day of April the rumour got abroad that the Queen had been safely delivered of a child, and the rumour was soon spread as a certainty. Church bells were rung, shops were shuttered for a holiday, and although it was daylight bonfires were lit; but later in the day the happy news was contradicted, and the period of waiting began again. Throughout the summer months the suspense continued, while the Queen, for much of the time, lay on cushions on the floor of her room trying to ease the pains she was suffering. Until July the doctors continued to tell her that she was with child; but before the month was out the Queen had to accept the melancholy truth. Hastily the Court moved to Oatlands, and all the preparations for the birth were swept away. The women returned to their homes, the cradle disappeared, and Hampton Court was cleansed of all the dirt and garbage accumulated during a royal residence of such unusual length. With this general exodus was extinguished the unfortunate Queen's most cherished hope.

The short spell of happiness which had transformed Mary's austere life was at an end. Philip's affection, which at best was tepid enough, had disappeared, and he was anxious to leave both his ageing wife and a country which was little congenial to him. For a full year he had been away from his own dominion, and only the prospect of fatherhood had delayed him from departing sooner. At the end of August, Mary accompanied him to Greenwich, and thence he set sail for the Low Countries. The Queen was once again alone, bearing the heavy burden of kingship, and with her personality embittered by the sorrows and disappointments of the past few months.

With the departure of Philip, there disappeared from the Court the Spanish element which had done so much to enliven the sober atmosphere which Mary spread around her, and the limited, provincial style returned, increased by the Queen's low spirits and indifferent health. But not all attempts at gaiety were at an end, for in the late summer of 1556 she gave a *fête champêtre* at Richmond Palace in honour of Elizabeth, with whom she was for a time on good terms. The royal barge was sent to conduct the Princess from Somerset House to Richmond, and in it Elizabeth sat in splendour beneath a green silk awning which was garlanded with flowers. Six boats followed the barge, containing the gentlemen attendants who were finely dressed in russet damask and blue satin, with caps of silver cloth decorated with green plumes on their heads. This elaborately dressed party disembarked at the gardens of Richmond Palace, was received by the Queen, and conducted to tables set in a pavilion hung with cloth of gold and purple velvet. After the banquet, the finest minstrels in the country gave an *al fresco* concert, and as darkness descended the Princess was escorted to her barge, and the procession of boats moved downstream back to London.

An exhibition of affection such as this was a rarity in the lives of these two women, and Mary was probably prompted to so unwelcome an entertainment by motives other than sisterly love. It was clear to Mary that no child of hers was to intervene between Elizabeth and the succession to the throne, and she hoped perhaps that a demonstration of benevolence might win Elizabeth over to her faith. It was a sharply contrasting treatment to that meted out to other supporters of the Protestant persuasion, who were suffering the intensest cruelties of persecution.

In the previous January Charles V had abdicated and Philip had succeeded as King of Spain. Had Mary until then harboured any expectation that she would ever see a resumption of a proper married life, these hopes must have ended; and it must have been with mixed feelings that she heard that Philip was coming once again to England in March 1557. She knew that the reason for the visit was political, and was not prompted by any affection for herself. Indeed in the eighteen months since they had seen each other she had become embittered both in character and in looks, and she can have appeared less than ever as a desirable spouse.

The visit was indeed no sentimental journey, but was designed to enlist the help of England against France. In this Philip achieved his purpose, but for the English it led to the loss of their last possessions in France—Calais was captured on 6th January 1558 and Guines surrendered a fortnight later. Having received a promise of support, Philip left England once more on 4th July, and he and Mary were never to meet again.

Their intercourse had not, however, been entirely confined to diplomacy, for after her husband's departure the Queen once again supposed herself to be pregnant, and this delusion persisted into the new year. Throughout the spring of 1558 she expected Philip's return, but in vain. With the beginning of summer all hopes of childbirth passed but her health did not improve, and by August it was clear that she was suffering from dropsy and intermittent fever. In September Cardinal Pole wrote to Philip: "Her hope of ... being soon consoled by your presence, is in fact the best and most efficacious remedy for all her ailments." But Philip responded only by a letter urging Mary to declare Elizabeth heir to the throne, perhaps bearing in mind the possibility of becoming the husband of a second, and younger, Queen of England.

Meanwhile Mary continued to move from one royal residence to another in the hope that a change of locality might relieve the fever which was exhausting her. From Richmond Palace she went to Hampton Court but, finding herself in no way benefited, passed on to St. James's Palace, keeping mistakenly to those low-lying places which were most likely to increase her malady. In addition to her personal sorrow at her separation from Philip, there was little in the condition of the country to cheer her spirits. The people were in a state of despondency, disheartened by epidemics and bad harvests, while the cruel persecutions had engendered bitterness amongst all classes. The Queen was intensely unpopular, and in her illness the people were inclined to pray for her death rather than her survival.

Early in November, Mary realised that her miserable life could not be prolonged, and she was reluctantly persuaded to accept the advice of both her Council and her husband to nominate Elizabeth as her heir. On 8th November the Master of the Rolls, accompanied by the Comptroller, journeyed to Hatfield and announced to Elizabeth that she was to succeed to the Crown, and that the Queen asked for only two conditions—that the old religion should be maintained and her debts be paid.

Having made this last attempt to ensure the perpetuation of her faith, an attempt of whose success she can have had little confidence, she gave up the struggle to live, and early on the morning of 17th November 1558 she died at the age of forty-two years and nine months. Those nearest to the Queen were convinced that her unreturned love for Philip had at least greatly accelerated her death, but there was little public sympathy for her in spite of her sad solitude. Many agreed with John Foxe, the martyrologist, that under no other reign in English history during peacetime had "so much Christian blood, so many Englishmen's lives been spilled . . . as under the said Queen Mary".

# Chapter 5

# ELIZABETH I

It was a strange coincidence that the lives of the two principal monarchs of the Tudor dynasty should have been dominated by the problem of matrimony. The public and private lives of both Henry VIII and Elizabeth for the greater part of their reigns were obsessed by the question of the conjugal state, while the archives of the Courts and the despatches of foreign envoys are devoted to a vast extent, an extent even greater than that of purely political affairs, to the fascinating and supremely intriguing question of the monarchs' matrimonial intentions.

The attitude of Henry was translucently clear: he was an uxorious man, and he passionately needed children, and above all a son, to solidify the position of the Tudor line. The extraordinary and far-reaching events which devolved from these simple instincts were largely fortuitous. Henry never consciously used his marriages as a counter in international affairs, yet they affected his relations with foreign powers more drastically than could have any dynastic match.

With Elizabeth the position was different. She realised as soon as she ascended the throne, as she had doubtless divined long before, that the question of her marriage deeply interested all the great Continental powers, as well as being of paramount importance to the people of England. No sooner had her coronation taken place than Parliament begged her to consider the matter without delay, while foreign ambassadors thronged the Court, advancing the desirability of some prince of their respective countries. Until Elizabeth was fifty years of age the intrigues and manœuvres continued, with the Queen herself an active participant in the game and becoming with years increasingly adept at keeping the ball in play.

The game was amusing as well as rewarding, but Elizabeth's inner feelings remained hidden. It was as important for her to have children as it had been for her father. The next heir was her cousin Mary Queen of Scots, who would bring Catholicism back to the country and thus probably reopen the religious dissension and persecution which had darkened the reign of Mary I. To a parliamentary delegation which waited on her to urge her to give immediate attention to the question of marriage, she replied: "I am already bound unto a husband, which is the Kingdom of England." It was one of those brilliant but baffling answers in which she excelled, and it brought the audience to an inconclusive end.

But there was truth in her words, she *was* wedded to her country, and it could never be questioned but that she gave up her whole life to its well-being. In only one direction did she fail it, and that was in producing an heir; and there seems little doubt that, however reluctant she may have been to endure any male domination, she would have accepted that risk had she not known she was incapable of child-bearing. It is sometimes suggested that her father's treatment of her mother, and of Catherine Howard who had shown her much kindness, had been so severe a shock to her young mentality that the very thought of matrimony had become invincibly repugnant to her. This complex, had it existed, would probably have shown itself in an antipathy to the opposite sex; but this was far from being the case, and it seems more probable that, while she was mentally drawn towards marriage, she was physically incapable of it. This cruel dissension within herself led to those outbursts of hysteria, so out of keeping with her iron will, and to the mysterious blood-lettings to which her slim and indefatigable body was constantly subjected.

Whatever mental struggles Elizabeth may have endured on the constantly raised question of matrimony, she quickly discovered on her accession how invaluable an asset was her potential marriage; and the clear-cut words, "I shall never marry", which she uttered when young, were transmuted later into phrases of the greatest possible ambiguity. She came to enjoy the game of leading her many suitors to suppose they had some chance of success, and this subterfuge, with her naturally disingenuous character, must have been some recompense for the conjugal happiness which she could never know.

She was a natural actress, and one in whom great intellectual gifts were added to an inborn talent. The contrasts and difficulties of her early life had taught her the necessity for reticence and dissimulation, and that these were sometimes more useful qualities than truth. It might have been expected, when she was suddenly brought from obscurity into the dazzling light which illuminated the holder of the throne, that her early experiences would have made her shy and gauche; but the absolute contrary was the case. On 14th January 1559 when, in magnificent procession from the Tower to Westminster for her coronation on the following day, she made her first appearance before the people of London she carried through her ordeal—for ordeal it must have been—with a grace and gentle dignity which brought the critical populace in enthusiasm to her feet.

9    Elizabeth I in procession to Blackfriars, 9 June 1600
*Detail from the painting by Marcus Gheeraerts the Younger*

10  James I hawking
*From the title-page of "A Jewell for Gentrie", 1614*

11  Nonsuch Palace in the time of James I
*Detail of a painting by David Vinckeboons*

How great an asset are good looks to a new sovereign. Henry VIII had immediately won the hearts of his people by the glamour of his appearance as a young King, and his daughter had inherited a share of his beauty, though in her it had a delicacy and transparency lacking in her father: in neither had it any durable quality. Elizabeth closely resembled her father in colouring, in her pale skin, in her red-gold hair, and also in her aquiline nose. The long oval of her face she inherited from her mother, and it had none of the rather coarse rectangularity of her father's. She was twenty-six years of age at the time of her coronation, and probably in the prime of her good looks; a few years later the thinness of her cheeks and the prominence of her nose was to give her face an austerity which even the flattering portraits of contemporary artists could not entirely conceal. Had there existed in England a sixteenth-century Goya, posterity might have had a clearer insight into how time and temperament had affected the Queen's appearance. But it is improbable, had an artist dared to paint a revealing and truthful portrait, that either he or his canvas would have long survived.

It was a subject on which Elizabeth was extremely sensitive. She was clearly so highly dissatisfied with the representations of her appearance which were available that she ordered a proclamation to be issued forbidding anyone to "draw, paynt, grave or portrayit her Majestie's personage or visage", until such time as the perfect portrait had been painted, which could then be copied by others. The proclamation went on to make it clear that it was not the Queen who took exception to indifferent representations, but "that her Majestie perceiveth that a great number of her loving subjects are much grieved, and take much offence with the errors and deformities allredy committed by sondry persons". In this atmosphere there was obviously no place for a candid royal limner.

However, in 1559 there was softness and charm in the young Queen's face, and dressed in gold brocade with an ermine-lined cape she appeared like a romantic figure from the Arthurian Legends as she was carried in her litter through the narrow, decorated streets from the Tower to the coronation ceremony at Westminster. Although the national exchequer was in a state of depletion, no indication of economy was allowed to mar the magnificence of the procession on this glorious day, and foreign visitors might have deduced from the lavishness of the display that the country was at the height of prosperity. Private wealth certainly existed, and it was this which was partly drawn on for the festivities. It was to be several years before the national finances were soundly based, and this was largely achieved through the Queen's personal astuteness.

In each reign the pre-coronation processions from the Tower to Westminster followed ancient precedent. There were the individual embellishments of the houses in the narrow streets, with carpets, coloured cloths and brocades hanging from the lattice windows and enlivening the sombre timbered elevations. At intervals along the course of the procession highly decorated archways spanned the streets, and here and there some set-piece would be staged—perhaps from beneath the portcullis of some mock mediaeval castle, the piping voices of children dressed as angels would deliver an eulogistic ode of welcome, or there would be a dramatic scene of young girls representing the eight beatitudes, each with a piece of verse to declaim. Children, indeed, on these occasions were much to the fore, singing songs, reciting poems, handing bouquets, and so forth.

But for this procession a novel tableau was staged which may well have caused some embarrassment. In "Gratious street ... a stage was made which extended from one end of the street to the other, richly vaulted with battlements conteining three ports". Holinshed goes on to describe how in the first "port" were seated figures of Henry VII and his Queen Elizabeth, the former being seated in the red rose of Lancaster, the latter in the white rose of York. They were regally dressed and held crowns and sceptres. In the next stage was the robust figure of Henry VIII and by his side the figure—ill-used or erring according to the sentiments of the beholder—of Anne Boleyn. Here indeed was a controversial intrusion, but as the mother of the Princess about to be crowned as Queen, who appeared in the third "port", she could hardly be omitted. From that time forward, however, it seems to have been thought wiser to allow Anne's name to rest in obscurity.

The spirit of showmanship, which had been so highly developed in Henry VIII and had been so effective in raising his personal popularity amongst the common people, had descended on Elizabeth in full degree. But she had a more difficult task than her father in putting it into effect. To stage a spectacle such as the Field of the Cloth of Gold, with the resources of a well-filled Treasury behind one, was not exceptionally difficult: to make a fine parade on a shoe-string—even a string of golden thread—needed far greater subtlety and scheming. The Queen's method, in short, was to make the rich of the country contribute to the support of the Crown, and to the maintenance of a regal way of life, by inducing them to pay for the honour and pleasure of having a royal visit to their houses. In the course of these visits she would be seen during her splendid progresses by the people of the country-side. It amounted almost to a levy on the well-to-do, but was a more agreeable means of emptying their money-bags than by imposing crippling taxes. It soon became apparent, too, to both Englishmen and foreigners that presents, preferably in the form of jewels, were particularly acceptable to the Queen, and were received without demur or embarrassment.

An admirable example of the grace with which she would receive a valuable offering occurred on a visit to Norwich in 1579. She was met by the Mayor, attended by his aldermen, who presented her, to the accompaniment of a fulsome speech, with "a faire standing cup of silver and guilt". Inside the cup was a gratuity of one hundred pounds in gold. The Queen in accepting—not declining—this valuable gift said: "Princes have no need of money: God hath indued us abundantly, we come not therefore, but for that which in right is our own, the hearts and true allegiance of our subjects, which are the greatest riches of a Kingdom." It was a noble sentiment, but one which no one was expected to accept too literally.

Mary, partly owing to ill-health, had been reluctant to make constant changes of residence; but Elizabeth, following as so often in the steps of her father, was constantly moving through the southern parts of her kingdom, and staying as often in the houses of her subjects as in royal residences where the expenses of maintaining the large retinue with which she moved would have to be met from her own resources. But the economic advantages were not the only ones which devolved from this plan: she also by this means came much closer in contact with the people than had her predecessors. The citizens of London had been afforded many opportunities of seeing their ruler in the flesh, but even Henry VIII, who was so conscious of the advantages of personal popularity, had not shown himself to such a wide section of his subjects as Elizabeth.

Her progresses generally followed a very similar pattern. Setting out from one of the royal residences, she and her retinue would pursue a zigzag course through the country-side, seldom travelling very far in a day, and staying two or three nights in each of the houses of various country gentlemen. The people she favoured with her company were by no means always men of great wealth or importance, nor were their houses of great size; but no doubt the humbler the host, the greater the flattery of being privileged to entertain the Queen. By this leisurely and devious course she would reach her ultimate objective, perhaps the Earl of Essex's splendid castle at Kenilworth or the Marquess of Winchester's battlemented house at Basing, where she would make a stay lasting a week or two. Then, by the same slow stages, she would return to Greenwich, Hampton Court, or Windsor.

John Stow, in his continuation of Holinshed's *Chronicles*, describes a progress the Queen made through Kent in the summer of 1586. He explains that his reason for paying particular attention to this journey, which was of no greater significance than any other, arises from his affection for his own county.

"Of which the queenes progresse into that countrie (wherein my selfe was borne and bred, and wherein I have both manie friends and kindred whome this progresse toucheth) I must as well (for the love which I naturallie beare unto it, as for the courtesie I dailie receive in it) leave some memorie to posteritie."

So now a humble member of posterity is taking note of his description, and endeavouring to help in perpetuating his words.

On 14th July the Queen set out from Greenwich on horseback, accompanied by the inevitable train of attendants, and rode nine or ten miles up the valley of the little river Ravensbourne to the market town of Croydon, where she stayed a night or two in the house of the Archbishop of Canterbury. Thence she moved eastward for ten miles across Bromley Common to the hamlet of Orpington to spend three days with Sir Perceval Hart, a former courtier; and so on to Knole, which was then royal property, an easy journey of under eight miles. At Knole Elizabeth remained five days before riding on to pay a double visit to Lord Abergavenny, firstly at his house at Burling, and then at Eridge Castle. For nine days in all she enjoyed the hospitality of Lord Abergavenny, who must have found himself a considerably poorer man at the end of so long a visitation. From Eridge she went on to stay with Thomas Culpeper at Bedgebury, and thence to Hampstead the house of Thomas Gilford who received a knighthood—at no expense to the sovereign—for the trouble to which he had been put.

From Hampstead the royal cortège moved down to the coast to Rye, where the gratified inhabitants affirmed that Elizabeth was the first monarch to visit that ancient port. For three days they basked in the sunshine of the royal presence, and on 14th August the Queen journeyed on to Sissinghurst Castle, where the owner, Richard Barker, was also rewarded with a knighthood. Her next host, Thomas Wootton of Bocton Malherbe, surprisingly refused the favour of the accolade "rather seeking honour by vertue of life"; and "Maister Tufton" at Hetfield, the following stop, was not offered the honour—the general principle being, seemingly, that a knighthood would be given for a stay of three days or longer, but not for a shorter visit. Almost always the Queen would present her host with some little personal possession, which he could treasure for its sentimental rather than its intrinsic worth.

After Hetfield, Elizabeth rested for four days at Westinghanger, a house of her own, before reaching Dover, where she was given a tremendous reception. On the hill above the town she was greeted by John Whitgift, Archbishop of Canterbury, and the Lord Warden of the Cinque Ports, accompanied by a bevy of 300 knights and gentlemen of

12    Queen Elizabeth's Entertainment by the Earl of Hertford at Elvetham, 1591

*From a contemporary print*

Kent. For six days she was splendidly entertained in the town "with delights answerable for the time", and then left for Sandwich, and so to the principal objective of her progress, Canterbury. For fourteen days, which included the anniversary of her fortieth birthday on 7th September, she was the guest of the Archbishop, who provided a series of splendid banquets and amusements for his somewhat exacting patron.

It was after being entertained by a previous Archbishop that the Queen delivered her famous parting broadside at his unfortunate wife. Elizabeth made no secret of her disapproval of the married state in bishops, but she had overcome her prejudice in Matthew Parker's case partly, perhaps, because he had been her mother's chaplain. On the occasion in question the Archbishop and his wife stood together to receive Elizabeth's farewell thanks which she expressed to her host "with gracious and honourable terms". Then turning to his wife her tone altered alarmingly: "And you", she said, "Madam I may not call you, Mistress I am ashamed to call you, so I know not what to call you, but yet I do thank you."—thus placing the blame for the Archbishop's deviation from chaste celibacy squarely on the head of his unlucky spouse.

The cost to the Archbishop of the Queen's visit must have been very great indeed, but from the vast stipends of his office he was fortunately in a better position to support the expense than the majority of the peers of the realm. Not only did His Grace entertain the Queen in a most sumptuous style, but he did not fail to remember to load her with elaborate presents on her departure. These consisted principally of horses and jewels, but also included a magnificent salt made of gold with a large diamond in the lid. Inside the salt were gold coins, and two agates, one finely carved with a portrait—suitably flattering, no doubt—of the Queen, and the other with a representation of St. George killing the dragon. The more important members of the royal entourage also received handsome gifts, and £500 was distributed amongst the officers of the Queen's household.

With this agreeable booty in the bag, the cavalcade started the slow return journey to Greenwich, stopping, as on the outward journey, at a number of country houses *en route*. It was an admirable system for a queen of Elizabeth's temperament, who adored the adulation which she received in full measure for the whole length of her journeys. The sight of their monarch gave infinite pleasure to the country people, and stimulated a loyalty to the Crown which became a great strength to the country. A few country gentlemen may have found themselves in financial straits when the rapacious legion left their houses, but at least there was the expensively earned knighthood, and some little memento

74

to hand down as a family heirloom, with which to console themselves; while the Queen had passed a useful and highly economical holiday, and returned bearing—with luck—enviable additions to her jewellery and treasures.

There was a touch of genius, the brilliance of inspiration, in the conception of the progresses. It was a system by which the glamour of the Court was brought into the countryside at a time when the reverse process presented impossible difficulties. Thus they were as effective in their way as the life which was carried on in the royal palaces in and around the metropolis, and the common people were solidly united in their support of the Crown to a degree which had not been reached in any previous reign. James I's progresses were almost entirely designed for his own and not his people's pleasure, and no subsequent monarch attempted to stabilise the position of the Crown by emulating Elizabeth's example; indeed none of the Stuarts—with the possible exception of Charles II—nor the Hanoverians possessed the character to make the enterprise a success, so that the progresses must be looked on as an individual triumph of the Queen's personality and ability.

The demonstrations of public enthusiasm which greeted the Queen's appearances became increasingly sweet to her. It was a form of flattery even more warming than direct speech; and flattery was a commodity which she demanded from those about her to an astonishing degree. It was not so much compliments on her intellectual abilities that she particularly prized—she was in no need of reassurance on that score—but rather on her physical attractions. This might be looked on as a not unusual feminine weakness, but in Elizabeth it was developed into a complex, and one which became stronger with age. In her later years, when all trace of the ethereal good looks which had charmed the public at the time of her coronation had disappeared, and her face had the frightening appearance of a death's-head, with rouged cheeks and blackened teeth, she would receive the most extravagant compliments on her beauty with the utmost satisfaction. It was indeed a strangely blind spot in one with so incisive and penetrating a mind.

Henry VIII had been a vain man; but physical vanity was far less highly developed in him than in his daughter, and had anyone risked an insincere compliment on his prematurely aged and bloated person he would have received a rough response. But both father and daughter shared a sense of jealousy towards their principal political rival. Henry, as a young man, had wished to be assured that he was a superior physical specimen to François I of France, that he had a more graceful and athletic body, a better turned leg; while Elizabeth was intensely anxious to be told of her superiority to the cousin whom she had never seen, Mary

Stuart. To the embarrassed Sir James Melville, Mary's representative at the English Court, she put the most ingenuous questions about their respective appearances and musical gifts, though she seems to have hesitated to ask directly whether she was more beautiful than Mary. Melville extricated himself from the cross-questioning with considerable aplomb by speaking in highly flattering terms of both ladies, but this was probably not entirely the response for which Elizabeth had hoped.

The contrasts in the Queen's moods were as violent and as unexpected as the contrasts in her character, and a Court dominated by a monarch of such unpredictable behaviour must have been in a constant ferment of uncertainty. The grace and erudition of her speech would give way on the smallest provocation to violent words, coarse abuse, and even blows from the delicate white hand, while the constant vacillation and irresolution in her decisions and the ambiguity of her replies put a burden on her ministers which they found it difficult to support. Nevertheless she was well served, and William Cecil—the patient, industrious Cecil—remained her devoted servant, in spite of the monstrous manner in which she behaved to him on occasions. In Cecil's last illness, the Queen showed that the devotion was not only on the Minister's side: she visited the dying man constantly and helped to feed him when he was unable to do so for himself. For some time after his death she would weep whenever his name was mentioned.

Elizabeth's relationships with those Englishmen to whom she was physically attracted were often on a highly emotional level. Her four principal lovers—if such a word can be used without suggesting that any were admitted to the royal bed—were William Pickering, Leicester, Christopher Hatton, and Essex, and of these it would seem that Hatton was the one who had the most genuine and unselfish love for his mistress. Pickering, "a wise, comely English gentleman", soon disappeared from the scene; but her feeling for Robert Dudley, who was created Earl of Leicester in 1564, lasted from her accession for thirty tempestuous years till Leicester's death in 1588. It was said that the Queen and Dudley had been born on the same day, and certainly they had been acquainted from an early age; but the strong emotional link which joined them for the greater part of the reign did not exist until Elizabeth was on the throne. Their relationship followed no gentle, level path but alternated between heights and depths in a manner which would have been intolerable except to two people to whom an almost hysterical relationship was agreeable. While Dudley still hoped to marry the Queen he behaved with some degree of discretion, but later—in his two clandestine marriages for example—he made little attempt to avoid actions which he knew would enrage his royal mistress. And yet Elizabeth never lost her affection for him and was overwhelmed with sorrow at his death. She kept the last letter he had written to her in a casket at her bedside for the rest of her life.

As a means of maintaining the favour of the Queen, Leicester arranged a magnificent entertainment for her at Kenilworth Castle during her summer progress of 1575. It represented a return for important emoluments amounting to £50,000 which had been bestowed on him—and also, perhaps, was designed to ease the guilt of his conscience on account of his secret marriage, of which the Queen was still in ignorance. It was anyhow fitting that Elizabeth should be entertained at the Castle, for it had been royal property until she granted it to her favourite in the fifth year of her reign.

Leicester had greatly increased the size of the building, and thus was able to house the Queen and her ladies, with forty earls and seventy other important gentlemen, within the Castle. The royal party arrived on 9th July, and the revels continued with little pause for twelve days. The approach to the Castle was lined with a number of dramatic tableaux, and, as the Queen crossed the bridge over the wide moat, a nymph standing on a floating island lighted by torches delivered a long, welcoming poem. At the moment the Queen entered the Castle all the clocks were stopped, and as she reached her chamber cannons were fired and fireworks exploded, making such noise and flame that they could be heard and seen for twenty miles around.

Each day brought new amusements—many cruel, such as bear-baiting, many probably tedious, such as endless pageants and masques—while several mornings were given up to hunting, of which the Queen was passionately fond. Various sights were provided for the royal amusement, such as an Italian tumbler, a local six-year-old fat boy who was five feet tall, a huge sheep; and the Coventry men produced a play which included a realistic "slaughter of the Danes", the knockabout style of which the Queen so greatly enjoyed that she asked for it to be repeated. And so the days passed to the constant accompaniment of music, singing, reciting, dancing, and copious eating and drinking. No other subject, not even the Archbishop of Canterbury and his regrettable concubine, could produce so lavish a diversion, and Leicester, while his secret was kept, remained high in royal favour.

Christopher Hatton was a man of less flamboyant personality, and at the same time a much more profound character. He first entered the Court circle as one of the Gentlemen Pensioners, a sort of royal bodyguard, for which he had been chosen for his height and good looks. His legal abilities came to light later. He soon became an intimate of the Queen, and developed a very real love for her—perhaps the only man who ever did. He was thirty-one, the Queen seven years older and her evanescent beauty was fading, but in Hatton's eyes she was still Gloriana. It seems to have been no feigned passion to help his career; but help it, it indeed did, and with the Queen's warm interest (to put it at its lowest) he quickly climbed to the position of Lord Chancellor, a post for which he was adequately equipped. The depth of feeling he allowed himself to show in his letters was remarkable. "Bear with me, my most dear, sweet lady; passion overcometh me. I can write no more. Love me, for I love you", he wrote. But the Queen's feelings had cooled into a platonic affection. To Hatton, however, Elizabeth remained the one love of his life, and he never married.

Robert Devereux, Earl of Essex, was a very different character. He first came to the Queen's notice in 1587 when he was twenty and Elizabeth was fifty-four. The young man's good looks and agreeable and intelligent address created an immediate effect: before the year was out he had been appointed Master of the Horse. But within a few months his irrepressible self-conceit and the arrogant quality of his character became apparent, so that the Queen, who was accustomed to a humble approach in her courtiers, was more than startled by Essex's lack of deference. "By God's death," she cried, "it were fitting someone should take him down and teach him better manners, or there were no rule with him." However, this was no more than a passing annoyance: the young man was far too attractive to provoke sustained anger in his ageing patron. The quarrel of the first few months set the pattern of their relationship during the whole of Essex's life, with Essex becoming increasingly truculent, and the Queen becoming less ready to forgive as the attraction cooled. The terrible scene in 1598 in a dispute over the appointment of the Lord Deputy in Ireland, when Essex was heard to say "her conditions are as crooked as her carcase", to which the Queen replied with a violent blow on the ear, marked the end of any emotional relationship even on Elizabeth's side. From that time Essex seems to have abandoned all attempt at discretion, and there came, firstly, his sudden return from Ireland against the Queen's express instructions and his equivocal behaviour while there, for which he was tried by a special court but acquitted; and secondly his lunatic plot to raise support in the City of London, to seize Whitehall Palace, and compel the Queen to discharge all her existing advisers. The attempt to provoke a rising was a complete failure, and Essex was condemned and executed on 25th February 1601 without, it would seem, the Queen suffering any great sorrow—perhaps rather relief—at the death of her once intimate friend. The romantic story of the ring seems to have had no basis in fact.

Whether the Queen had ever any intention of marrying any one of the four Englishmen to whom she was obviously so strongly attracted, it is impossible to say: equally her intentions towards the Duc d'Alençon remain an enigma. For ten years, until the year before the Duke's death in 1584, marriage negotiations continued intermittently, while every Court in Europe—including the English—remained in a state of continual anxiety as to the outcome. There seems no doubt that Elizabeth developed a genuine affection for her graceless suitor—her *grenouille*, as she called him—who was twenty-two years her junior. But, as with her sister Mary, distinction of birth compensated for lack of physical beauty, and she was clearly flattered by being courted by the brother of the King of France.

In the spring of 1581 the negotiations seemed at last on the point of fructifying. A large and distinguished embassy set out from France to make a formal offer from Alençon and to receive the Queen's definite acceptance. Tremendous preparations were made for their reception and entertainment at Westminster. Throwing, for once, financial discretion to the winds, the Queen ordered a banqueting room to be erected adjacent to Whitehall Palace at a cost of almost £2,000. It was a vast structure of canvas and glass 330 feet in length, with a roof supported on thirty tall wooden columns. The exterior walls of canvas were painted to look like stone, while the interior was festooned with great swags of artificial foliage and fruits, spangled with gold and set against the rich blue depths of a painted firmament.

Within this gaudy shell a succession of elaborate entertainments took place, designed to impress on the distinguished members of the embassy the importance of the great Queen of England. The banquets were followed by complicated masques and pageants in honour of the Queen, but, if their meaning was clear to the French envoys, their allusions in the long and enthusiastic descriptions of Holinshed are now darkly obscure. At least the envoys seem to have been impressed and to have realised that these rather childish revels were designed to do honour to the important mission which they represented, while the graciousness of Elizabeth gave every expectation that they would bring their negotiations to a quick and successful conclusion.

But in this they were disappointed. To their surprise and chagrin the Queen seemed unwilling even to discuss the matter which was the purpose of their visit, and when pressed would give only evasive and temporising replies, so that eventually after this expensive display the envoys retired baffled to France, with the position about the marriage remaining exactly as when they set out

In spite of this reverse, Alençon did not give up hope of bringing off the match, for which he was clearly eager; and in the following year he came over in person, sailing rather furtively up the Thames to Greenwich with none of the bombast which had attended the abortive embassy. Within two days he had left again, but returned in October of the same year on a more formal visit. Elizabeth was at Richmond, and there Alençon was received with the greatest warmth. He was given rooms in the Palace, and he was constantly in the Queen's company. So intimate did they appear that the despatches of foreign ambassadors were once again enlivened by the spiciest pieces of court gossip, the Venetian Ambassador even reporting that the Queen went to the Duke's room every morning before he was out of bed.

Towards the end of November the Queen and the Court moved to Whitehall, accompanied by the patient Alençon, who was lodged in a part of the Palace known as the garden house. A few days later she told the French Ambassador that she and Alençon were definitely to marry, and in token of this she kissed the Duke on the lips, and they exchanged rings. The Ambassador was overjoyed, and immediately informed the French king that after a decade of effort the desired objective had at last been achieved, and that the Spanish King, who had always opposed the match, had been outwitted. But he spoke too soon: the Queen advanced only to retreat; and so the farce continued with Elizabeth blowing first hot then cold, and mingling protestations of love with offers of help for Alençon's campaign in the Netherlands—both of which remained unfulfilled—until almost the day of the Duke's death in Paris on 11th June 1584. The Queen was then fifty years of age, and it was no longer possible to renew the delightful farce, of engaging in a political marriage, which she had played with such pleasure and success for the past quarter of a century.

Almost from the day of her accession as a friendless princess, the greater part of whose life had been passed in a dark and shadowy world of danger and seclusion, Elizabeth diffused a romantic glamour which remained with her for the whole of her turbulent life. It was a glamour which radiated from her remarkable personality, and infected the Court, the Ministers, and to some degree the country as a whole. It stemmed probably from her conviction of her divine right to Kingship. Though indecision was an inherent, and often useful, characteristic of her political dealings, there was not an iota of indecision about her confidence in the justice of her own position. There may have been murmurs about the legitimacy of her birth, and the intriguing Queen of Scots might claim to be the true holder of the Crown, but neither of these considerations gave her even a momentary doubt about her absolute right to the throne.

Elizabeth realised, as fully as had her father, that it was essential for the unity of England that the Court should be the hub round which the country revolved, and that to achieve this it was necessary to attract the greatest possible number of the nobles and important gentry into its orbit. In this she was highly successful. Not only was the Court the centre of fashion and culture, but it was—in the person of the Queen— also the bountiful source of material benefits. Henry VIII had been able to keep important subjects loyal and devoted by distributing the spoils of the monasteries. This invaluable cornucopia was now empty; but nevertheless an extraordinary number of sinecures and emoluments remained in the gift of the Queen, while the distribution of tracts of Crown lands and the granting of wardships of rich minors almost equalled in value the ecclesiastical spoils, and were very profitable to the recipients. But there was unfortunately a limit to the available rewards, and towards the end of her reign, as the prizes became rarer and less valuable, the devotion of the courtiers noticeably cooled.

And yet the Queen was remarkably successful in surrounding herself with a golden haze of sovereignty, and retained an astonishing personal *panache* until almost the end of her days. This is clear from contemporary records, but few accounts of the Queen and the life of her Court seem quite to catch this elusive quality of grandeur. Innumerable poets dedicated their works to the Queen, but the flattery they indulged in was so fulsome that all effect of creating a genuine picture was defeated; while the descriptions written by Holinshed and Stow of Court amusements and the appearance of the Queen at these revels are so long and complex, and so fawning to the sovereign, that they seem to have little connection with reality. A different aspect of Court life, however, is disclosed when John Harington, of whom more will be said later, writes of the "ill breeding with ill feedinge, and no love but that of the lustie god of gallantrie, Asmodeus". But this sour view seems to have been transitory, as he remained a fairly constant frequenter of the royal sphere; though his wife was left at his Somersetshire home, presumably so as to have no contact with the demon destructive of matrimonial happiness.

Perhaps the most revealing descriptions of the Elizabethan Court come from foreign observers, who brought a fresh and objective eye to the scene and accepted no ceremony as so natural as not to merit recording. Such a one is Paul Hentzner, a German who came to England in 1598, apparently as tutor to a young nobleman of his country. Through the influence of a friend, he received permission from the Lord Chamberlain to come to the presence chamber at Greenwich Palace and watch the Queen pass through to her chapel. Greenwich was always the favourite palace of Elizabeth: here she had been born on 7th September 1533, and throughout her life she spent as much time as possible—particularly the summer months—here, by the tidal waters of the Thames where she was closely in contact with that element which brought both fame and prosperity to her kingdom.

The Palace in Elizabeth's reign was a long irregular building, standing close to the river bank, to which all her Tudor predecessors had made rather random additions as more accommodation was required. Elizabeth's own desire for expansion was economically achieved by expelling in 1559 the Observant friars from their building, which adjoined the Palace, and using it to house her retinue. The long elevation to the river was punctuated by towers, the largest of which projected forward so that its foundations were washed by the water at high tide. The whole structure was crowned with battlements, but the necessity for these defensive features was belied by the wide transomed windows, which looked northward up and down the broad curve of the river as it wound past the shore of the Isle of Dogs. There was no symmetry in the structure, such as there was at Hampton Court and Nonsuch, and perhaps it was the essential "Englishness" of the architecture, untouched by any hint of foreign-inspired Renaissance, which appealed to the Queen, as much as the charm of its position.

It was to the presence chamber in this building, then, that Hentzner and his young pupil came to have a view of that fabulous figure, the Queen of England. The walls of the chamber were hung with tapestry and the floor was strewn with what seemed to him to be "hay", but was no doubt the rushes which were still used to cover the floors of public rooms. The hall was crowded with the nobility and counsellors, and the Archbishop of Canterbury and the Bishop of London were also present. At length the doors at the end of the room opened and the royal procession, with gentlemen, barons, earls, Knights of the Garter all in exact precedence emerged; then followed the Lord Chancellor with the seals of state and two gentlemen bearing the sword of state and the royal sceptre; lastly came the Queen with a train of ladies. She was then sixty-five years of age, her long pale face was wrinkled, and her hooked nose appeared more prominent than in youth, her eyes were small and dark, and between her thin lips could be seen the blackened teeth. Her head was covered with a wig of red hair on which rested a small golden crown. In her ears were pearls, and her white silk dress, decorated with pearls "the size of beans", was cut very low showing an expanse of bosom across which hung a necklace of magnificent jewels.

The reactions of a foreigner to this strange bedizened figurehead might well have been jocular, particularly as the record he wrote was not intended for English eyes; but on the contrary, oblivious of the gaudy trimmings, he was immediately impressed by the overwhelming dignity of her bearing. And this feeling of awe was increased as she moved along the gallery, and spoke graciously in a number of different languages to those who were presented to her in the course of her transit to the door of the chapel. In whatever direction she turned her short-sighted eyes, the assembled company fell on their knees as though dazzled and overcome by the presence of majesty. Sixty-five was a considerable age in the sixteenth century, but even as an old woman, Elizabeth had lost little of the histrionic gifts which served her so well throughout her life.

While the Queen was at her devotions in the chapel, the astonishing ritual of setting the royal dinner-table took place. Firstly two ushers entered the hall, one bearing a rod, the other a tablecloth, and kneeling three times with the utmost veneration they approached the empty table and laid the cloth; they then withdrew making the same obeisance. They were followed by others who with the same ceremony set salt, bread and plates on the table. It was then the turn of two peeresses who moved forward with the deepest curtsies, and rubbed the plates with the bread and salt. The table was then ready for the food, which was brought in by Yeomen of the Guard in scarlet uniforms. Each course consisted of twenty-four dishes in silver and gold plate, and each of the Yeomen was given a mouthful of the dishes he had brought in as a test for poison. When this long and complex ceremony was ended the Queen's ladies entered and removed some of the dishes to the private room, where the Queen ate sparely and alone.

The rigid ceremonial with which the royal life was conducted seems singularly exaggerated, and far exceeded that at any other European court; but Elizabeth understood the temperament of her people, and she knew that to be treated almost as a divinity gave her great power in the country. To her intimates—to the devoted Cecil and to the men to whom she was so strongly attracted—she may have appeared as a woman, and one who had infuriating qualities to equal any of her sex; but to the mass of the people she seemed a goddess, the invincible Gloriana.

This pageantry might suggest that the Court was conducted on lavish and extravagant lines but, making allowance for the period, there was considerable control. The Queen's Household Book lays down exactly how the domestic structure of the palaces was to be ordered; and, since the same household moved with the Queen to the various royal residences, the same rules applied at Greenwich, Whitehall, Richmond, Windsor, Nonsuch, and so forth. Each domestic department—Kitchen, Bakehouse, Pantry, Cellar, Spicery, Larder, Accatry (the butchery), Poultry, Pastry, and the many other offices required to nourish the Court —was organised on similar lines, with a staff consisting of a sergeant, a clerk, and yeoman. In general the first of these received the very precise sum of £11 8s. 1½d. a year, and the second £6 13s. 4d., and both had also

1s. 4d. a day board-wages. The yeomen were less generously rewarded. Only in the kitchen department was a higher salary paid, for here the head clerk received an annual stipend of £44 6s. 8d., 1s. 8d. a day for board, and in addition a number of "dishes of meat"; but in return for this he controlled "the direction and appointment of all meates, drinkes, and breade, spent in the Queene's house". The domestic structure was indeed highly complicated, but nevertheless was regulated on strict lines.

In spite of her mental abilities, Elizabeth was not a deeply intellectual character. She was well read in the classics—while at Windsor in the autumn of 1593 she translated Boethius *De Consolatione Philosophiae* in seventeen days—she had a remarkable gift for languages, she had a prodigious memory, and, like her father and her sister, she was an admirable musician. These qualities might well have been the foundation for making her a great patron of the arts. But this was not outstandingly so; men of talent, of whom there were a fairly large number during her reign, certainly were to be seen at Court, but it was men of action whom she preferred. If the two coincided, as occurred for example in Walter Ralegh and Philip Sidney, so much the better. She recognised Edmund Spenser's talent, and showed her appreciation by granting him an annuity of £50 in 1591, but some of his later works, such as *Mother Hubbard's Tale*, which cast reflections on the more frivolous aspects of Court life, were not received with approbation. The Queen enjoyed the plays of Shakespeare, but the slapstick farce of *The Merry Wives of Windsor* made a greater appeal to her robust humour than the drama of his early historical plays. Falstaff was an entirely congenial figure. Undoubtedly Shakespeare, and to some degree the young Ben Jonson, benefited from the royal patronage. The visual arts, however, received rather meagre encouragement. Nicholas Hilliard was an admirable choice as Court painter and jeweller, and it was perhaps in the latter capacity that he was of particular interest to the Queen. Though his jewels have disappeared, his miniatures remain one of the finest and most sensitive productions of that robust age.

Unlike her father, Elizabeth made no attempt to encourage foreign sculptors and architects to come to England in order to bring these arts up to the standards of Italy and France, and only a few portrait-painters, who could be guaranteed to produce a flattering royal likeness, were admitted to the Court circle. Her Court was thronged with foreigners, but they were present on political or commercial business and had no cultural ends in view. Never in the course of her life did Elizabeth leave the shores of England, and this may partly account for the little interest she seems to have taken in the development of the arts in other countries. That English talent was good enough for England, one feels, was her firm opinion; and the fact that this country lagged so far behind the Continent in the visual arts may have appeared to her to be more than counterbalanced by its importance in the political sphere, and its ever-increasing commercial prosperity.

Architecture was perhaps hardly a woman's subject in the sixteenth century, and indeed it made small progress during the four and a half decades of Elizabeth's reign; while the fumbling attempts of English architects during her last years to produce a rendering of the Renaissance style were seldom successful. Her own ventures into building were not very extensive, but at Windsor, which held next place after Greenwich in her affections, she constructed the great north terrace with a garden lying below it. On the terrace she would walk each day for an hour during her regular autumn visits, which often lasted until Christmas. She also built in 1572 the massive gateway nearest the town, and a few years later carried out alterations to lessen the intense discomfort in which the ladies and gentlemen of the Court lived, but the latter consisted of little but essential repairs. Altogether she is said to have spent about £1,000 a year from 1569 to 1577 on the decaying mediaeval structure of the Castle.

In the sphere of personal adornment, in which the Queen had a deep interest, objects were created of the greatest beauty. Perhaps owing to Hilliard's genius, the elaborate jewels and ornaments produced by the goldsmiths were often of the finest quality, a quality to rival any Continental production. Not only was the jewellery worn by the Queen of an almost Bizantine splendour, but the craftsmen's art was directed also into the making of exquisite ornaments of gold, enamel, and precious stones. At Hampton Court the Queen kept a collection of these objects in a little cabinet known as Paradise, which dazzled the spectator with the glitter of gold, silver, and splendid jewels.

With a love of jewellery went also a fantastic passion for dress. It was a family trait, but in the last of the Tudors it developed almost into a mania. The Queen's dresses were not distinguished by refinement of taste: it was rather at a magnificent display that she aimed, and her predilection was for gowns richly embroidered and sewn with jewels, so that they were as encrusted with ornament as the buildings of the early English Renaissance. This passion became no less as she grew older, and at her death her wardrobe is said to have contained "more than two thousand gowns, with all things answerable".

The Queen was one of the few women in the country to wear silk stockings. The first pair were made for her by her "Silk woman", Mistress Montague, in the second year of her reign; and in ordering further pairs to be made she expressed her delight, saying, "They are pleasant, fine, and delicate, and henceforth I will wear no more cloth stockings." Some years later the Earl of Oxford presented the Queen with some perfumed gloves trimmed with coloured silks which he had brought from Italy, and Sir Philip Sidney came with the offering of a "smock" trimmed with gold and silver lace and embroidered with black silk. Fulke Greville brought a similar garment enlivened with roses and "letters", and a "night-coif" as well. Presents of embroidered handkerchiefs and pairs of sleeves were constantly received. Such delicate additions to the gorgeous panoply of her dress gave infinite pleasure.

There was one very real disadvantage to jewel-encrusted dresses. Sometimes, after some festivity at which she had been wearing one of these precious gowns, the Queen would discover that some of the gems were missing. Perhaps they had become unstitched, or perhaps some Courtier had been able to obtain surreptitiously a useful perquisite. The ornaments which disappeared in this way were many and varied, and advertisements would appear detailing these exotic royal losses.

"Lost from her Majesty's back . . . one small acorn and one oaken leaf of gold at Westminster. Lost . . . two buttons of gold, like tortoises, with pearls in them, and one pearl more. . . . Lost, at Richmond . . . from her Majesty's back, wearing the gown of purple cloth of silver, one great diamond out of a clasp of gold."

Sir John Harington, Elizabeth's lively godson, who was quick to observe any amusing incident in the life of the Court, noted that the Bishop of London when preaching before the Queen had the temerity— or perhaps the thoughtlessness—to enlarge in his sermon "on the vanitie of deckinge the bodie too finely". It was a *faux pas* of the worst order and the Defender of the Faith was furious at this tactless animadversion on her little weakness. "If the bishope helde more discorse on such matters," she cried to her ladies, "she wolde fitte him for heaven, but he shoulde walke thither withoute a staffe and leave his mantle behind him." It would seem that neither the Bishop nor any other prelate was rash enough to touch on this controversial subject on any future occasion.

Although Elizabeth retained the astonishing vitality of her spirit until the end of life, and did not allow physical infirmity to lessen her energy, nevertheless the glamour of her Court inevitably diminished as the central figure advanced towards old age. For the first half of the reign the glory of both country and Court had been in constant crescendo, the apogee being reached perhaps at the time of the Armada in 1588. From that point until the Queen's death a slackening of the pace seemed to set in. There was less splendour at Court, and the general tone began to lose that fresh brilliance which had been so marked while the Queen was young.

During the first decades of her reign, Elizabeth had exercised an extraordinary control over the robust characters who formed the Court circle; but with increasing years her hold relaxed, and rival factions— such as those of Essex and the younger Cecil—arose which she had no power to reduce into submission. At the same time the economic condition of the country was deteriorating fast, and the Treasury, which she had been so astute in replenishing during her early years, was emptying. The bright light of the Elizabethan era was flickering out, but whether the Queen was fully aware how far the scene was darkening is doubtful.

In any case there was little change in the routine of the Court. Elizabeth still moved constantly from one royal residence to another, often spending no more than a week in any one house; the progresses through the countryside continued, and there were important ceremonies at the universities; but the enthusiasm which the appearance of the Queen had evoked during the first thirty years of her reign began to lose its warmth and spontaneity. At Court, too, there became evidence of a less deferential spirit towards the royal person, a greater reluctance to treat her as an almost divine being. There was the highly shocking incident, for example, of Lady Marie Howard, one of the Queen's gentlewomen, who refused to bring Elizabeth her cloak "at the hour her Highnesse is wontede to air in the garden", and when she was rebuked by her mistress, answered back rudely. There were other derelictions of duty which incensed the Queen, who swore she would "out with all such ungracious flouting wenches".

This little domestic insurrection took place in 1598: twenty years earlier, any young woman who had dared to behave so disrespectfully would probably have found herself removed to a cell in the Tower. During the last few years of her reign, the Queen must have realised that in spite of her mental vitality and nervous energy her control over her subjects was beginning to loosen. Essex disobeyed her direct orders, a chit of a girl like Marie Howard dared to be insolent to her: it was not surprising that her temper became exceedingly bad. During the last years of the Queen's life Sir John Harington noted with great distress her increasing physical frailty and mental perturbation; in addition he observed that she suffered at times from embarrassing lapses of memory, and blamed her counsellors for matters which were due to her own forgetfulness.

Harington had a genuine affection and admiration for the Queen, and he was intensely grateful for the kindness and generosity she had shown to himself and to his parents. They "have rootede such love, suche dutyfull remembraunce of her princelie virtues", he wrote to his wife— his Sweet Mall—on 27th December 1602, "that to turne askante from her condition withe tearlesse eyes, would staine and foule the springe and founte of gratitude". And the Queen's condition at this time was, indeed, deplorable. In the previous year Harington had already found her "quite disfavoured, and unattired", and she was eating nothing but "manchet and succory potage", and had become very thin. Nevertheless her nervous energy remained with her, and she marched up and down her room and stamped with anger if she was brought any bad news. When in a particular rage, she would thrust the rusty sword she kept with her into the tapestry—wishing no doubt that she was slaughtering some of the Irish leaders, who were disturbing her peace of mind at this period.

The Queen's death was not to be long delayed. In the middle of March 1603, while at Richmond, she became seriously ill, but obstinately refused to see doctors, to be carried to bed, or to receive any spiritual consolation. For several days she lay on cushions on the floor of her room, but as her end approached she gave way to the Archbishop of Canterbury's entreaties and prayed earnestly with him. On 24th March she died.

But still one further manifestation occurred of that disconcerting spirit which had been a characteristic all her life. Her body incased in lead and set in a wooden coffin covered with velvet was taken down the river in the royal barge to Whitehall. There, as her ladies were watching during the night, there was a sudden explosion, wood and lead were burst open, and the Queen's body was once again exposed to view. Next morning the coffin was hastily and soundly remade, and on 8th April, a month before the new King entered his capital, it was carried to Westminster Abbey for burial.

# Stuart
## Court Life

———

# Chapter 6

# JAMES I

*Come tryumph, enter church, court, citty, towne,*
*Heere James the sixt, now James the first, proclaymed,*
*See how all harts ar heald, that erst wer maymed,*
*The peere is pleasd, the knight, the clark, the clowne.*

With these words Sir John Harington opened an ode of welcome to James VI of Scotland on his accession to the English crown, and his enthusiastic sentiments reflected very truly the feelings of the English people. A love of change is perhaps less strongly developed in the English than in many other races, but inevitably they were stimulated by the thought of a new ruler, when at least three-quarters of the population can have known no other wearer of the crown than Elizabeth. The late monarch had remained a venerated figure till her death, but it was a pleasure and relief to all to welcome a King in the prime of life—James was thirty-seven in 1603—in place of the eccentric old lady whose vagaries during her last years had led to many difficulties. For the first time for more than half a century there was to be a man on the throne, and in addition the succession was at last assured, for James had two young sons.

On 27th March 1603, only sixty hours after the death of Elizabeth, Sir Robert Carey reached Holyrood house, having ridden almost day and night in order to give James the welcome but not unexpected news that he was now titular King of England, France, and Ireland, as well as of his own impoverished Kingdom of Scotland. No time was to be lost before coming into England and meeting the English Council and his new subjects. Ten days were spent in getting together his threadbare possessions, in bidding farewell to his family, who were to follow later, and in receiving the good wishes of the people of Edinburgh. Then, accompanied by a concourse of acquisitive Scottish noblemen and a few Englishmen, who wished to be the first to gain the favour of the new King, James set out on this exciting expedition to the south.

The new King had never previously crossed the border into England, he had never met his terrifying cousin Elizabeth, but he had been brought up to believe in the wealth and splendour of the kingdom over which he was one day likely to rule, and which contrasted so strikingly with the poverty and austerity of his own country. It was therefore with little concern that the cavalcade set out, although entirely lacking the essential commodity of money. Messengers, however, had already been sent to London explaining the financial difficulties of the new monarch, and at Berwick, the first town James entered over the border, emissaries were awaiting him bearing adequate, but not lavish, funds. This must have been the first indication to James that his new kingdom was no El Dorado.

However, tolerably supported by English gold, the great party moved southward at a leisurely and dignified pace. At the boundary of each county the King was met by the High Sheriff and the notabilities of the shire, who conducted him across his purlieu and then handed the security of the King over to the Sheriff of the adjacent county. In all the towns through which the King passed he was rapturously greeted, while at great country-houses, where stops were made, he was splendidly entertained, and time was allowed for him to indulge his overwhelming passion for hunting. On 23rd April James reached Burghley, the great house near Stamford built by William Cecil, Lord Burghley, and then the property of his eldest son. It was when riding from Burghley to Exton that the King was heavily thrown from his horse. The accident caused the greatest agitation to everyone in his train. Was this heaven-sent figure to be removed from the scene so swiftly? But fortunately it was no fatality, and James recovered within a few days.

From the magnificence of Burghley, the cavalcade passed on to the almost equally lavish entertainment provided by Sir Oliver Cromwell at Hinchingbrooke, where the little nephew, also Oliver, then aged just four years, must have had his first, and perhaps disillusioning, glimpse of royalty. A few days later, on 3rd May, James reached Theobalds on the borders of Hertfordshire and Middlesex and only thirteen miles from the City of London. It was a house which was to play a great part in his life, and was to become his favourite residence. There, twenty-two years later—a gloomy, unpopular figure—he was destined to die.

Theobalds at this time was the property of Sir Robert Cecil, second son of the first Lord Burghley, but four years later James persuaded Cecil to exchange it for the royal property of Hatfield, which then became the seat of the Cecil family. Cecil must have relinquished the place with reluctance, for the house and surrounding gardens were the creation of his father, who had begun building in 1564. Over the following twenty years a splendid house of brick and stone had arisen enclosing numerous spacious courtyards, and with balustraded towers crowned with cupolas at each corner. Part of the ground floor was arcaded, and on the upper floors tall, mullioned windows admitted a flood of light into the high, handsome rooms. The house was large enough to accommodate a retinue of even royal dimensions. Round the house Cecil had laid out an elaborate formal garden of avenues and topiary, which was one of the wonders of the age. Altogether Theobalds was looked on as one of the finest country-houses in England.

However, it was not the beauty of Theobalds which appealed to James—his unaesthetic character was untouched by such manifestations of the visual arts as domestic architecture or gardens—but the fact that the park and adjacent forests provided the best hunting within easy distance of his capital, and for this reason the place was to him highly desirable. Perhaps it was in order to prepare the way for the cession of the property that in 1605 James created Robert Cecil Earl of Salisbury, a few hours before he created his elder brother Earl of Exeter, thus giving the precedence to the younger man.

At Theobalds James met the members of the late Queen's Council, the Lord Keeper, the Lord Treasurer, the Lord Admiral, and others of importance, and the first of these made a "most grave, learned, briefe, and pithie Oration to his Majestie". Their reaction on seeing the unimpressive figure who had come to rule over them has not been recorded, but it seems that James made an adequately gracious reply, though as his Scottish accent was very strong it is unlikely that much of it was understood.

After a few days of relaxation, the King, accompanied by a cavalcade which had grown to enormous proportions and included, in addition to the rough Scottish nobles, all the foremost figures in English Court and clerical life, set out for the capital. His destination was the Charterhouse on the northern edge of the City. The whole length of his route was thronged with people hoping to catch a glimpse of the new King, and the crowds and their noisy greetings increased as the long procession approached London. A contemporary account describes the scene very vividly:

"The multitudes of people in highwayes, fieldes, medowes, closes, and on trees, were such, that they covered the beautie of the fieldes; and so greedy were they to behold the countenance of the King, that with much unrulinesse they injured and hurt one another, some even hazarded to the danger of death; but uncivil as they were among themselves, all the way as his Majesty past with shouts and cryes, and casting up of hattes."

The popular enthusiasm was spontaneous and intense, and as great as it had been for any previous monarch; it must have been with relief that James reached the sheltering courts of the Charterhouse. For this graceless Scotsman had none of Elizabeth's dramatic gift, which had immediately and permanently touched the hearts of the people on her first appearance in public procession. However, on this initial occasion the populace had not yet discovered how unattractive a figure had come out the mists of the north to be their King, and they demonstrated without reserve their joy that the succession of the crown was now secure.

Behind this outburst of jubilation there was unfortunately a cloud, an ominous cloud. Early in the year an outbreak of plague had started in the City. This was no unusual event; but in this year, instead of dying down after a space of weeks, it was increasing in violence as the weather warmed. So malevolent had it become that it was clearly impossible to contemplate carrying out the usual ritual on the accession of a new monarch—the procession through the crowded streets from the Tower to Westminster, and the gathering of great crowds both within and outside Westminster Abbey.

James, no doubt, easily bore this reverse with fortitude, and willingly agreed to the curtailment of his public functions. Thus from the Charter-house he moved without parade to Whitehall, and so in the royal barge down the pestilence-free waterway of the Thames to the Tower, his entry into the ancient fortress marking his formal entry into his new kingdom. He was then free to leave for the country palaces of Greenwich and Hampton Court, and to pass a few weeks in his favourite pursuit until the time came for him to travel northward to meet his Queen on her journey down from Scotland.

Early in June Anne of Denmark, with her two elder children, Prince Henry and Princess Elizabeth, set out from Holyrood, and on the 25th of the month reached Althorp in Northamptonshire. The King, seemingly not unduly impatient to be reunited with his spouse, did not join her till she moved on to Easton Neston two days later. The Queen, however, was splendidly received by Sir Robert Spencer, and here had her first experience of a masque devised by Ben Jonson, a form of entertainment which was to become the single radiant feature of the dim Jacobean court.

On this occasion the fun began as soon as the royal party entered the park, when to the sound of horns a satyr appeared out of a grove of trees and delivered a few verses of elfin welcome. Then, blowing a tune on his pipes, he disappeared into the wood, while to the strains of soft music a bevy of fairies tripped out of the shade of the trees and danced in a circle as their Queen supplemented the satyr's welcoming words. Thus to the sounds of poetry and music Queen Anne made her way to the house.

After a Sunday of repose, the revels were renewed on the Monday with an entertainment of Morris dancers, with interludes of Jonson's verses spoken by a youth supported by "divers Gentlemen's younger sons of the country". Here an unfortunate *contretemps* occurred, in that

94

the press of people was so great and so noisy that not one word of Jonson's graceful panegyrics reached the royal ears.

The following day the King and Queen met at Easton Neston, and then with their united retinues they moved from one great country-house to another on a slow journey southward to Windsor. Hither came the great ladies of the kingdom to pay homage to the Queen, whose manner seems to have been considerably more gracious than that of the King. All who could, flocked to Windsor in the hope of making a favourable impression on the new monarchs, and the concourse was enormous. "There was such an infinit companie of Lords and Ladies and so great a Court", wrote Lady Anne Clifford, "as I think I shall never see the like."

From Windsor the Court moved to Hampton Court, where Wolsey's great house, spacious though it was, was filled to overflowing, and retainers had to be accommodated in an encampment of tents pitched in the park. But the plague, which during the hot weather of July had become increasingly intense in the crowded houses of London, was stretching out its fatal tentacles towards the bivouacs in the green meadows of Hampton, and each day two or three victims contracted the disease and died. Anne Clifford, then a girl of thirteen, who was housed with her mother in one of the round towers of the palace, fell ill, and there was consternation that the plague might have crept into the royal entourage. Fortunately it turned out to be an ordinary fever; but it had been a severe scare, and as soon as the child was reasonably well, she was sent away to the house of a relative.

However, it quickly became too dangerous for the royal family to remain at Hampton, and the great cavalcade set out into the uncontaminated countryside, but unfortunately brought the pestilence in its train as it moved to towns and country-houses. As Sir Thomas Edmondes wrote from Woodstock to Lord Shrewsbury: "The Court hath been so contynnuallie haunted with the sickness, by reason of the disorderlie companie that doe follow us, as we are forced to remove from place to place, and doe infect all places where we come."

Nevertheless, in spite of the menace of infection it was impossible to postpone the coronation indefinitely. The risk had to be taken, and on 25th July 1603 James and Anne were crowned in Westminster Abbey. It was a ceremony of restricted splendour, and designed with the intention of attracting as few as possible of the contagious populace into the streets surrounding the Abbey: within the protecting Gothic walls, however, there was considerable pageantry. But it must have been a sombre festivity in spite of the rich robes and handsome uniforms, with anxious glances for that sudden pallor and sweating which was the prelude to an almost inevitable death within a few hours. Poe's story of Prince Prospero with his courtiers and entertainers enclosed within the ramparts of his abbey-building might well have been inspired by James's coronation: "Security was within. Without was the 'Red Death'.' Fortunately the ceremony within the Abbey of Westminster had a happier termination.

James had now been in his new kingdom for three months, and the early popular rapture at the arrival of the new ruler was wearing off. There was indeed a distinct sense of disillusionment. It was becoming clear that the King possessed none of the graces which would endear him to the populace, and, furthermore, that he had neither wish nor ability to develop a charm or dignity of manner which would have stirred enthusiasm on his public appearances. He loathed crowds, and made no attempt to conceal his feelings: he was not stimulated by applause. He became irritated when people stared at him, and furious if he were watched during the many days he spent hunting.

Thus the people soon began to lose interest in their grumpy, unglamorous monarch who made so little attempt to please them, and who expected their loyalty without making any effort to excite it. The Tudors never behaved thus. It was a condition that was to intensify as the reign advanced. From the first, however, James employed a method of giving pleasure to that important section of the community which came in the social scale just below the nobility—the landowners and squires, whose influence in the country was an important factor in maintaining the stability of the Crown. On these men he conferred knighthoods freely: indeed he conferred knighthoods in hundreds during the early months of his reign. On his first journey southward between Berwick and London he dubbed no fewer than 237; at the time of the coronation there were 300 fortunate recipients, and as he moved about the home counties parties of worthy but undistinguished local gentry found themselves ennobled, and so became warmly attached to the royal cause.

He thus inspired gratitude at no cost to himself, or more accurately at no financial cost to himself, for such was his horror of a naked sword that it cost him great effort to use it even for the peaceful purpose of conferring a knighthood. Often the King would turn away his face from the blade, so that the manœuvre was sometimes quite dangerous to the recipient. Sir Kenelm Digby, for example, nearly had the sword thrust into his eye; and in order to avoid these little *contretemps* Buckingham would guide the royal hand while the King averted his gaze. This cannot have lent much dignity to the ritual.

It was not until 1611 that the King hit on the happy plan of replenishing the exchequer by selling titles, which were virtually hereditary knighthoods, in the form of baronetcies. The recipients were supposed to be men of standing, with an annual income from land of at least £1,000, and the cost to them of the honour was between £1,000 and £2,000. Officially the money so raised was supposed to be used for the maintenance of the army in Ulster, but in the event this useful cash was devoted to more pressing debts.

The prodigality in knighthoods raised no criticism, but the King's financial prodigality towards his friends was a very different matter. James had little sense of the value of money, and his attitude towards it was one that is often found in those who are naturally parsimonious. He had an aversion to giving money personally: he was intensely reluctant to spend in order to increase the glamour of his Court and surroundings, he added almost nothing to the architecture of the royal residences or to their contents, he carried economy on his wardrobe to such a pitch that his appearance became, at least in later life, positively squalid. And yet, on the happy assumption that the resources of the Treasury were limitless, he would hand out grants to those he wished to favour with reckless lavishness.

The Queen's jointure was fixed at £5,000 a year, which, though it sounds reasonable, was said "to be as much, or rather more, than hath ben grawnted to anie former Kinge's Wief"; but on the other hand, her frugal spouse expected her to make use of Elizabeth's extensive wardrobe of dresses, the greater number of which must have belonged to the fashions of thirty or forty years earlier. Having made this provision for his wife, James felt at liberty to give his handsome young friend Robert Carr, later Earl of Somerset, a draft on the Treasury for £20,000. The Treasurer, realising that the King had little notion of the value of his gift, arranged for the sum in sovereigns to be heaped on the floor of a room through which he would pass. The ruse was highly successful, and the King was overcome with dismay when told that this golden mound was the little sum for which his favourite had asked him. As a result the shower of gold on this male Danaë was severely curtailed.

James's proposed generosity to Robert Carr was on a more lavish scale than to his supporters for whom he had only a platonic friendship; but the greater number of the hungry Scotsmen who had accompanied him from Edinburgh expected some material recompense now that they had reached the land which they persisted in looking on as a true Land of Promise. "The whole wealth of England", wrote Arthur Wilson in his history of the reign published in 1653, "would not serve the King's vast bounty".

John Chamberlain's chatty letters to Sir Dudley Carleton show that the poor state of the royal finances was a subject that was often to the fore. In December 1613, for example, he alludes to this perennial scarcity: "The very guard that attends the King's person now at Roiston, and the poore posts that trot up and downe, are far behind hand, and besides clamouring and murmurring have made many fruitless petitions to the King himself for their pay."

With a King who was so insouciant about money, and clearly had no knowledge of its true value, it was natural that the financial restraint which Elizabeth had so successfully imposed on her Court quickly disappeared; and after only some months of James's careless rule it was found that the household expenses had doubled. "Our Souverain spends £100,000 yearly in his howse, w$^{ch}$ was wont to be but £50,000", wrote Lord Cecil in despair to Lord Shrewsbury. And perhaps the worst feature of this thriftlessness was that there was nothing to show for the great sums which had been squandered.

As in previous reigns, when it was found that household expenses were becoming out of hand, strict "Ordinances" were drawn up in the King's name, designed to limit extravagance and waste. It was essential for the royal table to set an example of economy, so the first of the new rules ran as follows:

"Whereas Our-selfe and Our dear Wife the Queene's Majestie, have been every day served with 30 Dishes of Meate; nowe, hereafter, . . . Our Will is to be served but with 24 dishes every Meale unlesse when any of Us sit abroade in State, then to be served with 30 Dishes, or as many more as We shall command."

With this splendid example of royal austerity before them, it was confidently expected that there would be no difficulty in cutting down the meals of all courtiers and retainers. Wine, too, was to be rationed. The allowance of "Spanish Wines, called Sacke" was to be reduced to twelve gallons a day, though in this case there was no mention of the King joining in the reduction. Indeed it is unlikely that he did, for an abundance of sweet wine was one of his weaknesses.

It appears, also, from the Ordinances that a good deal of pilfering went on at Court, which probably stemmed from the King's general laxness of behaviour:

"Wee likewise understand of the daily losse of Our Silver Vesselles, Wee straightly charge and command, that no person, of what degree soever, shall presume to send from Our Boarde or out of Our Privy-Chamber or Presence-Chamber, any Silver Dishes."

If, for any reason, food had to be sent elsewhere, it must be transferred into dishes of economical pewter.

Just a year after his accession, the plague in the City having been exterminated by the winter frosts, James found himself under the necessity of making the formal progress through London from the Tower to Whitehall which the people demanded of a new monarch. Although in

Wilson's words "he did not love to be looked on", there was no way of avoiding the great pageant of which he was to be the principal feature. It was said that "he endured the days brunt with patience, being assured he should never have such another". How different was this attitude to that of Henry VIII and Elizabeth who seemed to be raised on wings by the adulation of the populace.

On the morning of 15th March 1604 the King, riding on a richly caparisoned white jennet and assuming as gracious a countenance as he was able, emerged from the great gateway of the Tower and set off on the painful journey through the decorated streets towards Westminster. A canopy, borne by eight gentlemen of the Privy Chamber, swayed over his head, and behind him followed Queen Anne and his elder son, Prince Henry, a stalwart boy ten years of age. In the procession rode all the most important people in the country, including the bishops and representatives of the legal world. Behind the Queen followed a galaxy of peeresses, with the wives of knights and the maids of honour.

The houses lining the route were decorated in the manner usual to these occasions with carpets and rich materials hanging from the windows, while barriers had been erected along the sides of the streets to allow the procession free passage. Owing to the year's delay in holding this pageant, more time than usual had been available to design and construct the various devices which enlivened the route. Amongst other surprises for the King were seven elaborate triumphal arches which spanned the streets, each being the production of a different City company or body of merchants. Had James had an eye for architecture, he would have observed that in Gracious Street he passed beneath a massive arch designed in a style with which he can have had only the faintest acquaintance. It was a tribute from the Italian merchants who traded in and with England, and the pillared gateway they had raised was a purer rendering of the Palladian style than anything before built in this country. Had it been in Vicenza the design would have had a bucolic air, but amongst the gabled, timber-framed houses of London its effect must have been striking.

Slowly the grand procession made its way westward, the unfortunate King being greeted at every turn by some new delight of pageantry, by songs rendered in childish trebles, by interminable odes of welcome and adulation—some composed by Ben Jonson—delivered from maturer mouths, by statuesque female figures in elaborate fancy dress whose significance must have eluded the majority of beholders. Thus for more than five long hours the ordeal continued, until at last Whitehall Palace was reached, and the King was free from the noisy, shouting crowds. Never again did he submit to being the principal actor in a pageant arranged for the amusement of the people—nor, indeed, once he was better known was this ever desired—and, in Wilson's words, "afterwards in his public appearances the accesses of the people made him so impatient, that he often dispersed them with frowns, that we may not say with curses".

Fate had woefully miscast James in the role of King of England. Had he been born a simple country squire, his character and qualities would perhaps have seemed up to the average. He was naturally a kind man, enamoured of his hunting and happy with his books. If he ate and drank more than was good for him, this was little different to many others, while his sentimental attachments to young men would not have been subjected to the critical attention which was inevitable in Court life. He might indeed have existed happily in obscurity; but instead of this, Fate had thrust his ungainly and undignified person on to the conspicuous seat of a throne. Although he had been a titular King since he was one year old, it was a position to which he never grew accustomed.

It would have been a redeeming feature of James's character had he promoted the visual arts, but in this direction he showed little predilection: his interests lay only in words. Undoubtedly he had a gift of language which was above the average. His writings, and he was prolific on a variety of subjects, may not have achieved a very high standard; but monarchs have little opportunity to develop their talents, and it was rather in speech that he showed an unusual ability and wit. When in good humour he must have been an admirable conversationalist, though the frequent coarseness of his remarks was not conducive to elegance. Sir Anthony Weldon, who seldom indulged in a compliment, went so far as to say of him: "He was very witty, and had as many ready jests as any man living." Some of the King's sayings which have survived show remarkable wisdom, such as: "Very wise men and very fools do little harm, it is the mediocrity of wisdom which troubleth the world."

James's public utterances to Parliament and to his ministers were apt to be less happy, and he seems to have had a certain mental arrogance which made him rate the intelligence of his audiences too low; but when discussing literary or philosophical matters he was at his best. It is fitting that his name will always be connected with the new translation of the Bible. This was decided upon as the outcome of a conference which he called at Hampton Court in 1604. After unremitting labour for seven years by a number of scholars, the new version appeared in 1611; and full credit must be given to the King, who was the true inspirer of this tremendous work.

Although in many ways James had the mind of a scholar, he was greatly amused by coarse buffoonery. Some of the evenings he most appreciated were enlivened by "fooleries", when, after supper, some of the less refined courtiers would entertain him with their antics. The exact

13　Anne of Denmark, consort of James I

*reproduced by gracious permission of Her Majesty The Queen, from a painting by Paul van Somer*

*Devonshire Collection, Chatsworth.
Reproduced by permission of the
Chatsworth Settlement*

14 Costume for Charles I in Sir William
D'Avenant's *Salmacida Spolia*, 1640

15 Queen Henrietta Maria
as Chloris in Ben Jonson's
*Chloridia*, 1631

nature of these performances remains uncertain, but it seems improbable that they were very elevated or poetic.

In spite of having so little gift for inspiring public popularity, it is clear that James had endearing qualities in private from the fact that he was well served and well liked by his personal servants, who responded well to the King's familiar manner to them and overlooked his sudden rages. The story of the scene with the Scots servant Gib illustrates James's rather hysterical style. One day at Theobalds the King sent for some papers relating to the Spanish Treaty which he was convinced he had handed to Gib. Gib denied all knowledge of them and fell on his knees at the King's feet protesting that he had never seen them. James, however, gave way to an uncontrollable passion and kicked Gib as he knelt before him. This was going too far, and rising Gib said with dignity: "Sir, I have served you from my youth, and you never found me unfaithful; I have not deserved this from you, nor can I live longer with you with this disgrace; Fare ye well, Sir, I will never see your face more." He then left the house, and rode off towards London.

Shortly after Gib's departure it was found that the papers which had caused so much disturbance had in fact been given to Endymion Porter, who produced them. The King, intensely contrite, sent at once in pursuit of the faithful Gib, who was brought back to the Court. "As he came into the King's Chamber, the King kneeled down upon his knees before Gib, intreating his pardon . . . protesting he would never rise till Gib had forgiven him." This, after a slight demur, Gib consented to do.

This little domestic incident, which Wilson describes, is in itself of no importance, but it is revealing of James's character: it shows the lack of control, and of dignity, and yet at the same time a warmth of affection which was not bounded by class. It demonstrated the King's own aphorism: "I love not one who will never be angry; for as he that is without sorrow is without gladness, so he that is without anger is without love." But these were not quite the qualities which would make the possessor the centre of a brilliant and ceremonious Court, and thus the traditions built up by the Tudors crumbled fast under James's faltering leadership. So undistinguished was his demeanour that it was not surprising that he was scathingly spoken of as "the fiddler's son", though Rizzio might well have bequeathed more charm to a son than James possessed. Sometimes, too, it was suggested that James was not royal at all: that he was the son of Lady Mar to whom Mary Stuart had entrusted her precious infant, that this infant had died and had been replaced by Lady Mar's own child. However, neither of these two reflections on James's parentage received any general credence.

Meanwhile the people of the country accepted their monarch with resignation. Although enthusiasm had been quenched, the relief of having a King on the throne with two sons to support the succession, and no rival claimants of any moment, was very great indeed. Thus the present and the future seemed secure, and James at least was a man of peace and disinclined to embark rashly on Continental wars. These considerations could be placed against the fact that his personality was unstimulating and his conduct quite often unedifying. It was a very serious reverse, felt throughout the country, when the King's elder son, Prince Henry, died at Richmond in 1612. He was a youth of exceptional promise, outstanding both in character and physique, so that the dimness of the actual King had been made more bearable by this bright hope for the future. Charles, the younger son and at that time only ten years old, was a delicate, stammering child who seemed unlikely to develop the qualities of his brother.

The Queen bore the loss of her son, as she did the vagaries of her spouse, with calm. She was not a clever woman, but she was sensible in her acceptance of those things which could not be altered. She had as little true love for the King as he had for her, and, at least during the first part of her marriage, she was reputed to entertain a romantic affection for several of the more handsome courtiers. Though she had no rupture with the King, she found it more agreeable to have her own establishment, and this was set up at Somerset House which she renamed Denmark House—a transitory nomenclature. Here she was able to devote her time to the production of masques, which were as great an interest of her life as was hunting of the King's. In Wilson's words: "The Court was a continued Maskarado, where she and her Ladies, like so many Sea-Nymphs, or Nereides, appeared often in various dresses to the ravishment of the beholders."

It was remarkably fortunate that there were a number of talented men at hand to devise the entertainments which the Queen and her ladies so greatly enjoyed. There were Samuel Daniel, Thomas Campion, George Chapman, Aurelian Townshend, and above all the brilliant Ben Jonson, all of whom showed a rich virtuosity in writing masques on a variety of themes, many of which contained an unexacting part of sufficient dignity and importance for the Queen to fill herself. But these clever compositions would have been dead things without the genius of Inigo Jones to give them life and reality with his stage settings. Even Ben Jonson's poetry is now principally interesting for its period feeling, but Jones's drawings for scenery and costumes have a perennial brilliance that comes only from genius.

The collaboration between Inigo Jones and Ben Jonson was not a happy one, and was not born of the same deep friendship and intimacy as was that of their contemporaries Francis Beaumont and John Fletcher. Indeed their antipathy increased until their alliance broke, and thus their earlier productions were their best. Of these the *Masque of Blackness*, which was produced at Whitehall on Twelfth Night 1605 was their most famous. The setting was the banks of the mysterious river Niger which was thought to be in that vague region designated as Aethiopia, and this gave opportunity for rich and exotic scenes, with negroes and nymphs galore. The stage effects were ambitious. The scene opened with waves breaking on the shore amongst which sported tritons, sea-horses, mermaids, and monsters. Floating on the waves was a great concave shell in which were the Masquers, who were dressed in azure and silver with jewels and ropes of pearls.

The Queen, with the Court ladies, played the principal parts, and the complex symbolism was expressed in declamation, song, music, and dance. The King was said to have been "not a little delighted" by this elaborate pageant; but it was probably with relief that the next day he left Whitehall for the male atmosphere of his hunting-box at Royston, where he remained some time indulging in his favourite amusement and, as Mr. Chamberlain wrote to Mr. Winwood, "not interrupted or troubled with too much business".

The *Masque of Blackness* was successfully and decorously played; but this seemingly was not always the case, as is shown by Sir John Harington's account of the performance on the occasion of the state visit of the Queen's brother, King Christian IV of Denmark, in 1606. The theme of the Masque was the visit of the Queen of Sheba to Solomon, and it took place after "a great feast". This proved an error of timing, for not only his Danish Majesty—and probably his English Majesty too—but also the cast had drunk too much. Everything went wrong from the start. The Queen of Sheba fell over, scattering her precious gifts of foods all over King Christian, who anyhow was too drunk to notice, and had to be carried "to an inner chamber". The play, however, continued with the appearance of Hope, Faith, and Charity, who were also unfortunately so intoxicated that Hope and Faith had to be led away to the lower hall where they "were both sick and spewing". Victory and Peace, who were the next entrants, did little better, and the entertainment was brought to a close in confusion.

Harington, though he makes a good story of the evening, was clearly rather shocked by the general behaviour, which he puts down to the lax example set by the King, and remarks that in Queen Elizabeth's day "I ne'er did see such lack of good order, discretion, and sobriety, as I have now done". And another contemporary critic, Peyton, was even more censorious, and remarks that: "The masks and plays at Whitehall were used only as incentives for debauchery, therefore the courtiers invited the citizens' wives to those shows." The tone of the Court had indeed gravely deteriorated since the previous reign.

The production of masques was perhaps the only direction in which the Court of James and his Queen attracted men of talent, and by this means a large band of brilliant writers were enabled to achieve successful and prosperous careers, where otherwise they might have languished in poverty and obscurity. But Inigo Jones, on whose talent the success of the majority of the productions depended, would undoubtedly have come to the fore in any event, and it was undeserved good fortune for James that this great designer and architect should have reached prominence during his reign.

From his earliest years Inigo Jones had intended to make architecture his career, and his travels and studies in Italy were designed to this end: the theatrical work in which he found himself involved, though interesting and financially rewarding, must have been frustrating employment for a genius who wished to create noble buildings in stone, rather than pretty scenes in canvas and wood. It was a step towards his objective when in January 1611 he was appointed Surveyor to Prince Henry; but in the following year the Prince died, and it was not till 1615 that, on the death of the holder, he was given the post, for which above all he must have wished, of Surveyor of the King's Works and Buildings.

Had James been an ardent and extravagant builder, what splendid architecture might have descended to posterity. If the money he wasted on his favourites had instead been devoted to royal building, London might have possessed one of the finest palaces in the world. Charles I hoped to remedy this omission, but it was not to be, and one must be grateful for the little that there is. In 1617 the Gothic Banqueting House in Whitehall was destroyed by fire, and in 1619 a new structure from Inigo Jones's designs was begun. Within three years the first truly classical building in this country had arisen amongst the crowded courts and varied dwellings which formed the Palace of Whitehall.

A year earlier, in 1616, Jones had begun a house for the Queen at Greenwich, which adroitly joined the garden of the palace to the park lying across the road to Dartford. However, in 1618 the Queen became ill of dropsy, and work was stopped; it was not renewed until the following reign. In November of 1618 "a mighty, blazing comet" appeared in the sky. As Wilson observed: "These Apparitions do always portend some horrid Events." In this case the "horrid event", so far as England was concerned, was of no great moment, and turned out to be the death early in the following year of the neglected Queen Anne.

The obsequies did not take place until May, owing to the difficulty of finding money for a state funeral, and James did not attend it. He was in indifferent health, and the loss of a wife from whom he was so detached did not move him very deeply. Robert Carr, Earl of Somerset, had disappeared from the royal circle in a black cloud of disgrace and suspicion, and his place in the King's affections had been more than filled by young George Villiers. Villiers was twenty-two years of age when he was appointed Cup-Bearer to the King, and he rose swiftly up the scale until he was Lord High Admiral and Duke of Buckingham before he was thirty.

The King, though only fifty-four at the time of the Queen's death, was senile for his age, and was fast passing into his dotage. His love for Buckingham and his love of wine were becoming the principal supports of his life. These weaknesses did not escape the eye of the French Ambassador, who wrote cruelly to his master in 1622: "He feeds his eyes where he can no longer content his senses. The end of all is ever the bottle." The King's letters to Buckingham became increasingly maudlin, and contained such phrases as "God bless you, my sweet child and wife, and grant that ye may ever be a comfort to your dear dad and husband."

Fortunately, perhaps, the King's life of decrepitude was not very long drawn out. In March 1625 he came to Theobalds, the house in which he had known the greatest happiness and relaxation, having been taken ill with fever and ague while at Newmarket some days earlier. Several doctors were summoned, who tried the conventional remedies while Buckingham and his mother, possibly with good intentions but certainly with fatal results, applied plasters to his stomach, and added powders to his beverages. The King showed resignation and piety as his dissolution approached, and after a few days he died, his death causing as little public emotion as had the Queen's six years earlier.

Perhaps as a compensation for the general absence of grief the new King, Charles, ordered a state funeral of unparalleled magnificence. The embalmed body rested for some weeks at Denmark House, and on 7th May the long cortège passed along the Strand and through the Holbein Gate at Whitehall to Westminster Abbey. In order to provide a suitable crowd of mourners, black clothes were handed out to over 9,000 people, and within the Abbey a splendid catafalque designed by Inigo Jones in the form of a domed temple supported on pillars was erected for the reception of the body. The burial service, which must have been somewhat wearisome, included a sermon lasting two hours delivered by the Lord Keeper. The cost of these funeral pomps amounted, according to John Chamberlain, to the extravagant figure of £50,000; but seemingly the organisation was indifferent, for he adds: "All was performed with great magnificence, but the order was very confused and disorderly".

107

# Chapter 7

# CHARLES I

The death of James I at Theobalds did not come unexpectedly, and the Knight Marshal, Sir Edward Zouch, was at hand awaiting the moment to proclaim the accession of the new King. Within a quarter of an hour of James breathing his last the Marshal was at the gate of the house making his momentous announcement; but unfortunately in his nervous hurry he styled Charles "rightful and dubitable heir". For those who enjoyed seeing omens in the smallest detail, the little slip of omitting the prefix "in-" was looked on as distinctly sinister.

Nevertheless it seemed on 27th March 1625 that the new King was inheriting a throne as stable as that of any of his five predecessors, with the additional advantage that there were no rival claimants to create difficulties and uncertainties. But though the kingship to which Charles succeeded was to all appearances a secure and dominating structure, the foundations were already showing weakness, partly owing to the lax rule, and laxer way of life, of his father. The prestige of the ruler and his Court, without which strong government was impossible, had considerably diminished during the twenty-two years of James's reign; and while the power of the King had lessened, the strength of the gentry in the country, from which the Commons were drawn, was constantly increasing.

The condition of the throne in England at the accession of Charles was closely paralleled a century and a half later in France, when Louis XVI inherited a crown stained and tarnished by the misrule of his grandfather. In both cases the new King was unfortunately not endowed with the strength of character or the political ability to correct the disorder bequeathed by his predecessor, and it was principally on account of inherited troubles that these two well-intentioned men were sent to the scaffold.

Probably the single factor which deflected Charles's rule from the outset into the troubled paths leading eventually to civil war was shortage of money. James's singular lack of competence in financial matters and his careless extravagance had emptied the royal purse very thoroughly, and Charles found himself in a position of difficulty. Since the accession of Henry VIII, no English king had succeeded to a well-filled Treasury; and each reign, with the exception of the first bountiful years of Henry's rule, had been darkened by the necessity for extracting funds from a reluctant nation.

At this period there was no distinction between the private income of the King—income which was used for the maintenance of his palaces, his personal expenditure, and so forth—and income which was required for all the expenses of government, to pay for ships and their complements; to meet the pay of troops enlisted for Continental wars; to maintain embassies in foreign countries; and for innumerable other duties at home and abroad. There were no regular taxes in times of peace, and the only constant income which the King received came from Crown lands and forests, from customs dues, from wardships, from the heavy fines imposed on erring nobility and landowners, and from a few other sources of a like nature.

This income had shown no increase during the past decades: indeed the returns from the remunerative fines, so constantly levied by the Tudors, had diminished. Furthermore, lack of control during past reigns had led to dissipation of royal property and estates, and so to a reduction in revenue. The Dissolution of the monasteries, which might have been expected to bring vast estates and rents into the royal bag, had in the end benefited the Crown very little, for no sooner were the properties seized than they were handed out to acquisitive noblemen and others, who thus founded the fortunes of their families on the finest of all securities—landed property. The majority of statesmen expected to be enriched in return for their services, and many were singularly successful in this direction. The handsome Sir Christopher Hatton rose to wealth in the sunshine of his gracious employer, while William Cecil, Lord Burghley, found opportunity during his long and devoted service to Elizabeth to amass a huge fortune—a fortune which enabled him to build the two most splendid country houses in England.

The foregoing are only two examples of a tendency which had been in existence for the past century, and which had led to gradual impoverishment of the Crown and the enrichment of those families whose members had been astute enough to enter the royal service, and to profit from their position. At the same time prices had been steadily rising over many years, so that the King's expenses had been constantly increasing. The only method of augmenting the revenue of the Crown was by means of grants voted by Parliament; and it was this system—this time-honoured system—which led to the constant and disedifying wrangles between Charles and the Commons, and so eventually to the disaster of civil war and the virtual extinction of the power of the Crown in England.

Charles was still under twenty-five when his father died, and it is probable that he had little comprehension of the changing relations between the Crown and Parliament. He assumed that it was obligatory for him to behave as an autocrat, and it was to be many years before he realised that his attitude was exactly the one that was bound to embitter further his dealings with the Commons. In spite of his intelligence and cultivation, Charles was curiously inept in his contacts with human beings. Socially he was tactless and diffident, and his manner was not helped by his stammer and thick Scotch accent, while in public he was seldom able to make a happy impression. He was completely lacking in the common touch which even his father, in his peculiar way, had possessed to some degree, and which was so highly developed in his son Charles.

The first act of his reign, which was to order a magnificent funeral for his father, can hardly have inspired confidence in his wisdom. To spend the vast sum of £50,000 on this disorderly procession when the Treasury was hard pressed for money, may have been a testimony to his filial love, but it showed a singular lack of prudence. It was an early, but not the first, example of his unfortunate gift for making wrong decisions. The expedition to Spain with its humiliating climax was perhaps the first: many more were to follow in the course of his disastrous reign.

A perusal of the history of Charles's reign might give the impression that the whole of it was devoted with little intermission to quarrels with Parliament, and that there can have been almost no opportunity for him to indulge in the more gracious aspects of life. But this was not the case during the first fifteen years, and one is glad to think that at least some parts of his life were tolerably pleasant. Political troubles rose like mountain peaks above a layer of cloud and grew ever more formidable and more closely crowded, so that eventually they completely dominated the scene; but below the clouds in the peaceful valleys between the mountains, as it were, the life of the Court was carried on for some time with all its traditional ceremony, etiquette and amusements.

The King was still unmarried at the time of his accession, but some months before James's death a treaty had been signed in Paris agreeing a marriage between Charles and Henrietta Maria, the third daughter of Henri IV, who had been assassinated a year after her birth, and sister of Louis XIII. At the beginning of May 1625 the Princess, then aged fifteen, was married by proxy to Charles at a magnificent ceremony which took place on a platform erected in front of Notre-Dame, and was followed by mass celebrated in the cathedral. The Duc de Chevreuse represented King Charles, to whom he was closely related; but it seems that the traditional custom of the proxy husband placing his naked leg on the bride's bed was dispensed with on this occasion.

On 24th May the Duke of Buckingham accompanied by a number of English noblemen arrived in Paris, and a few days later the young Queen set out with a great retinue of Englishmen and Frenchmen for her new life in England. The journey across France was considerably delayed by the sudden illness of her mother, Marie de Medici, at Compiègne, and a further hitch occurred when Buckingham decided he must pay a last intimate visit to the French Queen, Anne of Austria, before he left the country. However, at last on 23rd June she arrived at Dover, but the crossing of the Channel had been rough and prolonged, and she at once sent a message to Charles begging him to give her time to recover before they met. On the morning of 24th June, then, Charles and his wife met for the first time. The tension of the meeting must have been almost insupportable, but it passed off highly satisfactorily, each appearing delighted with the other. On seeing her husband, Henrietta Maria fell on her knees saying: *"Sire, je suis venue en ce pays de votre Majesté pour être usée et commandée de vous."* It was a disarming and admirable sentiment, but not one which in the event was particularly in character with her future behaviour.

Later in the day the great cavalcade set off towards London, the first night being spent at Canterbury, where it was noted with satisfaction that the marriage was successfully consummated. Thence the procession moved on to Gravesend, where the King and Queen embarked in the royal barge and, followed by a concourse of decorated boats, made their way upstream to Whitehall. Towards five o'clock in the afternoon the barges passed under London Bridge accompanied by all the pageantry which the citizens of London were so adept at providing on these occasions of royal festivities, while above the sounds of music and cheering were heard the deafening reports of a salute being fired from the bastions of the Tower.

The seldom-failing English weather played its part by sending deluges of rain at intervals on the happy crowds; but this did little to mar the public enthusiasm, and the bells from all the steeples of the capital rang till midnight and hundreds of bonfires blazed dangerously in the narrow streets. A few years later the young couple must have looked back to this period of popularity with painful nostalgia.

It was not only their popularity which was transient: their mutual affection, which had blossomed so promisingly at their first meeting, quickly withered and died, and very soon there was complete estrangement between them. Each had bitter complaints to make of the other. The young Queen was mortified to find that she was not the most important person in the King's life. Charles was controlled and dominated by Buckingham, and all his acts were dependent on Buckingham's encouragement or approbation. Seldom in history had a ruler of adult years been so strongly influenced by a minister, or had so deep an affection for him; for Charles adored Buckingham, not in the doting manner that his father had done, but with the admiration a schoolboy might have for someone stronger, more capable, more handsome, than himself. It was not surprising that Henrietta Maria was intensely jealous.

The King on his side suffered constant irritation from the crowd of French courtiers, priests, and servants who had come to England in the Queen's train. It seems evident that they made no attempt to stimulate harmony in the marriage, and fostered the notion that the daughter of Henri IV was infinitely superior to the frail little King of the rough island to which she had come. They encouraged the Queen to make the public aware of her Catholic faith. The religious aspect of the marriage was in any case full of difficulties. A tactful approach could have smoothed the path: the French made it clear at once that from their side no tact at all was to be exercised.

The first major disagreement occurred over the coronation. The Queen refused to take part in it unless it was performed according to the rites of the Catholic Church. This was obviously an impossibility, and the King was eventually crowned alone on 2nd February 1626, while the Queen watched the procession from the gatehouse overlooking Palace Yard. There were many other occasions when Henrietta Maria was persuaded to make a display of her religion, when it must inevitably cause offence to her husband and to the people of England. An outstanding example was her walk barefoot to Tyburn to commemorate the "Martyrs" of the Gunpowder Plot; though she explained this as having been no more than a saunter through the groves of Hyde Park with a casual glance at the site of the scaffold. Furthermore the numbers of the Queen's retinue swelled prodigiously. It had originally been agreed that the number would be restricted to sixty: before long there were said to be over four hundred.

In these uncomfortable circumstances the King and Queen became entirely estranged, and Charles soon realised that if his marriage were not to founder permanently, and if he was to maintain any authority at the Court, the Queen's French retinue must leave. It was one of his few prudent decisions, and he carried it through with a determination that was highly uncharacteristic. From Whitehall Palace the bevy of French followers was ordered to go to Somerset House, where the King came in person and informed them that they were to return to France. Not till a month later, however, and carrying with them a *douceur* of over £22,000 and almost the whole of the Queen's wardrobe, did the cavalcade eventually leave for the coast, and set sail for France.

The Queen was thrown into a violent passion by this high-handed behaviour of her apparently meek husband, and for a time their mutual relations worsened, though the relief to the King by the removal of a continual source of irritation must have been great. For at least the first two years of marriage this seemingly ill-assorted couple led separate lives, being together only when they appeared in public. The Queen's jealousy of Buckingham, who she was convinced had prompted the King to dismiss her French followers, grew ever more intense. But in this direction relief for the Queen's feelings was at hand, for on the morning of 23rd August 1628 Buckingham was assassinated in the hall of a house in Portsmouth where he was lodging. The murderer, John Felton, was a crazy individual, who was convinced that the troubles in the country and the poverty of his own life were due to the Lord Admiral, and that it was his duty to kill him. He therefore purchased a dagger for tenpence from a cutler on Tower Hill, set out for Portsmouth, and put his project into successful execution. The enterprise, however, was far from being the triumph he anticipated: he himself was hanged, the death of one of the most able men in the country in no way improved the situation, and only in the single direction of marking a turning-point in the marriage of the King and Queen—an aspect which cannot have occurred to him—did his rash act do good.

Henrietta Maria had matured quickly during these first troubled years of marriage. The petulant child of fifteen had become an attractive and determined young woman of nineteen, and with one of those strange mutations of human feeling, she and Charles became suddenly in love. Within a few months of Buckingham's death the Queen was pregnant, and though this child did not live, a son born on 29th May 1630 lived to succeed as Charles II. As the family grew in numbers, the King became increasingly dominated by Henrietta Maria—just as he had been dominated by Buckingham—and some of those rash decisions which ruined his relations with the Commons were prompted by the Queen, who was determined that the King should rule in fact as well as in name.

While the King and Queen had been disunited their influence on Court life had been negligible; but once the fortunate change had come over their personal feelings, they became the true leaders of the society which surrounded them. The lax manners which King James had tolerated, and even encouraged, in his courtiers were no longer permitted, and a strict etiquette was imposed. Immorality amongst the courtiers, though probably not exterminated, was at least no longer publicly tolerated, and, with the King and Queen as examples of perfect conjugal bliss, all licence was strictly taboo.

The Court indeed underwent the edifying process of a moral

spring-cleaning, and even those who were bitterly opposed to the King politically could make no adverse criticism on this score. In the *Memoirs of Colonel Hutchinson*, the regicide and ardent supporter of Cromwell, his widow wrote: "The face of the Court was much changed in the change of the King; for King Charles was temperate, chaste, and serious, so that the fools, mimics, and catamites of the former Court grew out of fashion."

The improvement in morality was probably a little less thorough than these words might suggest, but at least those who erred were expected to keep their lapses from morality out of sight, and to comply with the more intellectual standards of the Court. For if baudiness was out, culture was definitely in. As Horace Walpole described it: "During the prosperous state of the King's affairs, the pleasures of the Court were carried on with much taste and magnificence. Poetry, painting, music and architecture were all called in to make them rational amusements."

In this salubrious atmosphere, so different from the foggy climate of the previous reign, the arts began to flourish in a way they had not done for many decades. Charles was an enthusiastic and perspicacious collector of all manner of works of art, but above all of pictures. In this the example of Buckingham had been entirely good, for during his short and busy life—he was only thirty-six when he was murdered–Buckingham formed a remarkable collection of pictures, marbles, and sculpture. Many of his finest works of art had belonged to Rubens, whose collection he bought for the moderate sum of £10,000, while that enigmatic figure Balthazar Gerbier, in the course of his secret missions to and from the Continental countries, made many magnificent purchases for his patron.

The young Prince Henry had begun to form a collection of pictures before his early death, and Charles enthusiastically followed the initiative of his brother and of his closest friend. Throughout the first decade and a half of his reign, before the dark clouds descended completely on his life, he bought, with the aid of agents on the Continent, continually and prudently. His largest single deal was the purchase of the collection of the Duke of Mantua, which was considered one of the finest in Europe. It was not, unfortunately, a transaction which was regarded with much sympathy by members of Parliament, many of whom looked on it as an unpardonable waste of public funds.

However, in spite of frowns from the Commons, the King continued to add to his collection with a passionate interest. Gerbier was as helpful to the King as he had been to Buckingham, and in 1638 received a knighthood probably more for his perspicacious purchases in the art world than for his work as a diplomatic agent. Gerbier's field of action was principally the Low Countries: for purchases from Italy—the richest source of all

—the King depended largely on an equally curious character named Panzani, whose true purpose in coming to England and forming contact with the King was to foster a revival of Roman Catholicism. Cardinal Barberini had sagaciously chosen a secret envoy whom he could recommend to Charles as a useful agent for procuring works of art. In the latter direction Panzani was highly successful, and the Cardinal was able to write: "The statues go on prosperously; nor shall I hesitate to rob Rome of her most valuable ornaments, if, in exchange, we might be so happy as to have the King of England's name among those princes who submit to the Apostolic See." However, the "exchange" which the Cardinal had hoped for did not materialise.

Another useful purchasing agent was Abraham Vanderdort, a Dutchman, who—according to George Vertue—was made Keeper of the King's "cabinet" at Whitehall with a salary of £40 a year. This gallery was built in the midst of the Palace, and extended from the river almost to the Banqueting House and had windows looking out over the Privy Garden. Vanderdort, who was himself something of an artist, was useful in making designs for the coinage, and the many payments to him that appear in the records of the Exchequer suggest that his services were highly considered. The end of this invaluable servant was sad, and had the pathos of that of Vatel, Condé's famous *maître d'hôtel*, in the following century. He had been told by the King to take particular care of a miniature by Gibson, and to this end he hid it so securely that he was unable to find it when it was required. He was so overcome by this misfortune that he hanged himself. After his death the miniature came to light.

It was not only Charles's interest in the works of the great masters of the past that made his Court a place of culture, but still more his appreciation of the work of contemporary artists. The name of Anthony Vandyke will always bring to mind Charles and his Court: indeed the sympathy with which he is remembered depends to a considerable degree on Vandyke's art in representing him as a romantic figure. The sad, sensitive face, seemingly destined for tragedy, which looks out from Vandyke's canvases has contributed materially to the legend of the Martyr King. The Queen, too, was an admirable subject for Vandyke's talent, with her delicate features and dark hair curling over her forehead, in the style fashionable in France and known as *tête de mouton*. A number of other portrait-painters were attracted from the Continent to the Stuart court, and of these Honthorst and Daniel Mytens were outstanding. The former painted portraits of Henrietta Maria which are as beautiful as any of Vandyke's, while the latter's pictures of Charles show him as a rather less refined figure than do those of the "Principal Painter of their Majesties at St. James's".

None of these artists, accomplished though they were, was of the stature of Peter Paul Rubens, who came to the Court as a diplomatic envoy from the Netherlands—not in the covert manner of Panzani, but as an accredited emissary. He was not only invaluable to Charles in advising on the purchase of works of art—it was on his recommendation that the Cartoons of Raphael were bought, which are one of the rare survivals from the Commonwealth dispersal—but he also painted while in England the splendid apotheosis of James I for the ceiling of Inigo Jones's newly finished Banqueting House. He fully earned the knighthood which Charles conferred on him, and he, on his side, spoke of the King as "the most art-loving Prince in Europe". This remark was no small compliment, with such ardent collectors in the market as Philip IV of Spain, Queen Christina of Sweden, and the Archduke Leopold, Regent of the Netherlands. It was said that the keen competition between Charles and Philip IV had a material effect in raising the prices of first-class works of art in Europe.

Had Charles's collection survived, England would now have possessed many of the finest pictures in the world; but to the Parliamentarians art stank of a discredited monarchy, and soon after Charles's execution it was decided that "the personal estates of the late King, Queen and Prince shall be inventoried, appraised, and sold, except such parcels of them as shall be thought fit to be reserved for the use of the State". The inventory survives, so that the tragic loss is known. Over the following two or three years works by Leonardo, Raphael, Titian, Tintoretto, Correggio, and a host of other superb painters were quietly dispersed, many of them finding their way into the royal collections of Europe, with the obliging Gerbier profitably negotiating the traffic in the reverse direction to hitherto. When all had been sold, with the exception of a few "parcels" which for one reason or another were retained, the pictures, the coins, the jewels, and the fine examples of the goldsmith's art, the Commonwealth had benefited by a total sum of £118,000. It would be impossible to estimate the present value of the collection.

The King had, too, the praiseworthy intention of raising the standard of artistic production in England, which was lamentably backward compared to the Continent, by the founding of a school devoted particularly to the study of the polite arts and sciences. It was named the Museum Minervae and was situated in the house in Covent Garden of Sir Francis Kingston, who was nominated Principal. The young pupils were to be instructed in "foreign languages, mathematics, painting, architecture, riding, fortification, antiquities and the science of medals". The only blemish on this otherwise admirable institution was that only entrants were admitted "who could prove themselves gentlemen". This proviso would no doubt have excluded such a pupil as Inigo Jones.

The academy, which was opened in 1636, prospered for about a decade, and then under the rising power of the Parliamentarians it suffered the same extinction as all Charles's other efforts to promote the more civilised aspects of life.

Undoubtedly painting was the art which appealed above all others to Charles; but he also had an interest in architecture greater than his father, and had there been more affluence, and hence less dissension, during his reign there would probably have been some splendid royal buildings to mark this era. Inigo Jones was fifty-two at the time of Charles's accession, but still full of vigour with twenty-seven years of life before him. He must have welcomed with enthusiasm a monarch who had a love of the visual arts, but in the event the work he carried out for his royal master was small. The Queen's House at Greenwich had remained unfinished since Anne of Denmark's final illness, and in 1629 work was restarted and the house was completed as a rural retreat for Henrietta Maria. For the Queen, too, Inigo Jones carried out improvements at Somerset House. But the work which would have been his *chef d'œuvre*, had it materialised, was the grandiose plan for a palace at Whitehall on the site of the conglomeration of buildings which formed the existing palace.

When the Parliamentarian Inventory was drawn up, the objects enumerated were said to come from twenty-four royal palaces. This sounds imposing, but many of them were no more than small hunting-boxes, while several were dilapidated, and none except Hampton Court was either grand or comfortable. Whitehall was straggling and inconvenient, St. James's was without splendour, Greenwich, except for the Queen's House, remained as Queen Elizabeth had left it, Windsor was a fortified castle with little domestic comfort, Richmond was becoming decayed, and Eltham and Nonsuch were in a similar condition. Woodstock and Oatlands, which were perhaps Henrietta Maria's favourite places of residence, were in better state, but they were not buildings on the grand scale of Hampton Court.

The time had certainly arrived for the building of a palace in the capital which could rival those of the rulers of Continental countries. The date of these first plans was 1638, but the country was already restless and the King's prestige was very low. There was no hope at all of the project being achieved. Jones's plans formed the basis for John Webb's revised schemes during the reign of Charles II, but they were not destined to fruition (not at least until the nineteenth century, when they were adapted by Sir Gilbert Scott for his designs for the new Foreign Office building).

Although the scheme for the new palace remained unfulfilled, Charles and Henrietta Maria carried out a considerable amount of refurnishing and redecoration at Hampton Court and Whitehall. The rush-strewn floors, which had persisted so long in England, were at last abandoned, and rugs lay on the stone flags and on the broad oak or elm floorboards of the upper rooms. The heavy oak furniture, which had not changed very materially in character since the reign of Henry VIII, was discarded for lighter and more graceful furnishings, and the squat four-poster beds of the Tudors gave way to beds of taller and more graceful design. Tapestry retained its popularity for covering walls; and the products of the Mortlake Manufactory, which the King had done much to promote, formed an admirable background for the new style of furniture, and for objects of decoration and utility in gold and silver. However, the principal ornament of the royal apartments was inevitably the constantly growing collection of pictures.

Charles carried out one improvement at Hampton Court of a highly practical nature. Until this period the Palace had depended for a water supply on the conduits formed by Cardinal Wolsey more than a century earlier. This was far from adequate, and in 1638 the King directed a commission to make plans for bringing water from the river Colne to the Palace. By July in the following year a channel twenty-one feet wide, two feet deep, and eleven miles long was carrying a plentiful flow to the Palace, and also to the fountains which Charles had set up amongst the formal hedges of yew and box in his new gardens. The King's less happy idea of forming a royal forest stretching from Hampton to Richmond and twenty miles in circumference, was reluctantly abandoned at the insistence of Archbishop Laud. The project would have entailed the destruction of several villages and the enclosure of much common land. The Archbishop had difficulty in persuading the King that this would make him somewhat unpopular.

The tradition of Masques, which had been the favourite pastime of Anne of Denmark, continued strongly in the court of Charles and his Queen, and reached during this reign the highest stage of development —the highest and the last stage, for there was no renewal after the Restoration. Charles II was fond of witnessing plays, though not principally for intellectual reasons; but he attended them at the public theatres where they were performed by professional players, and the expensive productions staged solely for the benefit of the Court circle were not attempted during his reign.

Jonson and Inigo Jones were still collaborating at the time of Charles's accession, but the tension and rivalry between them was mounting, and the masque *Cloridia* of 1630, in which the Queen and her ladies took part, was the last product of their united talents. In his subsequent plays and writings Jonson lost no opportunity of attacking the character of Jones,

16    Charles I and his Court, with Greenwich Palace and the Thames in the background
*Reproduced by gracious permission of Her Majesty The Queen, from a detail
of a painting by Adriaan van Stalbemt*

17   Charles II on Horse Guards Parade. The Banqueting Hall is in the background
*Detail of a painting by an unknown contemporary artist*

but seemingly the sympathy of the King and his Court lay more with the Surveyor than with the irascible Poet Laureate, and the latter went to his grave in 1637 having spent his last years in neglect and poverty.

However, a wealth of new talent came to the fore, and burgeoned in the royal sunshine, though it is doubtful if any of these younger writers had quite the talent of Jonson during his most productive years. There was Sir William D'Avenant, said to have been Shakespeare's illegitimate son, who succeeded Jonson as Poet Laureate, and Thomas May who had been, as it were, the runner-up; there were Aurelian Townshend and Thomas Carew. For the majority of the masques Inigo Jones continued to design the settings and the costumes, while the scenic effects he contrived achieved an ingenuity which had never previously been reached.

Masques were not entirely devised to divert: they had occasionally also a rather subtle educational value. During the first stormy years of marriage the Queen had made little effort to master English, and this had been one of the many causes of friction between husband and wife. However, she greatly enjoyed taking part in masques, and in order to do this successfully she had to learn by heart many poetic lines. Thus she became fluent in English and spoke it habitually to her children, so that her son Charles at least knew almost no French until he had lived for some time in exile in France during the Commonwealth.

It was not only the writers of Masques who came to the fore at this period; there was also a bevy of poets, whose verses in praise of the King and Queen usually ensured to them the material benefits of royal patronage. Several were men of great talent whose genius might not have developed without the support they received from the King, and it must have been gratifying to Charles that a number risked their lives, or at least their liberty, in his cause when adversity came upon him. William D'Avenant, Abraham Cowley, and John Denham all acted as secret messengers, principally carrying letters between the King and Henrietta Maria, who was in France. When they could do no more for Charles, all three joined the Queen in France. Later D'Avenant was captured by a Parliamentary ship when on his way to Virginia, and was brought back to England and imprisoned in the Tower. He was soon released, however, through, it is said, the intercession of Milton. After his death in 1668, his widow published a volume of his collected poems with a long dedication to Charles II which opened—a little infelicitously—with the following words: "Your Highness is no sooner returned from exposing your person for the honour and safety of three Kingdoms, but you are persecuted by a poor widow. . . ."

During the middle years of Charles I's reign, D'Avenant had been instrumental in fomenting the cult of Platonic Love which Henrietta

Maria had inaugurated at the Court, and his masque *Temple of Love*, which was performed by the Queen and her ladies on Shrove Tuesday 1635, extolled this special form of cerebral, as opposed to physical, adulation. It was a tradition which Marguerite de Valois, the first wife of Henri IV, had attempted rather unsuccessfully to establish at the French Court. The unity of Charles and Henrietta Maria's married life formed at least a sound basis on which to build this unattainable ideal; and once the thesis was accepted, it enabled the Court poets to write verses in passionate praise of the Queen without a hint of indelicacy.

The ideals of the cult were described very clearly in a letter written in 1634 by James Howell from Westminster to Philip Warwick in Paris. "The Court affords little news at present," he wrote, "but that there is a love called Platonic Love, which much sways there of late; it is a love abstracted from all corporeal gross impressions and sensual appetite, but consists in the contemplations and ideas of the mind, not in any carnal fruition." These were not ideals which would have provoked much enthusiasm in either the previous or the subsequent reign; but one senses here a very distant foretaste of the Aesthetic Movement of the eighteen-seventies and 'eighties. Unfortunately, in neither century were the charms of incorporeal love endowed with any very durable quality.

From this contemplation of the artistic sensibility of the Caroline Court, it is painful to turn to the political dissension which was mounting in the country. Soon the whole elaborate structure was to be shattered by the increasing storm; and with it the theory of kingship, epitomised by the notion of the divine right of kings, on which the English monarchy had been based, was swept away for ever. Thus the last Renaissance court in England crumbled and fell, and the reign which had come near to being the most fertile and favourable for the propagation of the arts since the culture of the Renaissance had reached these shores ended in sterile gloom and disaster.

When Charles II returned in 1660, his position as a ruler was very different to that of his predecessors, and from that time forward the power of governing passed from the Crown to the Ministers. It is vain to consider how different the history of these years might have been if Prince Henry had survived to wear the crown. But had he developed as he began, with his determination of character, uprightness, and love of the arts, his reign might have been one of the most productive in English history, and the tragedy that unfolded under the weak guidance of his brother might have been avoided.

# Chapter 8

# CHARLES II

While the political troubles of Charles I's reign would suggest that the King was so constantly embroiled in quarrels with his Parliament that he had little peace or leisure in which to indulge in the pleasures of tranquil pursuits, so a superficial view of the reign of Charles II is that the "Merry Monarch" spent his whole time in amusements, mostly of a dubious description, and that the affairs of State were left entirely in the hands of his ministers.

Neither one nor the other is a true picture. The previous chapter has endeavoured to show that there were intervals of sunshine between the storms which gathered over Charles I; while his son took a far larger part in directing the fortunes of the country than he is usually credited with. Charles II's courage, resource, and generosity in the three major disasters of his reign, which occurred within a space of three years—the Plague, the Great Fire, and the calamitous war with the Dutch—showed him a true leader of his people.

But it is naturally the lighter side of Charles's life which makes more amusing reading than his constant efforts to persuade Parliament to provide funds for equipping a fleet and for building coastal fortifications; and there is no lack of contemporary memoirs and journals to illuminate the highly frivolous aspects of his reign. In the writings of Evelyn and Pepys the descriptions of the King's frailties are introduced amongst more serious matters; but a study of Anthony Hamilton's *Memoirs of the Comte de Grammont* would suggest that the life of the Court was given up without intermission to amusements and amorous intrigues. And, though Hamilton is probably not far from the truth in portraying a hot-house atmosphere of moral laxity as pervading the Court, the King throughout his reign maintained a strong sense of duty.

The close contact he had with his ministers and Parliament appears even more clearly in the pages of Sir John Reresby's *Memoirs* than in the diaries of Evelyn and Pepys. Reresby, a turbulent figure involved in constant quarrels and disputes, was Member of Parliament for the little borough of Aldborough in Yorkshire, and was a supporter of the Court party. In return for his support, he was not hesitant in begging favours of the King; and in this he was no doubt typical of the many place-seekers who revolved in the royal orbit. But though self-interest was never far away, he was sincere in his devotion to the Crown, and he formed a useful contact between Charles and his obstinate Parliaments.

At the Restoration, Charles became the third out of four successive monarchs who had lost one of his parents at the hands of the public executioner. In the cases of Elizabeth I and James I this melancholy fact had not affected their position very gravely, but with Charles II the situation was different. His father had died ostensibly by the will of the people, and, though the English were hastily banishing this disagreeable truth from their minds, there was no doubt that the prestige of the Crown had suffered a blow from which it could never recover.

However, none of this was apparent amidst the intense jubilation which hailed Charles's return to his country. On 25th May 1660 he landed at Dover, accompanied by his brothers the Dukes of York and Gloucester, and was greeted by General Monck who had been instrumental in accomplishing the Restoration. Along beflagged roads lined with cheering peasantry he drove to Canterbury, and by slow progresses and amidst mounting excitement he reached Rochester on the 28th; on the following day, which by an agreeable coincidence was his thirtieth birthday, he set out on the last stage of the journey to London.

Every mile he advanced towards the capital the procession increased in volume. At Blackheath, where the army was arrayed to meet him and cheered him lustily, he left his coach and continued for the remainder of the journey on a charger, so that he was in full view of the crowds. At Southwark he was met by the Lord Mayor and Aldermen of London who presented him with the City sword, while the Recorder delivered a long speech of welcome. These formalities accomplished, he was entertained to a banquet within a magnificent tent hung with tapestry.

From Southwark the great procession passed over London Bridge, through the twisting streets of the City, along the Strand lined with the great houses of the nobility, and so out into the comparatively open country that surrounded Whitehall Palace. Everywhere along the route houses were hung with decorations of carpets, damasks, and garlands of flowers; music of all sorts mingled with the cheers of the multitudes, and from the Tower the inevitable deafening salvos submerged all other sounds. So great was the tumult that a number of people, more emotional or more frail than their neighbours, expired. Even the entry of Elizabeth into London had fallen short of this.

Although there had been no long time for preparation, splendid triumphal arches had been erected at salient points on the route. These handsome baroque structures were the work—at least according to his own writings—of the enterprising Sir Balthazar Gerbier, who has been seen in the last chapter acquiring works of art for Charles I and, when the situation unfortunately changed, selling them again to foreign potentates. In the magnificence of the setting and in the popular rejoicing, the appearance of the new King was fortunately no anti-climax, as had been that of his grandfather fifty-seven years earlier. Charles's tall, slim figure and dark, rather heavy-featured face was highly impressive, while the grace of his manners and the geniality of his speech made an immediate impression. By the time he reached Whitehall Palace he had won the hearts of the people of London.

The momentous day of his entry into the capital having been so brilliantly carried through, Charles was able to spend the evening contentedly in the company of Barbara Palmer, who as Lady Castlemaine was to dominate his life for the coming years.

No change of régime of the magnitude of the Restoration could have been carried out more smoothly and with greater public approbation. But once the cheers had died away and the decorations had been taken down, Charles found himself in a position more difficult than he may have anticipated. The first and most pressing trouble was lack of money, which for the time at least submerged the burning question of the national religion. The Commonwealth government had shown little financial aptitude. In spite of obtaining a useful source of wealth from the sale of Crown properties and Cavalier estates, there had for some years been an annual adverse balance of expenditure over income of £1,000,000, while at the moment of the Restoration the cash resources of the Exchequer were said to have amounted to just over £11.

The new government were therefore faced with problems of the utmost difficulty, while the personal position of the King became constantly more worrying. No sooner was he installed at Whitehall than an ever-growing stream of Cavaliers presented themselves, begging for compensation for the losses they had incurred in the royal cause. No body of men could have more richly deserved the royal bounty. Many had lost their estates, suffered wounds and imprisonment, and perhaps spent years in miserable exile separated from their families. The King was fully conscious of his debt to them, and with his generous nature would have been glad to reward them liberally, but this was an impossibility.

The bestowal of peerages and baronetcies cost the King nothing and brought satisfaction to some of the applicants: others were rewarded with various appointments which were in the gift of the King, but there was a limit to the number of these. Nor can it be said that the choice of candidates for some of the posts was always the happiest. Sir John

Denham, the Cavalier poet, for example, fully deserved the gratitude of his master, but he was singularly ill-equipped for the post of Surveyor-General of His Majesty's Works, with which he was rather casually rewarded. A sad failure he would have made of his office if the young Christopher Wren had not been appointed his assistant.

Many also flocked to Whitehall who had nothing to ask, and nothing to gain except the pleasure of seeing a King once more established in England. On Sundays particularly, the throngs were enormous, watching the King in the Chapel Royal, where the bleak services of the Puritans gave way immediately to the more elaborate ritual with music and vestments which had been usual during the previous reign.

For all these—for the needy Cavaliers, the prosperous citizens, and the country squires—Charles kept open house during these first ecstatic weeks of his restoration; and one loyal and gratified subject wrote: "The eagerness of men, women, and children to see his Majesty and kiss his hands was so great that he had scarce leisure to eat for some days." In an atmosphere of such warmth and enthusiasm he was at his best, and exhibited a never-failing ease of manner and geniality.

Charles had now to envisage two major functions before he could consider himself fully established in his kingdom: one he no doubt looked forward to with pleasure, the other with some foreboding. The first was his coronation and the second his marriage.

Perhaps bearing in mind the difficulties his Catholic mother had caused his father over the coronation, Charles decided to be crowned while still single. The day fixed for the ceremony was 23rd April 1661, and it was carried through with the customary splendour. Samuel Pepys was in the Abbey by four in the morning, and obtained a good seat on a scaffold in the north transept. Seven hours he had to wait before the entry of the King, but such was the magnificence of the ceremony that he felt well rewarded. Leaving the Abbey before the royal procession, Pepys made his way to Westminster Hall, and was thus able to enjoy the full spectacle of the coronation banquet with the Heralds and the King's Champion playing their traditional parts. The diarist's evening was given up to drinking loyal toasts somewhat excessively, and ended in unedifying confusion.

Marriage presented a more obstinate problem, and it was difficult to know where to find a princess possessing the three main desiderata—an attractive appearance, the Protestant religion, and a handsome dowry. Of these, the last was an absolute necessity for the impoverished Charles; and it was on account of the material assets which were promised that Catherine of Braganza was eventually chosen, although her claims to beauty were not great and her religion was definitely wrong.

The dowry offered by Catherine's mother, the Queen Regent of Portugal, was lavish—half a million pounds' worth of gold, the port of Tangier, the island of Bombay, and permission for the English to share the Portuguese trade with Brazil and the East Indies—this last a very valuable concession. It was a glittering endowment and one designed to make any bride attractive; but the Portuguese were, in fact, exceedingly anxious for the match, as it would add greatly to the prestige of their newly founded dynasty in the eyes of Europe. Moreover, Catherine was no longer very young, as ages in the royal marriage-market went; she was to have passed her twenty-fourth birthday before she arrived in England, and if this match failed it was unlikely that any other would eventuate.

The terms were satisfactorily agreed, and English ships set out to take possession of Tangier and to bring back the greatly needed gold—and of course the Princess. The normal procedure would have been for a proxy marriage to have been celebrated in Lisbon before Catherine set out for England; but here arose a difficulty. The mixed marriage could not take place without a Papal dispensation. The Vatican, however, had not recognised the new régime in Portugal, so that the Princess could only have been described as daughter of the late Duke of Braganza. This was not acceptable, and so it was decided that Catherine must leave without her marriage lines, and hope for the best on arrival. Meanwhile Charles wrote affectionate letters to his bride, ending them, presumably with his tongue in his cheek, "The very faithful husband of your majesty, Charles Rex".

In the middle of April Lord Sandwich with the English fleet arrived at Lisbon, having successfully installed a force at Tangier. Intense jubilations took place in the town, with fireworks, illuminations and bull-fights, and the 23rd of the month was fixed for the departure of the bride with her Portuguese and English train. But at the last moment there was a serious hitch: the promised gold did not materialise, and the Queen Regent explained with apologies that it had been used for the expenses of the war with Spain. However, instead of gold, merchandise for half the value would be sent with the fleet, and the remainder in gold would follow later. Lord Sandwich had no option but to accept this compromise, and the Princess set sail accompanied by ships loaded with sugar, spices, and other useful commodities, but without a single bag of gold. In spite of constant reminders over the following years, the second half of the dowry was never in fact paid.

On 14th May the fleet arrived at Portsmouth, but it was not till six days later that Charles, who was delayed in London by Parliamentary work, arrived in the town after journeying all through the night. The

Princess was slightly indisposed and received her husband in bed. "It was happy for the honour of the nation", wrote the King to Clarendon next day, "I was not put to the consummation of the marriage last night, for I was so sleepy, having slept but two hours in my journey, that I am afraid matters would have gone very sleepily."

The letter continued to describe Catherine's appearance with temperate warmth, saying, "there is not anything in her face that can in the least shock one". This was not enthusiastic praise, but Charles seems on the whole to have been adequately satisfied with his bargain. And perhaps there was a certain attraction in the fact that Catherine, with her excessively cloistral upbringing, was so very different from the young women with whom he normally consorted.

But in looks she undoubtedly fell short of the high standard of beauty prevalent at Charles's Court. The appearance of these ladies is well known from the canvases of Sir Peter Lely in which, clad in low-cut silk dresses, they stand before heavy draped curtains with the hint of a romantic landscape in the distance. Their faces are framed by the soft curls which were then the fashion, and their eyes look towards the beholder with a glance which is both quizzical and melting. That they have a curious uniformity of appearance is presumably due to Lely's desire to make them conform to an admired type.

Catherine also had fine dark eyes, as well as an agreeable expression, though this latter asset soon faded before the trials and jealousies of her married life. She was low in stature and her figure was not graceful, with a long body and short legs. At least, however, she shone amongst her Portuguese ladies-in-waiting whose singular plainness created much heartless amusement at the Court. Not only were they ugly, but also so virtuous that they declined to sleep in any bed in which a man had ever lain.

On the following day the marriage took place. There was firstly a Catholic ceremony held in private in Catherine's bed-chamber, and this was followed by a public service conducted by Sheldon, Bishop of London. Charles presented his bride with a gold toilet service valued at the high figure of £400, while the unfortunate Catherine's present to her husband consisted of that embarrassing consignment of merchandise which had to be sold for hard cash.

Charles and Catherine remained several days at Portsmouth and thence, passing by Windsor Castle, where works were already in progress to make the place more habitable, they proceeded to Hampton Court—arriving there on the second anniversary of Charles's landing at Dover. During these two years great improvements had been made at the Palace, and the building, which had been largely emptied of its contents during the

Commonwealth, once again assumed an air of splendour so far as the straitened condition of the Exchequer allowed. John Evelyn was enthusiastic about the appearance of the rooms. "There is incomparable furniture in it," he wrote in his diary, "especially hangings designed by Raphael, very rich with gold, especially the Caesarian Triumphs of Andrea Mantegna, formerly the Duke of Mantua's. Of the tapestries, I believe the world can show nothing nobler of the kind than the stories of Abraham and Tobit."

The States of Holland had presented a magnificent canopied bed hung with crimson velvet embroidered with silver, while the Queen-Mother had given "a great looking-glass and toilet of beaten massive gold". Charles had imported many mirrors from France, which were hung here and at Whitehall, while Catherine had brought with her a number of "Indian cabinets" such as had never before been seen in England and were greatly admired. For an impoverished monarch Charles had indeed made a fine show to greet his bride, and even Pepys, who was not much interested in the visual arts, was impressed by "the noble furniture and brave pictures".

Charles had made great efforts to provide a setting suitable for a Queen of England; and this, coupled with the devotion he was displaying, made the marriage begin under the rosiest auspices. Undoubtedly Catherine fell at once deeply in love with her charming and attractive husband. There was, however, one anxiety in the background of her mind. Before she left Portugal her mother had spoken to her of Lady Castlemaine, and had warned her that she was never even to allow her name to be mentioned in her presence. Fortunately, as it happened, at the time of Catherine's arrival in England Lady Castlemaine was employed in that task, so unwelcome to royal mistresses, of maternity, and a son was born to her a few days after Charles's marriage. The child was at first claimed as his heir by Lord Castlemaine, but the mother would have none of this, and Charles willingly accepted paternity.

Thus domestically employed, Lady Castlemaine was out of view at this important moment in Catherine's married life. The respite was not long. Within a few weeks of marriage, Charles, with an air of innocence, presented the Queen with a list of the ladies he suggested should join her household. At the head of the list was the fatal name of Lady Castlemaine. Catherine, who till this moment had been the most docile and submissive of wives, flew into a temper, refused to accept her, and said she would return to Portugal rather than support such an insult.

This distressing interview took place in July, about six weeks after the wedding, and, though the relationship of the King and Queen varied in temperature thereafter from cold to cool, the marriage never again rose to any normal degree of warmth. The cold-heartedness of Charles in eventually forcing Catherine to receive Lady Castlemaine showed a singularly unattractive aspect of a character which was generally supposed to be remarkable for a casual good nature. But with Catherine his emotions were never stirred, and while he was absolutely ruthless in imposing his wishes on this unfortunate and helpless woman, he supported, apparently without rancour, the violence and rudeness of Lady Castlemaine with whom he was, at least physically, in love. To poor Catherine, who was entirely ignorant of the vagaries of the male character, this must have seemed very baffling.

It took many weeks to break down Catherine's obstinate opposition to receiving her husband's mistress, and it is impossible to say what threats or endearments delivered in the privacy of the crimson velvet state-bedstead eventually induced her to give way. But having at last accepted the situation, she received her rival with a warmth by which many members of that profligate Court professed to be rather shocked. Thus the poor Queen received disapproval from all sides; but from this time forward, in spite of her lamentable failure to produce an heir, she was at least treated by Charles with a rather negligent consideration, and was allowed complete liberty to indulge in her own simple and harmless amusements.

One of the poor Queen's greatest pleasures was her annual visit of several summer weeks to Tunbridge Wells. The chalybeate waters of this little spa had been first recommended to her as beneficial to fertility; and though they signally failed in this purpose, Catherine found the informal life she led there so agreeable that a visit to the Wells became an important feature of the Court curriculum. Even the King consented to join his spouse in these pastoral pleasures. The Court was accommodated in numerous small houses scattered amongst the trees which surrounded the town, and the elegant company strolled along the shady paths and over the wide lawns, and enjoyed a freedom from the formality which was inseparable from normal Court life. "Intimacy ripens at the first acquaintance," wrote Hamilton in his *Memoirs of de Grammont*, "and the life there is generally delicious." No doubt some of the pastimes which were so popular at Whitehall were practised with equal pleasure in the rustic surroundings of Tunbridge.

Charles, on his restoration, made no attempt to follow the example of his predecessors in maintaining and inhabiting a great number of royal residences. The restriction of his finances made this an impossibility, and instead he prudently concentrated his efforts on restoring and embellishing a few of the more important palaces. It was a task that was highly congenial to him, and, as it happened, there were several brilliant architects available to carry out his wishes: had there been a well-filled Treasury, England would undoubtedly have benefited from much fine architecture directly due to the King's initiative.

The principal palace was inevitably Whitehall, that curious conglomeration of buildings which had grown up round Wolsey's York Place till it covered with its courts and gardens an area of twenty-four acres and stretched for half a mile along the river bank. Within its purlieu were included not only the royal and state apartments but also many private habitations and public offices. Indeed the Court and government were here welded into one amorphous and unwieldy whole. It must have been a fascinating and picturesque group of buildings, but it contained only two structures of great architectural merit—the tall Holbein gateway which spanned the road passing through the Palace, and Inigo Jones's classical Banqueting House which rose, chaste and serene, above the roofs and low battlemented towers of its humble neighbours. Though Whitehall had no true dignity as a palace, it was singularly well adapted to the life led by Charles and his Court. No structure could have been better suited to intrigue, while the Thames flowing past the river-stairs was a constant invitation to secret and nocturnal adventure.

The valuable contents of the Palace had largely disappeared during the Civil War, but were fortunately partly located and returned at the Restoration. As early as June 1660 Evelyn noted in his Diary that: "Goods that had been pillaged from Whitehall during the Rebellion, were now daily brought in, and restored upon proclamation; as plate, hangings, pictures, etc". If these valuable objects had not been looted, they would probably have been sold under the Commonwealth, and have disappeared from the country for ever. As it was, a number of fine pictures which were of a quality Charles II would never have been in a financial position to afford, were soon hanging once again on the walls. Evelyn noted that these were "divers of the best pictures of the great masters, Raphael, Titian, etc.".

In the first years of his reign Charles made no very important structural alterations to Whitehall; possibly he hoped that the new palace originally projected by Inigo Jones during his father's reign and now put forward again by John Webb would materialise in his lifetime. However, he called in his Serjeant Painter, Robert Streater, to decorate the walls of some of the apartments with the flowing allegorical scenes which were just coming into fashion.

Across the park from Whitehall lay the old Tudor structure of St. James's, where Charles had been born, but this early connection did not induce him to look on it with favour as a residence. It became the official home of the Duke of York, and the Queen had here her Catholic chapel.

131

18 (overleaf) Windsor Castle from the River (1724)
From "Nouveau Théâtre de la Grande Bretagne"

The park, however, was always a place of great pleasure to him. Here he formed a long canal stocked with waterfowl, and here he constantly walked in the mornings when unable to take exercise further afield.

Windsor Castle needed more drastic treatment than Whitehall, and since it became his favourite place of residence a thorough overhaul of the domestic part of the structure was undertaken. On the panelled walls of Charles's new rooms hung the long delicate swags so brilliantly carved by John Evelyn's protégé Grinling Gibbons, while the chapel and part of St. George's Hall were painted by Antonio Verrio, the Italian painter, with the magnificent murals which were inclined to eclipse the rather pedestrian work of Streater. Charles was pleased with his improvements, and showed them off with pride to his friends. Sir John Reresby visited the Castle and noted in his *Memoirs*: "The King showed me a great deal of what he had done to the house, which was indeed very fine, and acquainted me with what he intended to do more."

Windsor had indeed every advantage for Charles. It was satisfactorily distant from the Parliament, which was the plague of his life, so that he could live there in comparative peace and in privacy. Should he wish to give a great entertainment, the fine rooms lent themselves to this purpose admirably, and he was able to make a splendid display. Furthermore, within the mediaeval fortifications were many small houses and apartments where his women friends could be discreetly accommodated.

But it was probably the romantic wooded surroundings of the Castle which provided Charles with his greatest pleasure, for it was an unexpected side to his character that he had a devotion to the country and to country pursuits. "The King lived very privately at this time," wrote Reresby in 1680; "there was little resort to him, and he passed his days in fishing or walking in the park." He greatly improved the gardens and planted avenues, a work which was much admired by Evelyn, himself an enthusiastic gardener and forester. "There was now the terrace brought almost round the old Castle", he wrote, "the grass made clean, even, and curiously turfed; the avenues to the new park, and other walks, planted with elms and limes, and a pretty canal, and receptacle for fowl." In addition there was Sir Samuel Morland's remarkable invention by which a jet of pure water could be thrown as high as the Castle. The Queen, too, enjoyed these pastoral interests, and, with her erratic spouse in a genial mood, she passed some of the happiest days of her life at Windsor.

Almost the first work Charles undertook on his restoration was the rebuilding of the decayed Tudor buildings of Greenwich Palace. In the autumn of 1661 Evelyn was discussing the plans with the inexperienced Sir John Denham, and dissuading him from raising the new palace on piles on the very edge of the river. Fortunately the work was largely taken out of Denham's feeble hands, and under John Webb's direction the noble building, known as the King Charles's Block, arose at right angles to the Thames.

Greenwich, however, played no great part in the life of the Court, and Whitehall and Windsor were the principal palaces, with occasional visits to Hampton Court. Very important also to Charles was his small house at Newmarket. The Queen was not very welcome there, and the King would enjoy himself prodigiously in the company of his more sophisticated friends with long days on the Heath attending the races, and hawking, with evenings given up to a variety of amusements to which the Queen's presence would have been no desirable addition.

Henry VIII's fantastic palace of Nonsuch had long been in a state of decay, but it was still sufficiently weather-proof to house several government departments during the disastrous year of the great plague. Thereafter it was abandoned, and some years later Charles granted it to the rapacious Lady Castlemaine, having at the time no other means of providing a present of value. The royal mistress had this crumbling emblem of Tudor pride demolished, and the materials sold for what they would fetch.

Had Charles's life been prolonged by a few more years, it is probable that the palace at Winchester would have become one of his favourite retreats, situated as it was at an even safer distance than Windsor from the troublous Parliament. In 1682 the King decided to erect a splendid building at the top of the steep slope to the west of the town. So rapidly did Christopher Wren produce his plans that on 23rd March in the following year Charles laid the foundation stone of what he hoped would be his most carefree residence—a true Sans Souci. The work was pressed forward with great speed, but in the event the sudden death of the King occurred before the new palace was habitable.

Though Charles II never possessed the autocratic power in the direction of the affairs of State that had been enjoyed by his predecessors, his example and influence in the country was strong, particularly amongst the wide circle which came in contact with the Court. The King's interest in building and in the laying out of gardens and parks percolated swiftly to his subjects. Many of them found themselves in much the same position as the King—with their houses dilapidated and their purses straitened —and yet many managed to repair the decay which had fallen on their houses during the past twenty years, and to restore them in the style which had developed during those architecturally sterile decades.

John Evelyn was never happier than when superintending improvements at Sayes Court, his house at Deptford, where the garden was his special pride, or giving his sound advice to others with similar interests.

And Sir John Reresby, between brawls, his Parliamentary duties, and petitions to the King and the Duke of York, would retire to his house at Thryberg and carry out extensive works. The place had been allowed to fall into "ruin and decay" during his minority, and the garden had become a wilderness which had to be entirely remade. He tackled the situation with energy, rebuilding the north side of the house with stone where before had been lath and plaster, and laying out a formal garden in the style that the King was making the fashion. "I made this summer", he wrote, "the *jet d'eau* or the fountain in the middle of the parterre, and the grotto in the summerhouse, and brought the water in lead pipes." In addition he planted several avenues. The royal initiative was highly infectious, and before long similar works were in progress at many of the country houses of England.

It was at Whitehall and at Windsor that the principal life of the Court was carried on, and it is the former which is particularly associated with Charles's reign. It was here that everyone who hoped for preferment or amusement flocked in the conviction, which was usually disappointed, that benefits must flow from basking in the sunshine of the royal presence. London became at this period a body with two hearts. There was what Macaulay called "the metropolis of commerce" centred round the Exchange in the City, and "the metropolis of fashion" seething in the halls and courts of Whitehall Palace. The former, particularly since the trading concessions which had sweetened Queen Catherine's arrival in England, was in a condition of sound and increasing prosperity, while the latter, for all its raffish elegance, existed on a brittle financial surface which constantly threatened to disintegrate into bankruptcy.

Early in Charles's reign "Ordinances for the Government of the Household" were drawn up in the traditional way. But in this case the elaborate rules were designed rather for the proper organisation of the Court than in order to achieve economy. Furthermore it was apparently hoped that the example of a well-arranged household would be followed by others in the country, for the Ordinance opens with these words:

> "To establish good government and order in Our Court, which from thence may spread with more honour through all parts of Our Kingdoms."

Some of the rules would hardly have had a general application, such as that which ordered that there were to be in the precincts of the Court: "no places to be employed for tipling-houses, selling or taking tobacco, hott waters, or any kind of disorder". Or the regulation to the Porters: "not to permit any stragling and masterless men, any suspitious person, or uncivill, uncleanly, and rude people, or beggars to come within our

Court". The Court was, of course, constantly full of "beggars", but they did not belong to the class envisaged by the Ordinances.

The rules of procedure were highly exhaustive, and covered every department of the Palace. The picture they present of a court organised and regulated to the last detail, hardly tallies with the lax and easy atmosphere suggested by contemporary diarists, and it must be supposed that the Ordinances once drawn up were largely forgotten.

But undoubtedly Charles's Court maintained a distinct standard of elegance. Though lack of morals was considered normal, coarseness of speech or behaviour was looked on with disfavour. Had Queen Elizabeth, for example, returned to Whitehall, her expletives and broad conversation would have caused shudders of disapproval. This civilised tone was set by the King, who, it was generally agreed, had the most gracious manners imaginable. He had advanced a long way from the time of his early exile in France, when La Grande Mademoiselle had found him gauche and silent. He had indeed social attainments of a high order, with a quick and sparkling wit and a great gift as a *raconteur*. As he grew older this latter gift was seemingly rather over-indulged, and stories were told and retold rather for his own pleasure than that of his hearers. Bishop Burnet observed, with his usual unepiscopal malice, that though a room might be full when the King began one of his stories, it was generally almost empty before he had finished it.

As Charles's stories grew longer with age, so his temper grew shorter, and that imperturbable geniality which had been so agreeable a characteristic during the first years of his reign gave way to moods of unpredictable irascibility. This was perhaps not surprising in view of the constant rebuffs he received from Parliament, both the Lords and the Commons at times showing little loyalty for their sovereign, and treating him with grave discourtesy. Until the King reached middle age, these disputes seldom affected his peace of mind, and Burnet remarked that he could "pass from business to pleasure and from pleasure to business in so easy a manner that all things seem alike to him"; while Reresby noted the same insouciant quality as late as 1679. He wrote in his *Memoirs:* "I was at the King's couchée. I wondered to see him cheerful amongst so many troubles; but it was not his nature to think much, or to perplex himself." But this happy equability became less easy to practise with age.

No doubt Charles had developed a protective shield to his feelings, to ward off the many cares of state which would otherwise have assailed him. But in any case he was not a man of very sensitive feelings, as was clear from his treatment of some of his ministers. The abandonment of his Chancellor Clarendon after many years of loyal service, for example, not only showed that gratitude had little place in his personality, but it also undermined the confidence of the country in his honour.

He had, however, the engaging, if trivial, quality of wishing that those people he liked should like each other, and to this end he took pleasure in spending an evening in the joint company of several of his mistresses. The suppressed feelings of these ladies can be imagined, but it was an intimate party such as this that Evelyn observed at Whitehall with no little disapproval only six days before Charles's death. "I saw this evening", he wrote in his journal for 25th January 1685, "such a scene of profuse gaming, and the King in the midst of his three concubines, as I have never before seen—luxurious dallying and profaneness."

The three ladies who are so disparagingly described by the virtuous Evelyn were the Duchess of Cleveland (formerly Lady Castlemaine), Louise de Kéroualle, Duchess of Portsmouth, and Hortense Mancini, Duchesse de Mazarin; and it was a distinct achievement on Charles's part that they should all pass a cosy evening together. The King's plebeian mistresses, such as Nell Gwynn and Moll Davis, were naturally not admitted to these select circles. The former was not new to the position of a kept woman when she caught Charles's wandering eye: indeed she called the King her Charles III, the first and second having been Charles Hart, the great-nephew of Shakespeare, and Charles Sackville, later Earl of Dorset, respectively. She was well housed, first in Lincoln's Inn Fields, and later in a pretty house in Pall Mall, conveniently backing on to St. James's Park.

Moll Davis had first been seen by Charles in a revival of Fletcher's *Two Noble Kinsmen*, in which she sang a sad little song beginning:

> *My lodging it is on the cold ground,*
> *And very hard is my fare.*

The pathos of the words so moved the impressionable King that she soon found herself the possessor of a comfortable little house in the newly built and fashionable St. James's Square.

Behind the amorous intrigues which played so large a part in Charles's life appears the enigmatic figure of William Chiffinch. His official positions were Page of the Bedchamber and Keeper of the Private Closet, but his principal—if unofficial—function was to act as pimp for his royal master. Though he has not come down in history as a man of very edifying character, it has never been suggested that he was anything but a loyal servant to the King. For he had other duties besides the one of supplying suitable candidates for Charles's bed: he acted as secretary for communications which the King was unwilling to trust to more formal channels; it was he who received the annual pension which was paid to the

King by Louis XIV; having a convivial manner, he was often able to obtain useful information for the King by staging drinking-parties for those who were normally guarded in their speech; it was he finally who introduced Father Huddleston to effect Charles's conversion to Catholicism on his death-bed. William Chiffinch, indeed, was a personage of importance in the Caroline Court, although his functions lay chiefly in the dark passages and narrow stairways surrounding the King's apartments at Whitehall.

Flamboyant women figured so largely at Court that they tended to obscure a more serious side to Charles's character, which certainly existed. He took an unexpected interest in science, and fitted up a laboratory at Whitehall close to his own apartments; here he took pleasure in working with the assistance of his chemist, Le Febvre. He became the first patron of the Royal Society, which was started under the aegis of Dr. Christopher Wren and others learned in the sciences. It was the King's initiative which led to the building of the Royal Observatory high on the hill above the old Palace of Greenwich, which was designed to facilitate the art of finding a measurement of longitude at sea.

Everything which had to do with ships lay close to Charles's heart, and it must have been very mortifying to him that, in spite of his really earnest endeavours, the parsimony of Parliament would not allow him to maintain a first-class fleet. The defeats which the better-equipped Dutch were able to inflict on the English fleet were a bitter humiliation to Charles and to most of his countrymen.

Charles's interest in embellishing his palaces and in laying out their surroundings has already been mentioned, and it may be supposed that if less of his scarce cash had been absorbed by his mistresses he might have bequeathed a finer legacy of architecture to posterity. But even given the most austere continence, it is unlikely that the great new Palace of Whitehall would ever have materialised.

Throughout his life Charles had been on the whole careful of his health. He adored exercise, whether playing tennis in the court at White-hall or Hampton Court, or walking for many miles in the park at Windsor or on Newmarket Heath. He rose exceedingly early in the morning, and endeavoured to dispatch the tedious work of government before the day was well begun. He was reasonably abstemious in eating and drinking, though Reresby mentions one occasion when Charles "was in good humour and drank very hard", and another when he rested "after a debauch".

And yet his life was not a long one. He was still a few months under fifty-five when he was suddenly attacked by his last illness, and four days later, on 6th February 1685, he died. Inevitably poison was suspected, but Evelyn pronounced his death to have been the result of an apoplectic fit, and this is the probable truth.

# Chapter 9

# JAMES II

The popular opinion of James II's character is that he possessed most of the faults of his father and very few of his virtues. This is a conclusion based rather on his disastrous failure as a King than on a close analysis of his personality; for he had undoubtedly some excellent qualities, though not perhaps in very generous supply. They might, however, have been adequate—with a little good luck—to have procured for him a fairly successful reign. His principal assets were courage, honesty of purpose, frugal tastes, an integrity unusual in the Stuarts, and—an important feature for a monarch—a dignified presence.

Several kings in English history have had less to recommend them than these few, but solid, advantages, and yet have not had such brief, inglorious reigns as James II. The faults which led to disaster were not of the blackest, and yet they heavily outweighed and nullified his modest virtues. His inability to tolerate compromise, and his intense religious fervour, which grew stronger with the years, were his principal drawbacks; and these were enhanced by a formidable lack of tact, and an absence of that natural grace of manner which had added so much to his brother's popularity. Sir John Reresby, who was with the King at the jubilant time of the crushing of the Monmouth rebellion, and also in the dark days preceding the Dutch invasion, remarked that James "was of a temper so equal as not to appear transported upon any occasion". This rigid self-control should probably be counted a virtue, but some show of emotion would undoubtedly have been more engaging.

It was a tragedy of James's life that his highest point of success was reached while he was still very young. When he was nineteen years of age his mother, Henrietta Maria, and his brother reluctantly agreed to his serving in the French army under Turenne, and within a short time he had earned the high regard of that brilliant general, who was impressed by his fearlessness in battle and his coolness in danger. At the age of twenty-one he was promoted to the rank of lieutenant-general, a promotion due to his merit as a leader as much as to his royal birth.

Although during the forty-seven years of life that still lay before him there were periods of success, such as when he was in command of the English fleet, his career showed on the whole a steady decline in achievement from those two glamorous years of early promise; while after his succession to the throne at the age of forty-one, there was little but frustration and disaster to mark the passing of his life.

In view of his personal unpopularity, owing to his extreme Catholicism during the latter years of Charles II's reign, it was surprising that the populace greeted his accession to the throne without any show of disfavour. The people, it seemed, were so partial to a change of ruler that a new wearer of the crown was sure to be received initially with some warmth. The traditional ceremony of reading the proclamation took place at Whitehall, Temple Bar, and the Royal Exchange without raising any particular popular emotion. As Bishop Burnet wrote: "there were no tears for the last King, and no shouts for the present one."

The accession entailed for James and Mary of Modena a move across St. James's Park from the old Tudor palace, where they had lived very happily, to the sprawling buildings of Whitehall, which were still permeated by the *louche* atmosphere created by the late King and his many mistresses. It cannot be said that it was an atmosphere uncongenial to James, for his morals had been no better than his brother's—though his mistresses had been far plainer. But the sudden death of his brother and his own succession had made him determined to carry through the reformation of his private life on which he had been half-heartedly engaged for some years.

This praiseworthy resolution was not at first crowned with marked success, but at least he managed to improve the general tone of the Court. If James's morals remained frail, he was adamant in imposing a proper decorum on the raffish courtiers who still thronged the halls and galleries of the Palace. He made it abundantly clear that he would not tolerate bad language and drunkenness in the royal precincts, and he spoke publicly of someone "who had the impudence to appear drunk in the Queen's presence". These disparaging words were taken to be a reflection on the Duke of St. Albans, one of Charles's bastard sons.

In these endeavours, the King had the warm support of his Queen, to whom he was devoted in spite of his unfaithfulness, and who surprisingly enough returned his devotion, although she was twenty-five years his junior. Unfortunately, high-minded intentions and conjugal felicity were not sufficiently compelling to make him give up immediately his favourite mistress, Catherine Sedley. This unbeautiful, but seemingly amusing, woman was naturally delighted by her lover's advance in position, and pictured herself in the same rewarding situation as had lately been enjoyed by the Duchess of Portsmouth. The Queen was intensely jealous of her rival, but it was some time before her tears, combined with the admonitions of his spiritual advisers, persuaded the King to command Mrs. Sedley to leave Whitehall. In the event, however, the banishment turned out to be of no more than temporary duration.

Meanwhile active preparations went forward for the coronation, which was fixed for St. George's Day, 23rd April 1685. There was particular interest in the ceremony, since the crowning of a queen-consort was a rare event: Anne of Denmark had been the one queen so honoured since the crown had been placed on Anne Boleyn's unroyal head. The rites in the Abbey and the subsequent festivities in Westminster Hall were conducted on the scale of magnificence and pageantry usual on these occasions; but the traditional procession through the City from the Tower to Westminster, which gave the people an opportunity of acclaiming their new ruler, was dispensed with. This omission was ascribed to a commendable economy, and it was said that as much as £60,000 was thus saved, which, in view of the bleak condition of the Exchequer, was a valuable consideration. This may, indeed, have been the prime reason for James's decision; but an uncertainty as to how he and the Queen would be received in the long progress through the narrow streets may have been a secondary motive. A contrast to this frugality was the vast sum he spent on jewellery for the Queen: over £100,000 was expended in supplying a suitable regalia, for almost all the Crown jewels had been dispersed by the Roundheads, and the few that survived had gone to adorn the rapacious royal mistresses during the previous reign. Jewels, James may have prudently remembered, provide a useful commodity in emergency.

The coronation service was so adjusted as to cause no affront to the couple's Catholic susceptibilities, while at the same time conforming to the rites of the Church of England. The distinguished congregation, which included almost everyone of eminence in the country, was highly edified by the Queen's majestic deportment and air of sincere devotion, which contrasted very favourably with the King's rather casual manner. James had taken considerable trouble to see that he and the Queen were arrayed with a proper splendour, but had made one omission in his careful preparations: he had failed to have the crown fitted to his measurements. This led to an unfortunate *contretemps*. When the crown was placed on his head with due solemnity, "it came down too far, and covered the upper part of his face", in Bishop Burnet's words. To others it appeared that, on the contrary, it was too small and would not stay on his head. In any case it had to be supported in its proper position by a bystander, and inevitably many professed to see in the tottering crown a sinister augury for the future. In the midst of all the grandeur of the occasion, James was suffering a very real private sorrow: on that morning his infant son by Catherine Sedley had died.

On the whole, however, the accession and coronation passed off more smoothly than many, including probably James himself, had anticipated; and his first speech to his Privy Councillors, in which he expressed his high opinion of the Church of England, and his determination to maintain the liberty and property of his subjects, made a very happy impression. The King, who had no natural facility for composing or delivering suitable speeches, was so gratified by the obvious success of his oration that he repeated it to Parliament, and also found several other occasions on which to delight audiences with the same well-chosen sentiments. It was, however, in conformity with his singular obtuseness that he should almost immediately have vitiated the admirable effect of this well-worn speech by making a public parade of his Catholic worship. Within a few days of the late King's death, he heard mass in the Queen's chapel at St. James's Palace attended by all the panoply he could muster. In writing in his diary of this occasion, Evelyn no doubt expressed the feelings of many: "He (James), to the great grief of his subjects, did now, for the first time, go to mass publicly ... the doors being set wide open."

While these events were taking place in London, the Dukes of Argyll and Monmouth were actively plotting in Holland to raise rebellions in Scotland and England designed to oust James from the throne on which he had so lately taken his seat. In the event, their abortive campaigns had an effect exactly opposite to what they had hoped to achieve. James's position was strengthened by these efforts to overturn him, and the two leaders lost their heads—Argyll on 30th June in Scotland, and Monmouth fifteen days later at the Tower of London.

This moment of success was the only time during James's short reign that he can be said to have enjoyed any general popularity. It was not perhaps a very deep sentiment, but it temporarily existed and could have been fostered. Unfortunately for his own prospects, he was not sufficiently subtle to turn the circumstances to his own advantage, which could have been achieved by a show of clemency. As it was, the modest enthusiasm which had been aroused by the successful crushing of the rebellions was quickly extinguished by the horrors of Judge Jeffreys' Bloody Assize, in the course of which 330 victims were executed, nearly 100 transported to the West Indies, and many flogged.

How far the King had intended the Protestant rebels to be treated with such severity it is difficult to assess. The compiler of the Memoirs of the King adopted a rather defensive attitude, and wrote that Jeffreys "drew undeservedly a great obloquy on his Majesty's clemency". But it seems that daily reports were sent to Whitehall of the progress of the trials and of the punishments inflicted, so that the King cannot have been unaware of the violence which was being perpetrated in his name. Furthermore, on Jeffreys' return from his orgy of butchery, he was given a peerage as a reward for the successful accomplishment of his mission.

The reigns of James's father and brother had both been dominated and soured by a scarcity of money. The first had foundered largely owing to Parliament's reluctance to supply funds, and the second had come near to doing so for the same cause. James, during his short reign, was at least spared difficulties in this direction. Although Members of Parliament were little pleased at serving under a Catholic ruler, they realised that he had at least the advantage of being a thrifty man; they may also have realised that their refusals during the previous reign to vote adequate funds for the maintenance of the fleet and the militia had not proved a very successful policy.

From the very opening of James's reign Parliament was in a generous mood, and responded willingly to his initial application for a grant for the navy which, he said with all sincerity, was "the strength and glory of the nation"; and also, though probably with less fervour, for paying the heavy debts left by the late King. James, too, would seem to have felt little enthusiasm for the latter objective, for it appeared at the opening of the following reign that Charles's servants were still owed the formidable sum of £60,000.

To find the large sums required, it was decided to levy a tax on sugar and tobacco, and on wine and vinegar. On this occasion Parliament was spurred on by the threat of the Argyll and Monmouth rebellions; but a second application in November of that same first year of James's reign for £700,000 was also voted without opposition, part of which was to be devoted to a standing army, the necessity for which was at last accepted by Parliament. There was, however, a drawback to a well-filled Treasury which the loyal Commons had not anticipated. Having secured a fairly lavish supply of funds, the King was no longer dependent on Parliament; and somewhat to the surprise of members, they found themselves prorogued until the following February.

Although James was naturally frugal in his personal tastes, and at once stopped the work on his brother's half-finished palace at Winchester, he lost no time in instituting a number of alterations and improvements in the decayed Palace of Whitehall—a palace which the Queen described in later life as "one of the largest and most uncomfortable houses in the world". In the autumn of 1685 he began the reconstruction of a long range of buildings, facing the principal court and the gardens, which was to contain suitably handsome apartments for the Queen. There was also to be a new chapel. James thus showed himself an infinitely more considerate husband than the late King, whose wife's rooms had been far less sumptuous than those of some of his mistresses. A little over a year later Evelyn viewed the Queen's newly finished apartments, and approved of what he saw. He was particularly impressed by Mary's bed—a tall and elaborate four-poster—the hangings of which had cost the vast sum of £3,000. He also made a note in his journal that "the carving about the chimney-piece, by Gibbons, is incomparable".

As a true connoisseur of architecture he was greatly pleased by the fine quality of the work in the new chapel, "now first opened publicly for the Popish Service", although he regretted its purpose. The rich marble of the walls and pillars, the figures of John, Peter, Paul, and other saints of the Church delicately carved in white marble by his brilliant protégé Gibbons, created an effect of great magnificence, which was increased by Verrio's lavish frescoes on the ceiling. Also, he added, "the throne where the King and Queen sit is very glorious, in a closet above, just opposite to the altar". Clearly piety was not thought incompatible with splendour and comfort. But poor Evelyn was intensely distressed by the ceremonial of the Mass which took place in this beautiful setting. "I could not believe", he wrote sadly, "that I would ever have seen such things in the King of England's palace, after it had pleased God to enlighten this nation."

In the following month, January 1687, Evelyn went to the new chapel to listen to the singing of the famous eunuch, Cifaccio, who had come from Rome in order to exhibit his talent before the King and Queen. Evelyn admired his performance, but added with Anglican severity: "Much crowding—little devotion." Some weeks later Cifaccio was persuaded to sing before "a select number of particular persons" in Mr. Pepys's house. This was a rare honour, as he seldom consented to appear before "any but princes".

The creation of the fine chapel was no doubt very gratifying to the Catholic members of the Court; but unfortunately the King's private life was once again less elevating than his show of religious devotion might have given reason to suppose. James's intentions of reforming his way of life on his accession had been perfectly genuine, but they had not been enduring. After submitting to banishment for a few months, Catherine Sedley decided to return to Whitehall, where she had kept her rooms, and at once her hold over the King became again as strong as, if not stronger than, it had been before her brief retirement.

The Queen was naturally incensed, and her mortification increased when James, in January 1686, created Mrs. Sedley Countess of Dorchester, and awarded her a pension to support her new title. Mary saw herself immediately in the same position as the down-trodden and neglected Catherine of Braganza. It was, however, a position in which she had no intention of remaining. She had no hesitation in showing her annoyance in public, and Evelyn wrote in his diary: "for two dinners, standing near her, I observed she hardly eat one morsel, nor spake one word to the King". James, whose conscience was more developed than his brother's, must have felt extremely uncomfortable. But worse was in store for him.

A few days later the Queen gathered in her apartments her own and the King's confessors, and a number of Catholic peers. She then begged James to come to her. In front of this distinguished and saintly gathering she stated clearly that "either he must give up his mistress, or she would withdraw to a convent". To the Queen's ultimatum the rest of the company added their various appeals. It must have been a singularly humiliating occasion for the King, and it was almost impossible for him to do otherwise than to agree to return to a state of virtue.

James might make his good resolution, but the newly created Countess was not very easily disposed of. Proclaiming loudly that she was a victim in the cause of Protestantism, she at first refused to be evicted from Whitehall; but the offer from the King of an Irish estate eventually achieved the desirable end. However, it was hardly likely that this resourceful and mischievous lady would for long waste her charms on so remote a locality. Within a few months she was once again in London, but not living in Whitehall Palace—thus far the Queen had triumphed. Lady Dorchester settled in the highly fashionable St. James's Square, which had been laid out during the previous reign, and was conveniently on the fringe of the royal domains which she had graced for so long. If the King still visited her, it was at least an intrigue carried on with discretion, and the Queen could ignore it: she anyhow had no longer the humiliation of seeing her rival at Court.

During his short, calamitous reign, James can have had little opportunity for amusement. Indeed, apart from intercourse with Lady Dorchester and one or two other similar friends, there were only two directions in which he turned for recreation—hunting, and playing at soldiers with his standing army. The former was a passion he had inherited from his grandfather, and until his life was disrupted by the cares of state, he gave up many days to this pursuit, showing an energy and stamina which reduced his companions to a condition of exhaustion. Richmond was a good centre for this purpose, and during the first two years of his reign he often repaired there for one or two days a week, spending the night in the old Palace.

His interest in his army was a more important affair, and to it he brought the enthusiasm he had previously lavished on the fleet. During the three summers of his reign, which the Court spent at Windsor, he would come over with the Queen, the Queen Dowager, and all his Court to Hounslow Heath, where his troops—for the most part under the command of Catholic officers—were assembled for his inspection. A special pavilion was set up for the King, and a gallery was built from which the two Queens and their ladies could watch the review. The whole army—horse, foot, and artillery—passed before the gallery with the King, an imposing figure, riding at the head of his troops. The artillery then discharged their cannon, and following this martial display there was a banquet in the King's pavilion, and feasting and carousing in the tents of the military.

It was all very splendid, and it must have given satisfaction and a sense of security to the King to see the glittering panoply of the army which he maintained largely at his own expense. In the event, when he was in need of its support, it lamentably failed him; while the country at large, so far from sharing the King's enthusiasm for his military machine, looked on it with dark suspicion. These highly trained troops, so rumour had it, were maintained, not for the defence of the country, but for the suppression of the liberties of the people, and for the enforcement of the Catholic religion on reluctant Protestants:

> *Now pause, and view the Army Royal*
> *Compos'd of valiant souls and loyal*
> *Not rais'd (as ill men say) to hurt ye*
> *But to defend, or to convert ye.*

Thus a vulgar rhyme expressed concisely the anxiety of the citizens of London, to whom a regular army was an innovation, at the spectacle of this efficient weapon maintained within a few miles of their gates.

The year 1686 saw a serious deterioration of popular sentiment towards the King, though it was less marked than during the two that followed. The brief popularity that devolved from the suppression of the Argyll and Monmouth rebellions had been entirely extinguished, and the hostility which was gradually developing in the country permeated into Whitehall, where constant subterranean bickerings between Catholics and Protestants cast an atmosphere of gloom over the Court. Not that James seemed aware that his personal popularity in the country was slumping dramatically: this was not a condition that he fully appreciated till the last months of his reign.

His efforts to give a little glamour and brilliance to his Court seem to have been unrewarding. On the occasion of his birthday, 14th October, for example, there was a parade of troops in St. James's Park, followed by a ball at Whitehall in the evening. A royal ball in the previous reign would have been attended by everyone who could possibly get to it: at James's rout there was a very poor attendance of the nobility.

However, the last day of 1686 was illuminated by a happy and encouraging little ceremony. On 31st December there was erected in the great court of Whitehall Palace, in front of the new chapel, a handsome bronze statue of the King dressed in Roman costume and standing in a noble and commanding attitude, as if directing the movements of his cohorts. It was the work of Grinling Gibbons, and survives as one of the finest statues in London. But there was more to it than the beauty of the modelling, for it was cast and erected at the cost of one Tobias Rustat, a former Page of the Chamber to Charles II and James, as a testimony of his loyalty to, and affection for, his masters. Thus there was at least one person in the royal entourage to whom the King appeared the epitome of princely virtues.

This was perhaps the last occasion on which there was any genuine demonstration of affection for the King—a demonstration, that is to say, which was not designed to promote a valuable return. During the following year James blundered forward, making continually a more public parade of his Catholic worship, and being either oblivious of the effect he was creating or considering it his duty to make no compromise in this direction. The reception given to the Papal Nuncio was an occasion for a display of deep devotion by the King and Queen, and so caused great offence to the Protestant members of the Court. The Nuncio was consecrated as titular Bishop of Amasia in the new chapel at Whitehall, and when he later came to the Queen's apartments both James and the Queen knelt to receive his benediction. That the King of England had knelt to the representative of the Bishop of Rome was soon widely known, and was looked on almost as a submission of the country to the authority of the Pope. The public reception of the Nuncio took place at Windsor a few days later, and caused an even greater commotion.

In these matters the King and Queen acted in the normal manner of good Catholics, while the special regard they showed for the Nuncio may have been intended in the best interests of the country to mollify the Pope, Innocent XI, with whom James was on extremely bad terms in spite of his devotion to the Church. The Pope, more subtle than the King, foresaw that James's extravagant demonstrations of Catholic fervour, so far from winning the country to the Catholic faith, would irretrievably lose it. In any case any act of devotion by the King was carefully magnified by the Protestants in order to increase his unpopularity with the people.

However disturbed the Protestants may have felt, they had at least one comforting reflection—the King had no son by Mary of Modena to carry

19  "The last Horse Race run before Charles the Second of blessed memory, by Dorsett (Datchet) Ferry near Windsor Castle", 1684

*From an engraving by Francis Barlow, 1687*

20  Charles II touching for the "King's evil", 1679

*From an engraving by F. H. van Hone*

21  (*overleaf*)  James II and Queen Mary at a banquet in Westminster Hall on the day of their coronation, 23 April 1685

*From an engraving by S. Moore in Francis Sandford "The History of the Coronation of James II", 1687*

22   Mary of Modena, consort of James II, lying in
*From a contemporary Dutch print*

23   James I and his son Charles (later Charles I) feasting the Spanish ambassadors,
18 November 1624
*From a Spanish Broadside of 1624*

on a Catholic dynasty. Five children she had brought into the world, the last more than six years earlier, but none had survived, so that the Protestant daughters of his first wife, Anne Hyde, remained the heirs apparent. The King, however, was endeavouring by every possible means to extinguish even this relief. In August 1687 the Queen went for several weeks to Bath, where the waters were thought to be particularly beneficial for promoting conception. Meanwhile James, who was making a progress through Wales, undertook a pilgrimage to the holy well of St. Winifred, and drank of the water which was credited with bringing about the object he so passionately desired. Early in September he joined the Queen at Bath.

Whether the credit lay with the mineral waters or with the saint must remain uncertain, but before the year was out the rumour circulated at Court that the Queen was pregnant, and on the 23rd of December the report was confirmed by a royal proclamation. The delight of the royal couple was intense, but it was by no means widely shared. To Mary of Orange and to Anne it caused the gravest displeasure and anxiety.

James remained singularly unaware that public opinion had turned firmly against him, and that his tenure of the throne had become precarious. Indeed he was hardly to be blamed, for, following his well-intentioned but unconstitutional efforts to establish the liberty of conscience, he received a number of addresses of loyalty and devotion from various sects of Dissenters. That he was misled by these dutiful words, which were in fact without significance, seems clear; and he appears to have looked forward with confidence to wearing the crown for the remainder of his life.

With a long reign in view, a matter which very naturally engaged his attention was the repair of some of the royal houses, the majority of which had been falling into decay since the opening of the Civil War. As has been seen, he had undertaken improvements at Whitehall as soon as he came to the throne, and he had also carried out a few repairs at Richmond Palace. At the latter he had spent some of his earliest years, and since his accession the Queen had taken warmly to the country retreat which stood so peacefully by the waters of the Thames. Thus, with his humiliating flight only a few months in the future, James commanded Sir Christopher Wren to prepare plans for a drastic restoration of the Palace. Work, it seems, had just begun when the King abdicated, and it was at once stopped. Thus Wren, who had seen his fine palace at Winchester abandoned owing to the death of one monarch, now saw his plans for Richmond extinguished owing to the deposition of another. He was to be more fortunate in his third venture.

This is no place to describe the religious dissensions which marred the spring of the fatal year of 1688, but throughout his troubles the King was buoyed up by the hope that the Queen would give birth to a male heir. Mary had decided that her child was to be born in St. James's Palace, the tranquil atmosphere of which had always been congenial to her, and was infinitely preferable to the crowded, gossiping world of Whitehall. When the time came, there was some delay in making ready her rooms, but late in the evening of 9th June she was carried in her chair across the park, accompanied by the King who walked beside her. At ten o'clock on the following morning, Trinity Sunday, an infant prince was born, and by command of the King the demonstrations usual on the birth of an heir to the throne took place in the form of the firing of cannon at the Tower and the ringing of church bells. But Evelyn's laconic entry in his diary caught more closely the public feeling: "A young Prince born, which will cause disputes."

And disputes there were indeed from the very moment of his birth. Dark stories were widely circulated that he was no child of the Queen at all; that she had never in fact been pregnant; that the infant had been introduced into her bed in a warming-pan; and—a few weeks later— that the child had died in Richmond Palace, whither he had been taken for his health, and had been replaced by a changeling.

All these rumours were carefully retailed by Princess Anne to her sister in Holland, with a wealth of circumstantial detail. Indeed the birth of a male heir so transported the two Princesses with anger and jealousy that they showed themselves in a singularly unamiable light. They achieved, however, their desired objective of confirming William of Orange in his conviction that England must be saved from Catholic thraldom.

So persistent and generally credited became the gossip that the King was unable to ignore it, and at the end of October he summoned a Council to which were called all those most eminent in Church and State, including the Queen Dowager, to give their testimony that the birth was genuine. The women of the bedchamber and the doctors gave evidence of a highly intimate description, so that no doubt can genuinely have remained but that the Prince of Wales was indeed the Queen's legitimate child.

While this rather undignified scene was taking place, William of Orange was waiting with his fleet for an east wind—a Protestant wind —to waft him to the shores of England. The delay was not protracted, and on 5th November, a week after the Council had met, he landed at Torbay. A few more weeks as monarch remained to James, whose reign is taken to have ended on 11th December, eleven days before he finally escaped from Rochester to France. But they were weeks of disaster and indignity, and have no place in a history of Court life.

# Chapter 10

# WILLIAM AND MARY

During the first twenty-six years of Mary's life her prospects of eventually wearing the crown of England varied dramatically and constantly. When her mother, Anne Hyde, died in 1671 she left James, Duke of York, four children surviving from the large number she had brought into the world —three daughters, of whom Mary was the eldest, and a single precious son, Edgar. At this point Mary's prospects were not brilliant; but the young Prince and the third daughter, Katherine, soon followed their mother to the grave, and thus Mary at the age of nine became the second heir to the throne.

Two and a half years later, however, James, who was still youthful and extremely amorous, married Mary of Modena, then aged fifteen, and there seemed every likelihood that one or more male heirs would intervene between Mary and her prospects. With commendable promptitude the Duchess of York produced her first child in January 1675. It was a daughter. Thus Mary's position remained unchanged, and so continued, although the first child had died and a second had been born, at the time of her marriage to William of Orange on 4th November 1677. Three days later the Duchess gave birth to a son, so that the duration of poor Mary of Orange's status as an heiress was singularly short.

Within a few weeks the infant prince was dead, but as Waller wrote:

> *The failing blossoms which a young plant bears*
> *Engage our hopes for the succeeding years;*
> *Heaven, as a first fruit, claimed that lovely boy,*
> *The next shall live to be the nation's joy.*

These were emphatically not sentiments shared by William of Orange; and indeed the poet was optimistic, for only one other child, a daughter who survived only a few weeks, was born before James succeeded his brother on the throne in 1685, while the elder daughter had already proved to be another "failing blossom".

Thus, with James on the throne, William could congratulate himself that his marriage had turned out to be a highly successful gamble, and that although at the time of his marriage the odds had seemed poor, his obedient spouse was now next heir to one of the most important thrones in Europe. Mary of Modena's health was indifferent, and it seemed highly probable that her years of child-bearing were at an end. The consternation, then, at the Dutch court when in December 1687 it became known that the Queen was once again with child, as has been described in the last chapter, was understandable, and the rage when she gave birth to a healthy son in June of the following year was boundless. Mary's stock as an heiress slumped overnight to an unprecedentedly low level. But the slump was not prolonged: before the year was out William had landed at Torbay, he and Mary had been accepted as King and Queen of England, and what Bishop Burnet termed the "double-bottomed monarchy" had begun.

The first years of Mary's married life had not been particularly happy. When she had first been informed by her father that she was to become the wife of the unattractive cousin whom she hardly knew, but to whom she had taken a marked aversion, she had burst into tears; and in this lachrymose condition she had remained throughout the marriage service and during the journey to her new home. Mary was a handsome girl, nearly six feet tall, and now she was linked for life to this insignificant and graceless man, four and a half inches shorter than she, and often in ill-health from asthma and other complaints which made him peevish and irritable. He had, moreover, decided notions about the subjection in which a wife should be kept. Thus Mary's life in Holland, as the consort of a not very important prince, was far from being gay and glamorous.

And yet, as the years passed, she became intensely attached to William, and her letters to him which have survived, after they succeeded to the English crown, show that this apparently charmless man had somehow inspired a positive adoration in the heart of his very feminine wife. "My impatience for another [letter] from you is as great as my love, which will not end but with my life..." was a typical ending to the many letters she wrote to him while he was out of England; and there is no doubt that these expressions of deep affection were genuine.

But if William was somehow able to inspire love in a wife, he was absolutely devoid of the graces which were necessary in order to become a generally popular king. "He neither loved shows nor shoutings", wrote Burnet, and he made this apparent from the moment of his entry into London. In pouring rain the people had lined the roads to St. James's Palace in the hopes of catching sight of the courageous defender of the Protestant faith, but after a prolonged wait they heard that William had reached the Palace in a closed carriage by a different route. Thus the first opportunity of stimulating a little personal popularity was cast away.

William III with Princess Anne (later Queen Anne) and Prince George of Denmark (*left*), and William, Duke of Gloucester, their only son. The plaque is of Queen Mary

*From a contemporary French print*

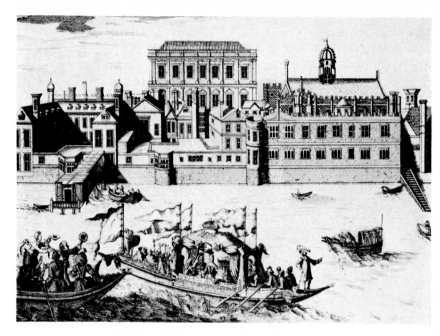

25   William III and Mary leaving Whitehall by barge
*From a print by de Ram*

26   The coronation of William III and Mary, 11 April 1689
*Detail of a print by R. de Hooghe*

Mary's arrival was arranged with a greater sense of the dramatic importance of the occasion. On 12th February 1689 she landed at Gravesend, where she was met by a number of distinguished courtiers who conducted her to Greenwich Palace where Princess Anne, with her husband Prince George of Denmark, awaited her. In the exultation of the moment, the royal sisters met "with transports of affection, which", as Lady Churchill wrote, "soon fell off, and coldness ensued". From Greenwich Mary came slowly up the river, followed by a large retinue, to Whitehall. She was, indeed, so elated by her good fortune that the frivolity of her behaviour caused considerable surprise. A more restrained demeanour, and one which showed some compassion for the afflicted father whom she was ousting would, it was thought, have been more appropriate.

But no such reflection seems to have entered Mary's mind. On the contrary she showed all the joy of a child—and she was indeed only twenty-six—in being back again in the old Palace of Whitehall. With disapproval Lady Churchill observed her running happily and inquisitively from room to room, "looking into every closet and conveniency, and turning up the quilts of the beds just as people do at an inn". And Evelyn wrote: "She came into Whitehall laughing and jolly, as to a wedding, so as to seem quite transported. She rose early the next morning, and in her undress, as it was reported, ... went from room to room to see the convenience of Whitehall." The levity was perhaps ill-placed, but curiosity was natural, as she was no doubt anxious to discover how much of the fine furnishings of the Palace had survived the departure of her father and step-mother.

On this score Mary need have had no anxiety, since such was the hurry and secrecy of their flight that they had been unable to take more than a few possessions with them, and most of their personal belongings remained in the Palace. A little later James sent an emissary begging his daughter to allow his clothes and other small things to be sent to him, but this request, as Clarendon remarked, "was utterly neglected".

The day after Mary's arrival, she and William walked in procession through the galleries of Whitehall to the Banqueting House for the important ceremony of the declaration by the Lords and Commons that the Prince and Princess of Orange were now King and Queen of England, France, and Ireland. A few weeks later their sway over the last of these countries was to seem almost as nebulous as that over the second. The appearance of the unfortunate King, coughing with asthma, and with a weak and twisted body, stirred neither enthusiasm nor confidence for the future; but the Queen, with her tall and handsome presence, made an immediate appeal. Once again, however, her cheerfulness was considered a little unseemly, and it was murmured that a dignified gravity, as if assuming the Crown as a duty, would have struck a more becoming note.

In any case, whether the Lords and Commons were entirely satisfied or not with their new rulers, there was now no going back, and a date was fixed for the coronation—11th April. This was only two months ahead, but with the previous wearer of the crown lurking across the Channel, it was essential that the position of the new monarchs should be regularised without delay.

Eight weeks was perhaps hardly long enough to prepare adequately for so elaborate a ceremonial, particularly as there were to be details about it for which there was no precedent. Charles II had been unmarried when he was crowned, James II's Queen had been only a consort; now there were two heads of equal importance to be anointed and crowned, and this added complications to the ritual. Moreover, this important day opened under the most disastrous auspices. On that morning it was learnt at Whitehall that James had landed some days earlier in Ireland, and that almost the whole of the country was in his hands. On that same morning, too, a letter from her father was delivered to the unfortunate Queen in which he poured the most formidable maledictions upon her for her want of filial duty. The news from Ireland and the arrival of the letter led to distressing recriminations between husband and wife as to which had been responsible for the revolution, which now seemed so likely to founder.

These unpropitious events led to a serious delay in the start of proceedings which had been timed for eleven o'clock: it was not till half-past one that the ceremony began. The elaborate ritual then rumbled forward with a number of unexpected halts and embarrassments, like some complicated and outmoded machine. An unfortunate *contretemps* occurred when the royal couple kneeling at the altar rail should have placed twenty guineas in a basin. The basin was offered, but the guineas had been forgotten. Neither the King nor the Queen had any money on them, and the Chamberlain and the Lord Treasurer were in the same state. "A long pause ensued, which everyone began to deem excessively ridiculous", till Lord Danby stepped forward and offered money from his purse.

At length the service reached its end, and the procession moved into Westminster Hall for the traditional banquet. At the end of the repast the King and Queen's Champion, clad in armour and on horseback, should have entered the Hall and cast his gauntlet to the floor as a challenge to any who opposed the monarchs. But the Champion was as elusive as the guineas, and it was not till nearly two hours after the appointed moment that he made his appearance. Whether the missing warrior was reluctant to come forward in case his challenge was literally interpreted was never disclosed; but owing to this unexplained delay dusk had already fallen in the great hall when he eventually appeared, and his traditional gesture was invisible to the company. It was hardly surprising that on this trying occasion the solemnity and decorum of the Queen's demeanour brought favourable comment.

Whatever hopes had been entertained that the opening of the new reign would bring brilliance to the life of the Court were quickly and effectively extinguished by the King. Social amusements had no part in his life, and he preferred working quietly and industriously in his closet at the many matters involving his two countries to spending his time on the sort of amusements which lent glamour to a Court. The two previous Kings, in spite of many faults, had been extremely accessible to those who wished to see them, and Charles at least had the invaluable gift of spreading an atmosphere of geniality around him. William, on the other hand, in Burnet's words, "was not easily come at, nor spoke to". Indeed, he was highly ungregarious.

With her lord so disinclined for any sort of festivity, it was impossible for Mary, as an obedient wife, to embark on those entertainments and receptions which might have been invaluable in forming an agreeable contact between the sovereigns and the nobility. Instead, a gloomy air of disappointment and distrust pervaded the halls and galleries of Whitehall, which only a few years earlier had echoed rather excessively with gaiety and laughter. The King was made to realise that his seclusion was unpopular, but he excused himself on the grounds of ill-health; and this at least was a welcome excuse to the unfeeling members of his Council, who saw here a hope that the throne might soon be occupied alone by the easy-going and expansive Queen.

In spite of his seclusion, William managed to exercise some degree of control over the concourse of intriguing and treacherous courtiers who surrounded the throne, and in this he was assisted to an unexpected degree by the Queen. For at least half of the six years during which he shared the throne with Mary, he was out of England—at first in his successful campaign against the Jacobites in Ireland, and later on the unrewarding wars in Flanders which were so wasteful of English blood and English money. The campaigning season, which was as precious to William as the hunting season to the average Englishman, generally occupied the spring and summer, so that at these periods Mary was left in control of the government. At first the ordeal to her must have been very great. During her married life she had been accustomed to give way in everything to her autocratic husband, and was never required—or indeed allowed—to make any decision of importance of her own. Now suddenly she found herself for months at a time alone at the head of a much divided government, few members of which she was able to trust.

D. Marot fecit avec Privileg

27  Hampton Court Palace.  A chimneypiece designed by Daniel Marot, "Architecte
de sa Majesté Britannique"

It was astonishing how quickly her character and personality developed. At first she had been a largely disregarded figurehead at the meetings of the Council, but once her preliminary diffidence had passed she became a person to whom members deferred for a sound and impartial judgement; and also one who was to be feared for her alarming insight into the duplicity which distinguished almost every one of her entourage. Had she survived her husband, it is not improbable that she would have gone down to history as one of the great queens of England.

Very early in his reign William decided that he did not intend to live in Whitehall Palace. The reason he gave was that a site so close to the river was bad for his asthma, but a more truthful reason was that it would have been impossible for him in that spreading conglomeration of buildings to lead the life of retirement he wished for. In addition, the *louche* atmosphere which his uncle had introduced had been by no means successfully eradicated by his father-in-law.

Hampton Court, then, was the place he decided should be the principal residence for himself and the Queen, though its low situation would seem to have been as little salubrious as that of Whitehall. There anyhow he could live in seclusion, coming to London only on Council days. The towers and battlements of Wolsey's spreading building were admittedly in a poor state of repair, but this, it might have been supposed, would have appealed to William since it made any parade or magnificence in his way of life almost impossible. But no, it was one of the contradictions of his strange character that he, so parsimonious in most directions and averse to display, decided that this old Tudor building should be transformed into one of the most handsome palaces in the world.

Fortunately the royal buildings were in charge of one of the most brilliant architects England ever produced, Sir Christopher Wren. He had been appointed Surveyor-General in 1669, and, at the age of fifty-seven when he was commissioned to undertake the transformation of Hampton Court, he had a wealth of experience behind him. The first task was to make part of the Palace suitable for habitation while the major works were in progress. This entailed transforming a number of the dark Tudor rooms into apartments which conformed to the improved ideas of comfort. To this end the narrow, mullioned windows were altered to sashes—probably the first seen in England—which admitted more sunlight and air; the Tudor fire-openings were replaced by marble bolection mouldings; and the linenfold panelling was removed to make way for the large panels above a chair-rail which were the taste of the age.

The Queen's own apartments were in the Water Gallery, a Tudor building standing near the river bank. Under Wren's supervision the rooms, though not large, were splendidly decorated by the highly accomplished artists and craftsmen who brought such incomparable richness to the late Stuart age. Verrio covered the ceilings with sublime scenes in which crowned heads and the gods of Olympus mingled in genial unity; Grinling Gibbons lightened the rigid lines of the panelling with his carved swags of extraordinary delicacy; and there was one room which was particularly personal to the Queen. This was the Delft Ware Closet. Here the decoration was Dutch rather than English, and was in fact the work of that highly versatile designer Daniel Marot, who came to this country in the train of William and Mary, and termed himself *Architecte de sa Majesté Britannique*. In this room, with its many little shelves and brackets, was arranged the Queen's collection of blue and white *faïence* which provided her, in her moments of leisure, with an absorbing interest. As the collection increased in size it spread into other rooms, and Daniel Defoe in his *Tour of Great Britain* wrote that: "The long Gallery . . . was filled with this China, and every other place where it could be plac'd with Advantage".

The Queen, indeed, started a fashion which Defoe suggests was carried to absurd lengths. He describes these ardent collectors as "piling their China upon the Tops of Cabinets, Scrutores, and every Chymney-Piece, to the Tops of the Ceilings", and adds that so much money was spent on this popular craze that many injured "their Families and Estates". Mary was not very fortunate in the fashions she introduced, for her other innovation—the painted calicoes and chintzes which were brought from the east and were used as hangings for beds and for covering furniture —became so popular that English manufacturers were almost ruined until an act was passed to prohibit the import of these foreign materials.

In addition to the elegant decorations of the Water Gallery the Queen had also installed here a rare comfort for the period, "a small Bathing-Room, made very fine, suited to either hot or cold Bathing, as the Season should invite". What a tragedy that this fascinating little building, which must have been a superb example of the decoration and furnishings of the period, should have been demolished when Wren's wings were completed.

When the King was in England, and Mary was not constantly summoned to Whitehall by affairs of State, she was able to go back to the domestic occupations which were her special pleasure. In the tranquil rooms of the Water Gallery she occupied herself with knotting fringe— a much favoured pastime of the period—and with the needlework at which she was highly accomplished. Early in the following reign, that observant traveller, Celia Fiennes, particularly remarked on the work of the late Queen which she saw at Hampton Court:

"The hangings, chaires, stooles and screen the same, all of satten stitch done in worsteads, beasts, birds, images and fruites all wrought very finely by Queen Mary and her Maids of Honour."

It does not appear that the Queen had inherited her grandfather's taste for pictures, but in addition to her interest in Delft ware she collected a number of fine oriental cabinets which were imported into England by the East India Company. In July 1693 Evelyn inspected the collections and was highly impressed: "I saw the Queen's rare cabinets and collections of china; which was wonderfully rich and plentiful, but especially a large cabinet, looking-glass frame and stands, all of amber, much of it white . . . esteemed worth £4,000". There were also "China and Indian cabinets, screens and hangings. In her library were many books in English, French and Dutch, of all sorts; a cupboard of gold plate". Only in one direction did Evelyn consider the Queen's passion for collecting was excessive, and this concerned a silver filigree cabinet which he felt sure belonged to "our Queen Mary", and so should have been sent to her at St. Germain. However, it shared the fate of James's clothes, and remained at Whitehall.

The Queen took a close interest in the design for a new layout for Wren's buildings at Hampton Court. Charles II had already replaced some of the rather cramped Tudor gardens by a more formal arrangement, and had thrown a long canal in the French manner across the park. But Wren's vast new wings demanded something on a much more majestic scale, and Mary supervised the construction, by the partners London and Wise, of a great *patte d'oie* of avenues stretching away from the majestic east façade which was gradually rising. In this she had the help of William, who was interested in garden design, and, in Defoe's rather excessively flattering words, "was allow'd to be the best judge of such Things then living in the World".

The King's ambitious project of converting Hampton into an English equivalent to Versailles was by no means looked on with favour by the government and Parliament. From their point of view there were two overwhelming objections: the King and Queen would become inaccessible, and a vast amount of money would be required from the depleted Treasury. As Burnet wrote: "This spread a universal discontent in the City of London". The unfortunate Queen, left alone to deal with the difficulties of the situation, wrote to the King in Ireland: "I hear of so much use for money, and find so little, that I cannot tell whether that of Hampton Court will not be the worst for it".

William, however, was not prepared to forego his dream of a great English palace, and with many troubles and delays building slowly proceeded. But he gave way to the opposition to his living constantly so far from London, and to remedy this, since he was obdurate in his aversion to Whitehall, he bought for £20,000 Lord Nottingham's house at Kensington. Standing on rising ground, close to an attractive little village and with a great area of wooded country stretching away towards Whitehall, it had the merits of being both healthy and reasonably accessible.

Naturally Wren was commissioned to convert this agreeable, but not very large, country-house into a suitable residence for the King and Queen; but it was to remain a domestic building, and not one adapted to large entertainments which the King so heartily disliked. William was in Ireland during the greater part of the time that the house was being rebuilt, and Mary was left to supervise and urge on the work. Her letters of 1690 show her constant anxiety as to whether it would be ready in time for the King's return. "The outside of the house is the *fiddling* work, which takes up more time than one can imagine," she wrote, "and while the schafolds are up, the windows must be boarded up, but as soon as that is done, your own apartments may be furnished." The smell of paint, however, still hung about the King's rooms, and it was some compensation for his return being delayed that this allowed time for the smell to disperse.

As it turned out, it was exceedingly fortunate that the Kensington house had been bought and the alterations pressed forward so fast, for in April 1691 Whitehall Palace was very badly damaged by fire. William had landed in England the same day, and he came up the Thames to find smoke still rising from the partly gutted buildings. Mary had escaped in her night clothes just before the flames had engulfed her rooms; but in spite of the danger to the Queen, the Jacobites accused William of having instigated the fire in order to put an end effectively to the traditional right of the public to have free entry to the Palace and watch the monarchs when eating in state. Although the fire was undoubtedly accidental it was highly favourable to the King's desire for seclusion. Seven years later the Palace was completely destroyed by fire, except for the Banqueting House and the Holbein Gateway.

As in previous reigns, Ordinances for the regulation of expenditure in the household were drawn up soon after the dual accession. In this case they are dated 1689, and every detail is tabulated with meticulous care. One perceives here the supervision of William's frugal eye, for, like his great-grandfather, James I, he was excessively careful about shillings and pence, but was willing to spend large sums on military campaigns and on bricks and mortar. Unfortunately the King's attempts at domestic economy seem to have been a singular failure, if Bishop Burnet's view is correct: "By some great error of management, though the Court never had so much, and never spent so little, yet payments were ill made, and by some strange consumption all was wasted."

There was anyhow no attempt at economy in the food for the royal table, in spite of the fact that hospitality was anything but lavish. The Queen, however, had a reputation for being greedy, and excessive eating led to her corpulence at an early age. The list of meat and game to be provided for "Their Majesties Diets" seems prodigious. At supper it was not quite so plentiful as at dinner, where mutton and beef jostled with turkey, goose, capons, pheasants, partridges, quail, and a number of other birds; while in addition there were "Desert Plates" of morelles, truffles, asparagus, artichokes and so forth. The wine was also in good supply—claret, champagne, Rhenish, and Spanish wine being available. A separate item was a bottle of the last "For washing the King's feet weekly"; it is obscure what beneficial properties the wine possessed when used for this curative purpose. Mary also liked ale apparently, for Elinor Franklin was allowed £45 a year for "providing ale for the Queen".

All the employees in the household are mentioned by name in the Ordinances, with the amount of their stipends. The King's Master Cook, Patrick Lamb, Esq., for example received an annual sum of £11 8s. 1½d., while Philip Drew, child, earned £2, and the turnbroaches, of whom there were five employed on this menial task, were given nothing except their board. The turn-broaches, seemingly, were not a very trustworthy lot, and were inclined to raise a little cash by selling their places in the royal kitchens to other unfortunates who were willing to work for nothing except the food they could obtain. For this reason special rules were drawn up: "For preventing great abuses practiced by the turnbroaches, scowerers, or doorkeepers. . . . Our pleasure is that none of those places be hereafter sold." In future new recruits had to be vouched for by two officers of "Our Greencloth".

The complex structure of the royal household, and the vast number of people employed in an incredible variety of capacities, emerges clearly from the Ordinances. William and Mary's Court was conducted entirely without *panache* and on what were regarded as frugal lines, while elaborate entertainments were events of great rarity; and yet the tradition of employing an army of retainers was kept up. Nearly 300 men and women ministered to the wants of their royal masters and of each other, and in addition to these there was a concourse of men engaged in the stables on looking after 102 horses; while the chapels at Whitehall and St. James's had choirs of men and boys as well as chaplains, "a Master of the Musick and organists", all of whom were paid from the Privy Purse. As long as a household on this scale was thought necessary, it was not surprising that William's efforts at curtailing expenditure were somewhat unsuccessful.

While William was battling against his father-in-law in Ireland, Mary had thought it right to give a few entertainments at Whitehall. Some small balls were arranged, which not only broke the monotony of her existence but also gave an impression of confidence and security which she was far from feeling: for in spite of successes against the Jacobites on land the situation at sea was lamentable, and invasion by the French seemed possible at any time. Nevertheless a particularly grand ball was envisaged to celebrate the return of the King after the victory of the Boyne; but in the event William was unable to leave Ireland as early as he had anticipated, so the festivities were first postponed and then—no doubt to the King's relief—abandoned.

On the whole, very little diversion or entertainment interrupted the sombre rhythm of Court life. When the King was in London all gaiety was extinguished by his taciturn presence, and his doting spouse—so anxious to please—made little effort to dispel the gloomy atmosphere which he created. He never felt at ease with English courtiers, and took no pleasure in their company. The only occasions, seemingly, when his reserve loosened was when he dined with Marshal Schomberg and Dutch friends such as Arnoud van Keppel, who as a youth of eighteen had come over with William in 1688 and at twenty-six was created Earl of Albemarle. About this friendship the Duchesse d'Orléans wrote: "The King is said to have been in love with Albemarle as with a woman, and they say he used to kiss his hands before all the Court". At these dinners, cheered by the gin of his native country, the King was reputed "to talk fast enough". But these were not little gatherings to which the Queen was invited.

When William departed for his campaigns on the Continent, the Queen's time was almost entirely given up to her very harassing duties. Each morning she would rise at six to spend two hours reading and writing; at eight there were prayers, followed by four or five hours of business until dinner. From four to seven there were audiences and receptions, and on most evenings she had a little time to play basset— a soothing card game which had a constant appeal. After supper she wrote her almost daily letters to the King, describing her actions and asking in the most humble manner for his approbation; and so to bed about midnight. Thus, with constant visits to Hampton Court and Kensington to inspect the progress of the great works, in which she clearly took a knowledgeable interest, she had small leisure for diversion.

She found few opportunities to visit her kingdom, and it was astonishing how little of the country she had ever seen, and how few of her subjects had set eyes on their Queen Regnant. How different was this from the Tudors, who had come in contact with their people all over the country in the course of their progresses. Mary accompanied the King to the coast on several occasions when he was leaving for the Continent, and on one of these spent several days at Canterbury; she once travelled to Lincolnshire and stayed a few nights at Belvoir Castle. That would seem to be the extent of her personal knowledge of her kingdom, except for the environs of London. William's travels in England were rather more extensive, particularly after the death of the Queen, when he visited the universities of Oxford and Cambridge, and stayed in a number of great houses in the Midlands.

Throughout the six years she reigned Mary had two constant sorrows. The first was the fact that she was childless. It was a condition which had afflicted the two preceding queens regnant, and had provided a major anxiety to several monarchs since Henry VIII. But this made her disappointment none the less keen. During the eleven years of marriage before she came to England she had had two miscarriages, and at the time of her accession there seemed no reason to despair. "I know the Lord might still give me one, or several, if it seemed good to Him", she wrote in her journal. But the Lord, it seemed, showed little enthusiasm for the perpetuation of the Stuart dynasty, and her constant prayers were not rewarded.

The second cloud in the background of her life was her quarrel with her sister Anne. While Mary had been in Holland they had carried on an affectionate correspondence, united in dislike of their stepmother, and to some degree of their father. Once Mary became Queen their affection, which had been warmed by distance, quickly disappeared, and turned eventually to an acute hostility. It lasted until Mary's death. This was caused by Mary's order to Anne to dismiss the Marlboroughs from her service; but the Princess refused to be parted from her beloved "Mrs. Freeman", and as a protest withdrew from all contact with the Court. Although Anne's lymphatic presence would have added little to the general merriment, Sarah Marlborough's acid wit might have struck some stimulating sparks. In any case the quarrel between the sisters cast a shadow over the royal family.

During her short reign Mary did little deliberately to court popularity, and yet with her fine presence and gracious manners she had won considerable esteem, so that the news of her death from smallpox at the age of thirty-two on 28th December 1694, at the newly finished Kensington Palace, caused genuine sorrow. William, who had never shown her much affection, was apparently overcome with despair; but this may have been due less to a sense of loss than to uncertainty for the future. Would this

169

28 (overleaf) Hampton Court Palace in 1724
From an engraving by L. Kniff after J. Kip

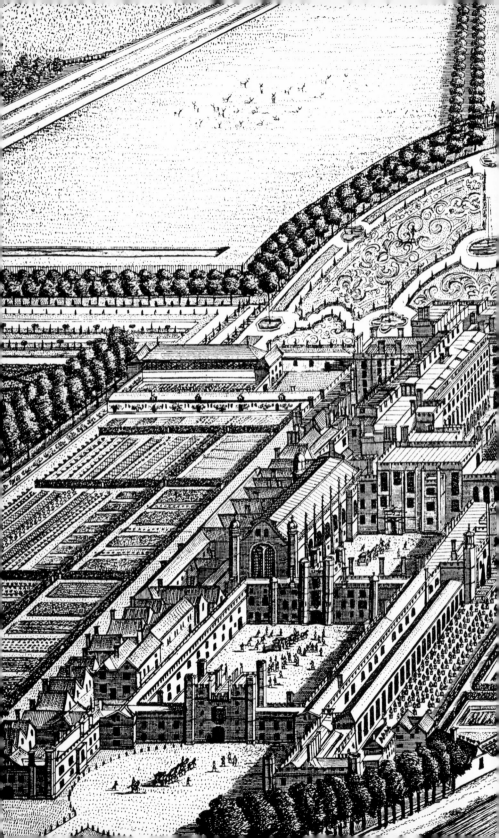

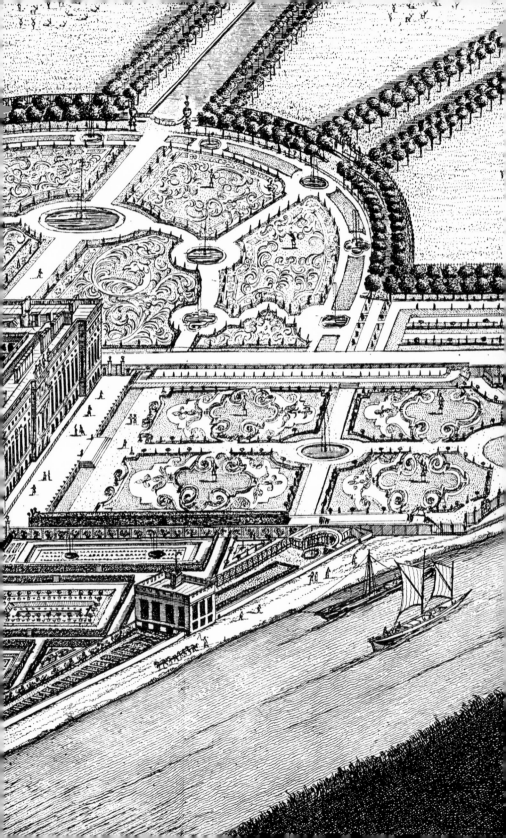

alien people, whom he had taken little trouble to conciliate, tolerate him as King without his popular Queen? Undoubtedly his situation would become difficult, and he would no longer have the liberty to spend half of each year in his own country. It was a becoming gesture, and one of rare prodigality, to provide for the Queen a funeral of unparalleled splendour, and no doubt it increased such esteem as the populace felt for the King. It was not until the pageantry was over and the body of the Queen had been laid in the vaults of Westminster Abbey that a letter in Mary's hand was found giving instructions that her burial should take place with the greatest simplicity. It was perhaps on this account, or more probably because William was soon consoled, that no monument was raised to her memory.

Amidst the general regret at the Queen's early death, there was at least one who shed no tears : that was her father. Elizabeth-Charlotte of Orléans was shocked by this lack of parental feeling and wrote to her aunt on the subject from Versailles: "King James of England, who is here with us, does not wish us to wear mourning for his daughter. He insisted very strongly on our not doing it. He showed no signs of sorrow at her death". In view of the complete lack of feeling Mary had shown for her father, it would perhaps have been surprising if he had shown any emotion on her death.

Work at Hampton Court was at once stopped, and both the King and Christopher Wren must have envisaged their joint dream of a magnificent palace fading into oblivion. To the latter this was no new experience: work on the new palace at Winchester had been halted on Charles II's death and the restoration of Richmond Palace had been abandoned on James II's abdication. The exact state that Hampton Court had reached at this anxious time was carefully noted by the observant Celia Fiennes in the journal of her travels: ". . . just the shell up and some of the Roomes of State ceil'd but nothing finished". The gardens, however, were further advanced than the structure and consisted—as they still do to some degree—of "great fountaines and grass plotts and gravell walkes and just against the middle of the house was a very large fountaine and beyond it a large Canal guarded by rows of even trees". In this direction at least the Queen had been able to complete her work.

Mary's unexpected death caused a wave of consternation, and inevitably Jacobite hopes were raised. But, although William was not popular with Parliament, he had gained their respect, and there was no move to unseat him. There was a good case for Princess Anne to succeed to the Crown, but few showed any wish to see her at the head of affairs before her natural time. Hopes, indeed, were concentrated on the Duke of Gloucester, the only one of Anne's seventeen children to live beyond infancy. At the time of Mary's death he was five years old and showed promise of living to maturity—a promise which was not fulfilled, for in 1700 he died and the last hope of the continuation of a Protestant Stuart dynasty was thus extinguished.

William's abilities were always rated more highly across the Channel than in England. To the English he appeared as an ungracious and unglamorous foreigner, and his mental qualities were disparaged accordingly. Few, however, even beyond the water would have been so fulsome in their praise as the Frenchman, Misson, who wrote in his *Travels over England*: "I do not believe there is in the world a more worthy man, a Sublimer Genius, nor a King so fit to govern".

Nevertheless there was a lessening of dislike, and the feelings of Parliament towards their King showed a gradual improvement. Financial grants, which were at first agreed with the utmost reluctance, were soon passed in a rather more gracious manner. Annually there had been an embarrassing haggle about the royal revenue, but in 1698 the King was granted an income of £700,000 per annum for life, and the very humiliating financial debates were over. On the other hand in 1699 a Bill was passed by the Commons ordering the standing army to be reduced to seven thousand men, which entailed sending back to Holland William's favourite regiment of Dutch Guards. The King was intensely mortified, and showed his spleen in a letter to Lord Galway in which he wrote: "God will punish the ingratitude of this nation".

In January 1698 the final fire at Whitehall Palace took place, and thus a good case could be made out for completing the unfinished shell of Hampton Court. In the following year work was resumed, and it was then so successfully hurried forward that the rooms were decorated and furnished before the King's death three years later. The full scheme, however, which entailed demolishing the remainder of Wolsey's building and raising a great edifice on the site in the same style as the south and east fronts, was abandoned.

It seems unlikely that William took much interest in the furnishing of his new palace, but Celia Fiennes's testimony after a second visit shows that it was carried out with the magnificence for which that period was outstanding. Pictures and tapestry hung on the panelled walls, and chandeliers were suspended from the high painted ceilings; crimson and gold velvet covered the chairs, and was draped in rich folds over the windows. In the long gallery the curtains and the covers of chairs and settees were in green and white damask, and on marble-topped console tables between the windows stood pots of orange and myrtle trees. The wizened, twisted figure of the King hobbling amidst this splendour must have seemed singularly out of place.

And yet this was the great palace of which he had dreamed as a worthy setting for the ruler of England; and he, an alien, had done this great work for his adopted country. Had the Commons been more lavish with their supplies, much more would have been done. Windsor might have undergone the rather strange metamorphosis that Wren had proposed, and perhaps the vast new palace at Whitehall, for which Wren also made designs, would have taken shape. But in spite of these grandiose building-projects William never intended to develop a Court on a scale commensurate with the setting. In the grandeur of his palaces he wished to rival his enemy Louis XIV, but the thought of a Court arranged on the elaborate and ceremonious lines of that of the French King was anathema to him. Once Mary's presence and her timid attempts at gaiety were removed from the scene, the life of the Court became dreary indeed. Formal entertainments were held, but the brilliance which had distinguished the Court of Charles II was for ever dulled.

Moreover, the atmosphere was little enlivened by the fact that William began to give way to excessive drinking, or as Burnet tactfully expressed it: "The King . . . was now falling under an ill habit of body." This was no doubt promoted by his ill-health and the annoyance of dealing with the obstinate and unsympathetic English. His little drinking-parties with Lords Pembroke and Wharton were inclined to develop into highly undignified carousals, and inevitably had the effect of reducing the King's poor constitution to a low state of debility.

William may have regretted the non-fulfilment of some of his projects, but he was at least satisfied with what he had achieved at Hampton. "He was so much pleased with the place", wrote Burnet, "that he went thither once a week, and rode often about the park." It was on one of these occasions that his horse fell with him, and his collar-bone was broken. He returned to Kensington in his coach, but he never fully recovered, and within a few weeks of his accident, on 8th March 1702, he died aged fifty-one.

To the people in general he had been too remote a figure to be widely mourned, but his good qualities were appreciated by those who came in contact with him, although he had inspired little personal affection. There were not very many, however, who would have echoed Celia Fiennes's enthusiastic description of him as "our glorious truely great King William". His body was carried to the grave in Westminster Abbey with a lack of magnificence which, in Burnet's words "was scarse decent".

# Chapter 11

# QUEEN ANNE

Many English monarchs have been miscast for the parts they found themselves called upon to play in history, but perhaps none possessed fewer of the qualities required to make a successful ruler than Queen Anne. She had inherited neither a natural sense of authority from her Stuart ancestors, nor the intelligence of her mother's family, the Hydes. On the other hand her simple, indolent nature contained few of the vices of either family, and she had the amiable quality of wishing to please—as long as the effort was not too great.

In spite of the contempt with which her sister had treated her, she had enjoyed her life as a royal princess—a princess of high position but without responsibilities. She was attached, in an unemotional way, to her bovine husband Prince George of Denmark, who appreciated a quiet country life as much as she did herself, and they shared interests in a love of gardens and horticulture, while their appreciation of the arts was limited to pleasure in listening to music.

A burden on her existence was the unremitting effort to produce an heir—an heir of either sex to carry on the Protestant line. The seventeen births which she contrived were a strain on her physique, but constant child-bearing was a duty which women of the period accepted uncomplainingly, since it was not to be expected that more than a moderate proportion of their offspring would grow to maturity. In this direction Anne was even more unfortunate than most of her contemporaries.

Left to themselves, Princess Anne and Prince George would have been perfectly content to carry on a life of gentle inactivity, but it was not a condition that the Princess's adored Sarah Churchill was prepared to accept for her mistress. Lady Churchill's singular powers of invective, which later were to be used against Anne herself, were at this period directed against the King and Queen. It was monstrous that they should deny the Princess the use of Richmond Palace, for which she wished; it was even worse that no really adequate financial provision was made for her. In the latter direction Sarah's efforts were effective and, much to the annoyance of the Queen, Anne was granted by Parliament an annual income of £50,000; while eventually, rather than accept a royal residence, and the supervision and control which would have gone with it, she rented for herself Berkeley House, in Piccadilly, and lived there in freedom.

The death of the Queen must have been an intense relief to Anne. She became indeed the heir apparent to the throne, but with her unambitious nature she was entirely content that William should remain as the occupant, and probably hoped that he would survive her. In any case her position improved, and after a tepid reconciliation with the King she was granted St. James's Palace as her residence. She became, too, a person of importance in the kingdom: not only was she the heir to the crown, but she was also the mother of the second heir, for the young Duke of Gloucester appeared to be a healthy child.

These were the happiest years of Anne's life, but they were not of long duration. In the summer of 1700 her son died aged just eleven years, and two years later the King's frail life was extinguished, so that she found herself forced, far sooner than she expected, into a position for which she knew herself ill-suited.

Her age was thirty-eight, not old even by standards of those days, but her wits had grown no sharper with the years, while her body, owing to its corpulence, had become far from mobile. No one could have been less generously provided with suitable qualities to deal with as crafty and self-seeking a body of politicians as any monarch had ever been called upon to control. It was remarkable indeed that she muddled through her reign without being overcome by disaster. Too little intelligence can perhaps be less of a drawback than too much.

Although always the less attractive of the two sisters, she had not when young been devoid of physical charms. Her tall figure, chestnut hair, and beautiful hands had been definite assets. But when she came to the throne she must have been aware that she was no longer a pleasure to the eye, and this increased her natural diffidence. Her figure had long since lost its youthful line, and she had become exceedingly stout. Like her sister, she was distinctly greedy, and in addition she had the reputation of drinking excessively. Elizabeth-Charlotte of Orléans wrote of her in 1701: "Princess Anne is delicate. They say that she drinks too much wine and likes too strong wines". No doubt she relied on alcohol to supply the animation which nature had not provided in her make-up.

One asset, however, she retained throughout her life: she had a voice of exceptional sweetness. This had been observed by Charles II when she was a girl and, anxious to make the most of the modest charms nature had provided for his niece, he had had her trained in speaking by the famous actress, Mrs. Betterton. It was time and money well expended, for when

176

she read her first speech from the throne the members of Parliament were unexpectedly charmed by her clear and musical voice and her shy manner. Bishop Burnet was particularly struck by it, and wrote of her "softness of voice, and sweetness in the pronunciation, that added much life to all she spoke". Long after Anne's death, when there can have been no cause for flattery, Speaker Onslow wrote: "I have heard the Queen speak from the throne and she had all that Bishop Burnet and others have noticed of the sweetness of her voice and manner. I never saw an audience more affected: it was a sort of charm."

Her words were the words of her ministers, but one phrase she brought in which may have been her own, for it expressed a fact of which she was intensely proud. "I am entirely English", she said, and indeed she could say it with more truth than any English monarch since Queen Elizabeth. Her sister sharing the Crown with a Hollander could not emphasise the fact with equal force.

The coronation was fixed for 23rd April. The long and complex ceremonial must have proved a grave ordeal for the Queen, not only on account of her bashful nature but also owing to the unfortunate fact that it coincided with an attack of gout in her feet, which made all movement for her both difficult and painful. However, a postponement would have been very undesirable, so it was arranged that the Queen should be carried in a special chair upholstered in crimson velvet; and on the occasions when it was unavoidable that she should leave the chair, her stout figure was supported by members of her entourage on either side.

Celia Fiennes was present in the Abbey, and noted every detail of the performance with her usual meticulous care. She was particularly impressed by the crown, which "was made on purpose for this cerimony vastly rich in diamonds, the borders and the globe part very thick sett with vast diamonds, the cross on the top with all diamonds which flamed at the least motion". Altogether the coronation passed off without the mishaps which had marred that of William and Mary, while at the subsequent banquet in Westminster Hall the Queen's Champion carried through his traditional challenge without hitch.

By eight o'clock in the evening the ceremonies were successfully accomplished, and the exhausted Queen could retire to bed at St. James's Palace. While she was seeking rest, and the populace was thronging the streets and giving way to the jubilations usual on these occasions, enterprising thieves entered the deserted Westminster Hall and removed all the plate, pewter, and even tablecloths—a satisfactory evening's haul.

With the coronation over, the Queen's life took on the pattern to which it was to conform till her death twelve years later: with little alteration she kept to the routine of moving to her various residences at set seasons of the year. In the early spring she would usually be at Kensington Palace, then, as the weather warmed, she would go to Hampton Court, and so in June or July to Windsor Castle, where she would remain for the hot season. In the autumn she would be back at Hampton Court, and when the high rooms began to grow chilly she returned to St. James's Palace for the winter; but her stay at the last would be varied by excursions to Kensington—sometimes only for the day, at others for a few nights.

Kensington was probably her favourite of the royal palaces: here she and Prince George were able to indulge their greatest interest, in extending and improving the gardens and planting trees in the park. The garden had been small during the previous reign, and to the north of the Palace an area of disused gravel-pits stretched up to the highway to the west. This unpromising terrain was converted by the royal pair into a garden, so successfully that it earned even Addison's critical approval. "It must have been a fine genius for gardening", he wrote, "that could have thought of forming such an unsightly hollow into so beautiful an area. On one side of the walk you see this hollow basin, with its several little plantations lying so conveniently under the eye; on the other side of it appears a mount made up of trees."

Between the new swards and the Palace, the Queen made one of her few additions to the architecture of the royal buildings. This was the orangery, of which Defoe wrote that she "often was pleased to make the Green House which is very beautiful, her Summer Supper House". It was designed by Wren, who had already passed his seventieth year, but nevertheless was to outlive the Queen by nine years. However, in this work he had the assistance of the far younger Vanbrugh, and the combination of Wren's experience and Vanbrugh's bold imagination produced a building of exceptional charm. The alcove containing a garden seat was also the product of this happy alliance.

It is unfortunate, in that age of brilliant architects, that Anne did not possess the normal royal urge to create new buildings. Her Lord Treasurers were no doubt thankful that during her reign there was no counterpart to William III's ambitious schemes, or to extravagances such as those of Louis XIV across the Channel. Nevertheless posterity has been the loser. Long after Anne's death the Duchess of Marlborough wrote of her: "She was never expensive, nor made any foolish buildings"—a strange compliment from the creator of Blenheim.

The Queen's residence at Windsor was enlivened by a diversion unexpected in one so immobile: she was passionately devoted to the chase—a love inherited perhaps from her great-grandfather, James I. She was far too unwieldy to mount a horse, but she followed the hunt in the Great Park in a little chaise which she drove herself. The fact that these sporting outings took place during high summer was looked on as no drawback. Swift, during a visit to Windsor in July 1711, was astonished at the Queen's activity, and wrote in his *Journal to Stella*: "She . . . drives furiously, like Jehu, and is a mighty hunter, like Nimrod."

So far as the royal residences went, the annual round was pleasant enough; but like many crowned heads both before and since, she felt it a necessity to have a small house in which she could escape from the formality of Court life. During her sister's lifetime, when no grace and favour house was put at her disposal, she had bought a cottage—a glorified cottage—on the edge of Windsor Park, and this she retained after her accession for occasional retirement.

Little would now be known about the internal appearance of this building were it not for the record left by Miss Fiennes. Her visit to what she calls "a little retreate out of the Palace" took place soon after Queen Anne's accession, and it is clear that the house, though small for a queen, was not inconsiderable. There was a guard-room in the cellar, offices and rooms for the ladies-in-waiting on the ground floor, and on the first floor apartments for the Queen and Prince George. These royal apartments were handsomely fitted up with marble chimney-pieces, pier-glasses with marble-topped tables below them between the windows, damask curtains in white, crimson, and yellow, furniture covered in the same material, and "little wanscoate tables for tea, cards or writeing". In the "Presence roome" hung a portrait of the previous Queen Anne—Anne of Denmark, wife of James I.

There was not only elegance here, but also convenience. Opening out of the Queen's dressing-room was "a closet that leads to a little place with a seate of easement of marble with sluces of water to wash all down". It may have been a slightly chilly contraption, but was far in advance of the general contemporary arrangement.

To this tranquil little house Anne brought her husband in the summer of 1708 when he was suffering severely from the recurrent attacks of asthma which were to lead to his death a few months later. The Queen's intentions were probably of the best, but Sarah Marlborough—her husband was created an earl in 1689 and a Duke thirteen years later—saw this retirement in a different light. The house which, she said, "though as hot as an oven, was then said to be cool, because from the Park such persons as Mrs. Masham had a mind to bring to her Majesty could be let in privately by the garden". This dark reference was to Harley and his Tory colleagues, whom the Queen was desperately anxious to see in office in place of the Whig family junta under the masterful leadership of the terrifying Duchess of Marlborough.

Here lay the tragedy of Anne's life—the incessant squabbles which went on beneath the surface of the smooth routine with which her life was ordered. Ever since her accession the domination which Sarah exercised over the Queen had increased, and her jealousy of anyone who had the Queen's confidence—particularly of Mrs. Masham—had de-developed into an intolerable mania. The days early in the reign when Anne would write four notes a day to her "dear, dear Mrs. Freeman", as she called Sarah, and sign them "Your poor, unfortunate, faithful Morley", had passed; and the sentiments of love and dependency were changed into fear and hatred of the domineering character against which she felt herself helpless. Few crowned heads can have had to support such insolent words as Sarah felt justified in using to the Queen, who in the face of a torrent of invective became so mentally paralysed that she was unable to reply. Her only recourse was to leave the room, but even this was sometimes impossible when the Duchess took up a strategic position with her back to the door.

The last terrible scene between the two took place in April 1710, at Kensington Palace, whither the Queen had withdrawn in order to avoid the interview which the Duchess demanded. The latter followed, however, and forced her way into the Queen's presence in an effort to avert a final break. As usual on these occasions, Anne was almost speechless; but she remained unmoved by both invective and floods of tears, and eventually the Duchess had to retire knowing that the domination she had exercised for thirty years was at an end. No word was ever exchanged between them again.

There was a particular bitterness to Sarah in her break with the Queen in that for some years past the affection and confidence, which Anne had lavished so profusely on her, had passed to a protégée of her own, Abigail Hill, later Mrs. Masham. Abigail was an impoverished cousin of the Duchess, and also of Harley, and had been thankful to accept a humble position in the entourage of the Queen. She had few physical advantages: she was extremely plain, with a prominent nose which seemed all the more pronounced owing to its redness. But she was highly intelligent, and in that Court of intriguers was more than able to hold her own. The fact that the redoubtable Duchess was eventually ousted was no small tribute to her capabilities. Furthermore she was an invaluable secretary to the Queen, many of whose more sensible letters appear to have been composed by her helpful lady-in-waiting.

Mrs. Masham was not of high enough social status to take over the Duchess of Marlborough's office of Mistress of the Robes: this elevated post was designed for the Duchess of Somerset, who was largely above the petty squabbles of the courtiers. Sarah, however, refused to give up her key of office, the golden key she is portrayed wearing attached to her dress by a blue silken ribbon, and eventually the Duke had to be instructed to obtain it from her. He received it—thrown on the floor at his feet, with a torrent of abuse of the Queen. The Duke was not unused to violent scenes, for, as he remarked to Lord Dartmouth, his "wife acted strangely, but there was no help for that, and a man must bear with a good deal to be quiet at home".

On 28th October 1708, two years before the final break with Sarah Marlborough, the Queen's husband, Prince George of Denmark, had died at Kensington—the third royal death to take place in the Palace since William III had bought it eighteen years earlier. For months the Queen had devotedly nursed her husband, often sitting up much of the night to support him during violent attacks of asthma. How deeply she was affected by his death, it is difficult to say. In Sarah Marlborough's view not unduly, for, as she wrote: "on that very day he died she (the Queen) ate three very large and hearty meals". Indeed nothing but illness could interfere with Anne's remarkable appetite.

The arrangements for the funeral of the Prince provided the Queen with an antidote to whatever grief she may have felt, as she busied herself in ordering the ceremony on the exact rules of protocol. This was one of the few subjects in which she took a deep interest, and now several days were happily occupied in deciding who should attend the interment, and the exact position which their rank and precedence should command. These were matters in which she always insisted on a rigid punctiliousness, just as she allowed no courtier into her presence unless he were wearing a full-bottomed wig. There was a most unfortunate occasion in 1712 when Prince Eugène had paid a ceremonial visit to the Queen bringing with him only tie-wigs. The Queen was incensed at this show of bad manners, and the goodwill-visit threatened to become a fiasco. But fortunately before the important function on the Queen's birthday, when presents of great value were to be exchanged, he obtained the necessary adornment; and probably this measure of concealment improved his appearance, for Swift wrote of him, "he is plaguy yellow, and literally ugly besides".

Anne's insistence on the small details of etiquette, combined with her limited intelligence and inability to carry on a conversation of the least interest, were not ingredients which induced a Court circle of any brilliance. It is probable that the Drawing-room which Swift attended at Windsor in the summer of 1711 was typical of these melancholy gatherings. There were so few people present "that the Queen sent for us into her bedchamber, where we made our bows, and stood about twenty of us round the room, while she looked at us round with her fan in her mouth, and once a minute said about three words to some that were nearest her, and then was told dinner was ready, and went out". Poor Anne! One feels for her, compelled to appear before the critical eyes of people who were much too clever for her, when she would have been far happier gossiping on some simple subject with the sympathetic Mrs. Masham.

Swift at least was compensated for the lack of amusement at this royal entertainment, for after it he was invited by one of the gentlemen-in-waiting to dine at "the Green-Cloth". "It is much the best table in England, and costs the Queen a thousand pounds a month while she is at Windsor or Hampton Court; and is the only mark of magnificence or hospitality I can see in the Queen's family: it is designed to entertain foreign ministers, and people of quality, who come to see the Queen, and have no place to dine at." One is glad to know that in this dreary Court there was at least one place where there was some lavishness and display.

Bishop Burnet, who was so often bitter and uncharitable about his contemporaries, was fairly just in what he wrote about Anne as a Queen. In his view she was always easy of access and prepared to listen to anyone who came to her, but her replies were so vague that little was gained by an audience. And he added: "She has laid down the splendour of a court too much, and eats privately; so that except on Sundays, and a few hours twice or thrice a week at night in the drawing-room, she appears so little, that her court is as it were abandoned." Swift's account of the poor diversion to be found at these Drawing-rooms suggests the reason for their being sparsely attended.

And yet Anne retained a personal prestige which was entirely lacking in her two successors. There survived a flicker of divine right in her ungainly body and slow mind. As she grew older she lost the modest allowance of beauty and intelligence with which nature had endowed her; but her inner conviction of the importance of her position never deserted her, and she thus retained a certain majesty and authority till the end of her life.

The Court, however, had fallen far from the position it had held in most previous reigns as the social and intellectual centre of the country, the centre to which all looked who hoped to make their mark in the life of the country or to reach fame as practitioners of the arts. Thus it had been as lately as the reign of Charles II, who, although no very intellectual character, had taken pleasure in gathering brilliant people round him and in furthering the arts. Now the cultural leadership had been decentralised from the Court into the country-houses which were springing up in all parts of England, and it was to the great landowners to whom the artists looked for patronage. For there was much private affluence in the country,

29  William III on his deathbed in Kensington Palace, 8 March 1702
*From an engraving by P. van den Berge*

30    Queen Anne and the Knights of the Garter
*Detail of a painting by P. Angelis, 1713*

although the Exchequer had been almost emptied by Marlborough's costly victories.

It cannot be said that the arts suffered from this shifting of the fulcrum, for Queen Anne's reign synchronised with one of the most brilliant and fruitful periods of artistic production in the history of the country. In literature, in architecture, and in music there was an exceptional number of outstanding figures, while even English painting, which had been slow to develop, was advancing under the leadership of Thornhill. In Grinling Gibbons the country possessed a carver whose genius in his particular line had no equal in Europe. But Queen Anne had no part in all this; she was satisfied with her royal residences as her predecessors had left them to her, and beyond installing some embellishments, she was content to leave the structures of her palaces as she found them. Only at Windsor, which had received little attention since early in the reign of Charles II, did she carry out material work, and there her outlay was largely confined to necessary repairs. However, these amounted to the substantial figure of £40,000.

With the gardens and parks she showed more enterprise. In addition to the extensive work at Kensington, which has already been mentioned, she commissioned Henry Wise in 1708 to create a formal garden and to enlarge an existing canal below the north Terrace at Windsor, at a cost of nearly £7,000. Also in the park there she planted an avenue which still bears her name.

Like her sister, Anne seems to have had no curiosity to see the country over which she ruled. As a girl she had stayed in Scotland with her father, when he was banished from the court of his brother; at the time of the landing of William of Orange she had deserted her father and fled to Nottingham—a defection which should have caused her much unease of conscience. But since her accession her excursions into the deep country-side had been confined to occasional visits to Newmarket, for she took some interest in racing, and to more frequent journeys to Bath for the sake of her own and her husband's health. To the populace of England she must have been an unknown figure. Perhaps she thought it better so, knowing that her ungainly appearance, her inability to make the gracious remark to put people at their ease, would detract from such prestige as she had. For, surprisingly enough, she was popular with the poorer classes. Her reputation for homeliness and diffidence made her a comprehensible and sympathetic figure, while the fact that she was much beloved by those who served her in a humble capacity was generally known and appreciated.

She was revered, too, for the contribution she had made to the comfort of a singularly ill-rewarded body of men, in inaugurating the Bounty which bears her name and which continued to help the poorer clergy till the present day. Only at last is it disappearing before the general reforms of Church finance. To mark her birthday in 1704 the Queen sent a message to the House of Commons announcing that she was willing to forego the "first-fruits and tenths" of every benefice—a tax which had originally been levied by the Pope, but which since the Reformation had been the perquisite of the sovereign—and with this money a fund was to be formed to help clergy who were in need. The amount was considerable, and represented a definite financial sacrifice on the part of the Queen. The memories of many far more brilliant monarchs have been recalled with less gratitude by posterity.

As in many weak and limited characters, the Queen had a streak of intense obstinacy, and in her case it was principally concentrated on a determination not to allow the heirs to the crown to come to England. On the death of the young Duke of Gloucester, Parliament had decided that the heritage should pass to the Protestant Electress Sophia of Hanover and her son. The Electress, as a grand-daughter of James I, was considerably older than the Queen, and also a far more intelligent and vivacious personality. Her son, Prince George, had come over to England many years earlier in 1681 as a possible suitor for Princess Anne of York, as she was then called. The affair had come to nothing, and it is possible that the Queen still harboured a sense of resentment from his unenthusiastic courtship in those far-away days.

However this may have been, Anne felt a deep jealousy of her heirs, and presented an adamant front to any suggestion that they should come to the country over which they were to rule. Some attributed this strange attitude to a secret hope of the Queen's that her half-brother might eventually succeed to the throne, but there is little reason to suppose that this was the case. It is more probable that her refusal was due to an aversion to sharing her modest popularity with an heir, for it is probable there would have been considerable show of enthusiasm for the Prince, had he appeared in London. In the event, the Electress died two months before the Queen, so that she was spared the responsibility of taking up her inheritance in old age.

Although the Queen's wish that the Whigs and the whole Marlborough clan should be ousted from government was achieved, she soon found that the Tories under Harley and St. John afforded her little personal tranquillity. At least, however, the country was at peace; but there was no peace at the meetings of the Council, where the ministers were constantly quarrelling violently, regardless of the presence of the uncomprehending Queen at the head of the table. Moreover, the two principal ministers were quite often far from sober.

186

As the Queen's already indifferent health declined, the strain of these acrimonious meetings increased until, at an unusually vituperative Council on 27th July 1714 at Kensington Palace, the unfortunate Queen suddenly complained of violent pains in her head and fainted. She had often exclaimed that the perpetual contention of which her Cabinet Council was the scene would cause her death, and it now appeared that her prognostication was correct. She was taken to her bedchamber and at first showed signs of recovery, but early on the morning of 1st August she passed into complete unconsciousness, and died between seven and eight o'clock. She was in her fiftieth year, and must have given up the burden of attempting to rule with the utmost relief. As her devoted Dr. Arbuthnot said of her: "Sleep was never more welcome to a weary traveller."

Soon after the Restoration a new vault had been formed on the south side of Henry VII's Chapel at Westminster, and there on the 24th August the body of the last sovereign of the House of Stuart joined those of Charles II, William and Mary, and George of Denmark. Owing to Anne's extreme corpulence, her coffin was almost square.

# Georgian
## Court Life

———

# Chapter 12

# GEORGE I

For some years before Queen Anne's death, the dust had been settling thickly on her Court. The amiability which had once brought some cheerfulness to the dark rooms of St. James's and pervaded the quiet gardens of Kensington had faded before the Queen's ill-health and depression of spirits. But nevertheless the tradition of glamour which accompanied the Stuarts throughout their dynasty was not fully extinguished even in their last, prosaic representative on the throne. In spite of manifold shortcomings, the Stuarts had inspired loyalty and sacrifice amongst sections of their subjects, and Anne was sustained till her death on a wave of popular affection, stemming perhaps from the romantic adversities of Mary, Queen of Scots, more than a century earlier. But the momentum ended at her death, and was not brought fully into being again by either of the Pretenders.

With the accession of George I the position of the Court radically changed. The quarrelling and corrupt ministers survived from the previous reign, and now that the faint authority of Anne was removed, they continued and developed their machinations regardless of the foreigner who was now technically their master. The new King was under no illusion about their probity, indeed he came to believe that almost no Englishman was honest; but he was ready to let them rule the country in their own way with little reference to the Crown. He fully realised that he had been called to the throne for his single merit of adhering to the Protestant faith, and that no one was inspired by any feeling of loyalty towards him personally.

The Hanoverian dynasty opened with no sense of security, and George hardly supposed that he would retain his uncomfortable and unwelcome seat till his death. Perhaps for this reason he made no attempt to learn the language of his new country, or to master the intricacies of its constitution. The majority of the ministers were worse linguists than the King, and spoke little French, a language in which he was fluent. With his Prime Minister Walpole he found a common tongue in Latin, which both spoke extremely indifferently, and misunderstandings were not rare, though about this Walpole cared very little.

George of Hanover was fifty-four when Anne died on 1st August 1714, and the moment had come which he had openly dreaded for several years, although his position as heir apparent to the Crown of England had given him a useful prestige on the Continent. He made no great haste to exchange his comfortable middle-class life amongst people who understood and revered him for the empty grandeur of his new situation. However, prolonged delay was impossible, and on 18th September he landed at Greenwich. The ship bringing him from the Dutch coast was fog-bound in the Thames estuary for twenty-four hours, and the new King was conveyed up the river in a barge, reaching the dilapidated palace of Greenwich after dark. In another barge came the Prince of Wales, who, arriving first at the steps, was mistaken for the King and was given a suitable initial welcome, which then had to be repeated for his father. It was one of those little *contretemps* which did nothing to improve relations between father and son.

The situation adjusted, the reception of the new monarch proceeded with tremendous dignity. An assemblage of the most distinguished people in the country, headed by the Archbishop of Canterbury, the Lord Chancellor, and the other members of the Regency Council which had been in control since Queen Anne's death, received the King as he stepped ashore. The royal party then made their way through crowds of onlookers to their apartments in the Palace, where the King and the Prince dined quietly in private.

The following day was given up to formalities. Many were admitted to the King's presence and allowed the doubtful pleasure of kissing his hand, while at intervals throughout the day George showed himself to the great crowds which had come from London to see him.

September 20th was a brilliant autumn day, and at noon in golden sunshine the King and the Prince of Wales entered the royal coach and, preceded by a concourse of nobility and gentry in resplendent carriages, set off towards London. It was dusk before the slow-moving cortège entered the courtyard of St. James's Palace. Along the route there was ever-mounting enthusiasm; homes were decorated, stands were erected, and loud huzzas echoed through the crowded streets whenever the King's homely face appeared at the window of his coach. These loyal demonstrations were evidence of the popular relief that a new monarch was coming to the throne without the civil disturbance which many had feared. Never again during his reign was George ever to stir anything but the most perfunctory enthusiasm.

Indeed nature had not endowed him with any of those graces of mind or body which could engender emotion in the people. He was slow in mind, and short and clumsy in figure, and he had inherited none of that sparkle which had illuminated the personality of his mother the Electress Sophia. He was not an ill-natured man, but his reputation had not been improved by the dark stories of the murder of Königsmark, and the banishment of his wife, Dorothea, to the Castle of Ahlden, where she remained a prisoner from 1694 till her death in 1726—a year before that of the King, who had divorced her.

A Queen might have brought gaiety and charm to a Court which George could do nothing to enliven. During the first two years of the reign the Princess of Wales, Caroline of Anspach, took to some degree the place of a Queen at court receptions; but when relations between the King and the Prince and Princess worsened until there was a complete break, the social atmosphere at St. James's depended solely on the King's indifferent presence. Even at Hanover, where he had felt at ease, he had failed to bring any sense of warmth or gaiety to his Court. This chilling atmosphere was mentioned by his first cousin Elizabeth-Charlotte of Orléans in her voluminous correspondence: "... the old gay good humour is no longer to be found at Hanover. The Elector is so cold that he freezes everything into ice", she wrote.

Certainly George had no wish for a brilliant Court. He had no interest in the arts, and clever people and intelligent conversation were not at all in his line. He felt comfortable and at ease with the two women who were his constant companions for the greater part of his life, and these with two or three of his German advisers were all he needed for company. The two mature women, who caused so much surprise to the English on their arrival, were Fräulein von Schulenberg and Frau von Kielmannsegge, who within a few years of the King's accession blossomed into the Duchess of Kendal and the Countess of Darlington respectively. The former, tall and gaunt, was nicknamed "the Maypole", and the latter, whose early beauty, which was reputed to have been considerable, had disappeared into extreme corpulence, was known as "the Elephant and Castle". Both were naturally reputed on their arrival in England to be the King's mistresses; and even Horace Walpole, writing his *Reminiscences* in 1789, accepted this tale without question; but as the second of these ladies was known in Hanover to be the daughter of the King's father by Countess von Platen, it is more charitable to suppose that George's relations with his half-sister were platonic.

A month after the King's arrival, on 20th October, the coronation took place, and the great body politic found itself officially surmounted by a foreign head. In several provincial towns riots took place in favour of the Pretender, but in London the day passed without unfortunate incident.

193

31 (*overleaf*) Kensington Palace (1724)
*From "Nouveau Théâtre de la Grande Bretagne"*

Thus George was able to settle down with his German entourage to enjoy as far as possible his new position. His heart, however, remained in Hanover, and at first at least he believed, and probably hoped, that he might at any time find himself on his way back to Hanover with the brief interlude as King of England in the past.

So long as he was not unduly troubled by the English ministers, chattering in a language he was unable properly to understand, and was allowed to spend quiet evenings in the company of the two new peeresses, he was tolerably contented. All public appearances were very uncongenial to him, and he took no pleasure in the parade which was expected of royalty. When he went to the opera, which was an entertainment he enjoyed as the language bar did not arise, he seldom took his place in the royal box, but would sit in some less prominent position, and was usually obscured behind the tall figure of the Duchess of Kendal.

A weekly occasion on which he acceded to public demand that he should show himself was when attending Sunday morning service in the chapel at St. James's. The torment anyhow was not of long duration, but it was conducted with the utmost dignity. There would be a splendid procession made up of members of the Court, the Yeomen of the Guard and the Gentlemen Pensioners, all in elaborate uniforms, conducting the homely person of the King on his way to pay dutiful homage to his celestial master. But this little gesture to the English love of pageantry fell far short of what the people expected of their monarch, and there was much public grumbling at his seclusion. Had he been constantly in the public eye, however, his graceless style would probably have added little to his popularity.

George found himself more than adequately supplied with royal palaces for his simple needs, and with his lack of interest in the visual arts he had little wish to alter or improve them. Earlier in life he had completed the rebuilding of his favourite palace of Herrenhausen which had been begun by his father, but he made very few alterations to the royal buildings in his adopted country.

St. James's Palace was naturally the new King's principal place of residence: its modest proportions and simple decoration were congenial to his love of seclusion. Here he established himself, living principally in only two rooms, in one of which he ate and slept, and in the other giving unavoidable audiences. The traditional levées, which had been a feature of the Court life of his predecessors on the throne, he did away with as far as possible, but when absolutely obliged he would appear fully dressed in his dining-room-cum-bedchamber.

A slightly exotic note was given to the King's otherwise very prosaic entourage by his two Turkish attendants, Mahomet and Mustapha. These two men had been taken prisoner many years earlier when George—then the Electoral Prince—was serving with the Imperial army, and they had remained with their Teutonic captor ever since. In England they were appointed Pages of the Backstairs, a post of some importance, and they were so closely in the confidence of the King that even the most influential ministers were sometimes glad to discover from them the direction in which the royal mind was working. Lady Cowper, the wife of the Lord Chancellor and a Lady-in-Waiting to the Princess of Wales, mentions in her *Diary* several pieces of gossip she heard from these two characters.

In addition to St. James's the three other royal palaces of Kensington, Hampton Court, and Windsor were available to the King, and of these the first two were in admirable condition; but Kensington was the only one to which he made any material alterations. Four years after his succession he relieved Sir Christopher Wren of the post of Surveyor-General of His Majesty's Works, which Wren had held for over forty years, and appointed an obscure figure, William Benson, in his place. On whose recommendation this change was made is not known, but it proved most unsatisfactory to the King, for the supposed improvements which Benson made in 1718 at Kensington had to be almost entirely obliterated by William Kent a very few years later. Benson's name, with his inept work, has passed into obscurity, but Kent's fine decorations at Kensington remain as a rare credit to the first Hanoverian King. His mural paintings still enliven the walls of the King's Staircase, and, although of no high quality, have charm and interest, for they show, through the painted arcades, various figures from the Court circle, including the Turkish pages.

In spite of his alterations at Kensington, George I did not use the Palace very regularly, and he made no attempt at all to maintain the elaborate train and pattern of life which had been habitual with his predecessors on the throne. The dignified progress of the whole Court from one palace to another at stated seasons of the year was a programme which had little attraction for him. He was moderately contented at St. James's, and found the rural surroundings of Hampton Court congenial. The latter, indeed, was the only place where he showed a little initiative in providing entertainment for himself and his courtiers, for here in 1718 he decided to have a theatre constructed in the great hall in which plays could be produced during the long summer evenings. The construction took longer than was expected, so that it was not until the autumn that the building was ready: on 23rd September it was inaugurated with a performance of *Hamlet*, and a week later *Henry VIII* was played. The latter was particularly appreciated by the King and was occasionally repeated during subsequent summers. These plays were produced in English, so it must be supposed that the King could understand the language in some degree, although he was unable to speak a word. Later in the reign even this pastime, which must have been very welcome to the courtiers, lost its interest for George and the theatre was seldom used.

His heart remained in Hanover, and it was to his palaces there that he wished to escape whenever it was possible for him to leave England for a few months. The first of these visits took place in the summer of 1716, when George had been less than two years in his adopted country, and on this occasion he nominated the Prince of Wales as Regent. It was a venture which he did not repeat on any of his subsequent absences. The Prince greatly enjoyed his new importance, but the general popularity he gained brought no satisfaction to his father, and it was at this period that the intense dislike between the King and his son began. Lady Cowper wrote in her *Diary*: "The King was no sooner gone, than the Prince took a turn of being civil and kind to Everybody, and applied himself to be well with the King's Ministers, and to understand the State of the Nation."

In addition to these praiseworthy employments, the Prince endeavoured to bring a little glamour back to the life of the royal circle by moving to Hampton Court and leading with the Princess a life of social brilliance by providing entertainments which were so sadly lacking in the dull round at St. James's when the King was in England. This sudden animation gave great pleasure in those circles admitted to these amusements, and Lady Cowper particularly remarked in her *Diary* on the "great Splendour" in which the Prince resided at Hampton during the whole summer.

The return to Hanover in 1716 was the first of the five visits the King made during his reign, the others being in 1719, 1720, 1723, and the last, during which he died, in 1727. Before he left on this first occasion there were rumours at Court that it was not his intention to return, and perhaps it was jealousy of the good impression his son was making in his place that brought him back to England at the end of six months.

But although he abandoned any thoughts he may have had of abdication, and sent his son back into a position of no influence, he himself made no attempt to attract popularity. He never travelled about his kingdom, and a very small proportion of his subjects can ever have had a sight of him. He had no contact with the common people, and even with the upper classes contact was not close unless they were able to speak German or French, which was not a very general accomplishment. The miserable failure of the Pretender's rebellion in December 1715 undoubtedly consolidated the King's position on the throne, but it brought him none of that personal popularity that James II had fleetingly enjoyed after the collapse of Monmouth's rising in 1685.

Thus the King remained insulated from the people of his kingdom within his circle of German favourites and German advisers. English place-seekers soon discovered that the surest way to advancement was by bribing the former, who always seemed in need of money, and showed no diffidence in accepting sums proportionate to the importance of the posts they were asked to obtain. One of the Duchess of Kendal's most successful—and best rewarded—achievements, was the restoration of Lord Bolingbroke to favour. He had been attainted on the death of Queen Anne and had fled to France; but a substantial *douceur* of £11,000 secured a pardon from the King, and he was allowed to return.

George probably welcomed these useful presents to the Duchess of Kendal and Lady Darlington, which relieved him of some of his financial responsibility to these avaricious women. He had already handed over to them the fine jewellery which had been bequeathed to him by Queen Anne, but cash, of which they were constantly in need, was not readily available. But these transactions naturally confirmed his belief that an honest Englishman was a rarity. His German advisers, Bernstorff, Bothner, and Robethon, however, would seem to have been but little less susceptible to bribery than the English, although they undoubtedly served their master faithfully in the difficult circumstances in which he found himself.

The atmosphere in George I's Court had at least in one direction much in common with that of William III: in both cases a foreign monarch with his foreign friends was grafted on to the existing Court circle. With the latter, however, the English Queen made the gulf between the two nationalities less pronounced, and she was able to bring about some mingling between the two circles. In the first Hanoverian Court, there was no personality to form a link between the two parties, nor, indeed, had the King any particular wish to be on terms of friendship with his English courtiers. In a situation such as this it was inevitable that jealousy should exist between the rivals, and conversation was apt to turn acrimoniously on the merits of the two nationalities.

The Prince of Wales, with unexpected tact, announced that he thought the English "the best, the handsomest, the best shaped, the best natured, and lovingest People in the World", and added that the finest compliment anyone could pay him would be to say he looked like an Englishman. It was a compliment he was hardly likely to receive without solicitation, and it was emphatically not a view that survived his elevation to the throne. These words, however, were very ill-received by the German courtiers, who voiced highly opposing sentiments. Baron Schutz, according to Lady Cowper, said that, "Nothing could make him believe that there was one handsome woman in England"; while Countess

Buckeburgh was of the opinion that "English Women did not look like Women of Quality". The English courtiers no doubt voiced equally outspoken views of their German colleagues, so that considerable tension pervaded the evenings at St. James's.

This mutual jealousy of the two nationalities must have made social occasions uncomfortable enough, with the two camps present but not mingling; early in the reign, however, a more serious crisis destroyed any harmony that might have survived the Court's jealousies. This was the violent quarrel between the King and the Prince of Wales. At the time of the accession there had been little sympathy between father and son, and, as has already been mentioned, the King's incipient dislike of his son was stimulated by his success as Regent in 1716. Thenceforward their relations deteriorated fast.

The climax of their quarrel came in the following year at the christening of the Prince and Princess's second son. The ceremony took place in the latter's bedchamber at St. James's, and the King had insisted that the Duke of Newcastle, a particular enemy of the Prince's, should be one of the sponsors. It can hardly have been a very happy or Christian baptism, for the Prince took the opportunity of insulting the Duke in the presence of the King, and the latter, in a rage, ordered the Prince's arrest. That, at least, is how Horace Walpole recounts the story.

The arrest was of very short duration, for that night the Prince and Princess left St. James's Palace for Lord Grantham's House in Albemarle Street. Soon afterwards they moved to Leicester House, a pleasant seventeenth-century building lying on the north side of the present square of that name. Here they carried on a rival and more interesting court than that of the King, in spite of the fact that they were deprived of their guard and of all official marks of distinction, while it was announced that no persons who paid their respects to them would be received at Court. In addition the Prince and Princess's three young daughters were kept at St. James's in the custody of the King. The eldest son, Frederick Louis, had anyhow remained in Hanover, while the infant son—the innocent cause of the rift—died at the age of three months, so that the Prince and Princess were bereft of all their children.

Alexander Pope visited Hampton Court Palace in the summer of 1718 at a time when the quarrel was at its height, and, although an atmosphere of contention was not uncongenial to him, it sadly reduced the already modest pleasures of Court life. To Lady Mary Wortley Montagu he wrote plaintively: "Our gallantry and gaiety have been great sufferers by the rupture of the two courts here: scarce any ball, assembly, basset-table, or any place where two or three are gathered together." Thus the Court was pervaded by a dull monotony at a time when many of the great country-houses, and to some degree the apartments of the Prince and Princess of Wales, were sparkling with the brilliance and wit of such men as Pope and Gay, Hervey and Chesterfield, Addison and Congreve, and a number of others, who with a little incentive from the monarch could have transformed the air of stagnation into one of life and activity —without perhaps raising the moral tone to an uncomfortable degree.

The squabbles in the royal family were exceedingly gratifying to supporters of the Jacobite cause, for it was clear to all that the stability of the Hanoverian régime was thereby weakened. Nevertheless, it was by no means easy to bring about a reconciliation between these two singularly obstinate men, and for several years efforts by members of the government were entirely unsuccessful. It was not indeed until 1720 that Prime Minister Walpole was at last able to open some negotiations between the opposing camps, but the King's stipulation that the Prince and Princess should return to live at St. James's seemed at first likely to wreck all hopes of family peace.

Eventually, after intense skirmishing on both sides, the Prince was induced to go to St. James's and see the King. The fact that the visit took place on St. George's Day may have been a good augury for some degree of harmony. It was true that the interview lasted only five minutes, and the King could only be heard to murmur crossly, by those who were carefully listening at the door, "*Votre conduite, votre conduite*"; but at least the ice was broken, and there was much rejoicing at Court at what was optimistically looked on as a reconciliation. Although there was no more than token unity in the family, it greatly eased the atmosphere, and the King and the Prince and Princess could appear at the same receptions, in spite of the fact that the King would often ignore both his son and his daughter-in-law, whom he called, "*Cette diablesse Madame la Princesse*".

The Prince and Princess once again attended the Drawing-rooms, those rather mournful weekly receptions which the King found himself compelled by tradition to hold. Their presence lessened the general boredom, and on the first occasion after the so-called reconciliation the King made an effort to show geniality. "*Vous êtes la bien-venue, Madame. Je suis ravi de vous voir ici*", he said to the Princess; but there were no such soft words for his son, and on this, as on many other occasions, there was "Dumb Show between the King and Prince", as Lady Cowper noted in her *Diary*.

At times these gatherings at St. James's were enlivened by unexpected incidents such as the occasion when a certain Mr. Mayo had to be removed for being "drunk and saucy". He came to fisticuffs with a fellow courtier and "in the Fray pulled him by the nose". Under the earlier Tudors the penalty for quarrelling in the presence of the King might have been the loss of a hand. But drunkenness under the Hanoverians was regarded with an indulgent eye, for even the King himself was inclined to drink, as well as eat, too freely, while it was not unusual for the Duke of Newcastle, the Lord Chamberlain, to appear at Court the worse for drink.

The King took so little interest in English tradition that it can hardly be supposed that he was in any way instrumental in the revival of the Order of the Bath. This anyhow took place in 1720, and Horace Walpole suggests that it was reinaugurated by his father, the Prime Minister, in order to provide an alternative to the many demands for the Garter—the intention being, as he put it, that "the red should be a step to the blue". Sir Robert Walpole was one of the first of the new knights, and put this purpose into practice by receiving the Garter the following year.

There were few people in the world for whom George I had any true affection. Towards his nearest relatives—mother, wife, son—his feelings varied from indifference to dislike, while to the Duchess of Kendal and Lady Darlington he was attached rather by habit than love. In their company he could pass easy, peaceful evenings, cutting paper or playing ombre without having to exert the least mental effort, an effort which was inevitable when he was in social contact with tiresome foreigners. But there was one person to whom this phlegmatic man was sincerely and deeply attached. This was his sister, the Queen of Prussia. When she died, this normally unemotional man gave way to uncontrolled grief, and was said to have spent five days without eating, drinking, or sleeping, and to have walked for this time about his room wailing and "hitting his toes against the wainscote". This passion of grief shows that the King's character contained more sensibility than would have been supposed from the stolid front he presented to the world.

Once the agitation caused by the animosity between the King and his heir had died down, Court life resumed its uneventful rhythm. However, between the King's visit to Hanover in 1723 and his last, four years later, an event occurred which gave the courtiers an agreeable subject for gossip. The King, who was nearly sixty-five years of age, took a new mistress, in this case an English woman, Anne Brett. In 1715 Lady Cowper mentions a Miss Brett, as a "Seamstress", a vocation less humble than it sounds, and this may be the same woman who a decade or so later was elevated to the more glamorous—if unattractive—position of physical favourite.

Anne Brett, to whom the German intimates apparently raised no objection, was given apartments in St. James's Palace, and here she remained when the King set out for Hanover in 1727. She took the opportunity of the departure of her royal lover to have a door opened from her rooms into the garden of the Palace. Princess Anne, the King's eldest granddaughter, who was also living in the Palace, at once ordered it to be bricked up again. How the dispute would have ended it is impossible to say, but in the event the King was dead within a few days of his leaving England, and Miss Brett's short reign of power was at an end.

The King was taken suddenly ill while passing through Holland, and, though almost speechless, insisted on driving on to Osnabrück knowing probably that his seizure was mortal and being determined to give up his soul in his own beloved land. That wish he achieved, dying shortly after his arrival in this ancient bishopric on 27th June at the age of sixty-seven. He was buried at Hanover, thus sharing with James II the distinction of being one of the only two kings since the Middle Ages whose bodies lie outside England.

George I made so slight an impact on his subjects that after his death there was no clamour to perpetuate his memory in any public place; but during his lifetime one of the most strangely placed statues ever erected was raised in his honour. This is the marble effigy which still surmounts Hawksmore's eccentric tower of St. George's Church, Bloomsbury. The King's prosaic form is much idealised, and is given additional nobility by the Roman dress in which it is portrayed. Thus the man, who so much disliked being in the public eye, looks out from this pillared and rusticated eminence over the city for which he had so little love.

# Chapter 13

# GEORGE II

During the thirteen years of George I's reign contact between the monarchy and the people of England had been so effectively broken that the death of the King, and the accession of his son, caused no more than a ripple of interest in the country at large. So drastically had the attitude to the monarchy altered that it seemed difficult to believe that the death of Queen Elizabeth I was no more than a century and a quarter in the past. In 1727 it mattered very little to the ordinary man whether the father or the son was on the throne: both were foreigners, and to the average Englishman all foreigners were inherently unimportant.

However, to the gilded individuals who were closely connected with the Court and government a change of sovereign was an important matter, and it was particularly so in the present case when father and son had been so bitterly opposed that the friends and supporters of one were automatically enemies of the other. Those who, with an eye to the future, had sided with the Prince of Wales in the quarrels with his father, and so had been banished from the King's circle, now looked for their reward; while the position of a man such as Sir Robert Walpole, whose political dexterity had kept George I safely on the throne, was obviously precarious.

How precarious became immediately apparent. No sooner had the news of the King's sudden death reached Walpole than he hoisted his corpulent body into the saddle and galloped down to Richmond to announce this highly acceptable news to the son. The first act of the new King was to order Walpole, whom he automatically detested as his father's Prime Minister, to go to Sir Spencer Compton at Chiswick and take orders from him. This impetuous dismissal of the most experienced and skilful politician in the country and his replacement by a man of little capacity might well have led to disastrous results.

If the first act of George II was to rid himself of Walpole, the first act of the new Queen was to effect his return, thus showing at once her political sagacity, and the subtle and tactful manner in which she handled her obstinate husband. For the days during which Walpole remained in eclipse, he and his wife were shunned and snubbed by the courtiers who had fawned and flattered only a short while before. As Lord Hervey wrote in his *Memoirs*, which throw so intimate a light on the Court during Caroline's lifetime, "his presence that used to make a crowd . . . now emptied every corner he turned to".

At the first Drawing-room held at Leicester House after the new King's accession Lady Walpole found herself jostled and ignored, until the Queen noticed her in the crowd and called for her. Then, as Lady Walpole wrote, "the torrent divided and shrank to either side, and as I came away I might have walked over their heads, if I had pleased". The courtiers, attuned to the subtle nuances of royal favour, correctly interpreted Caroline's distinction of Lady Walpole; while the King, strutting and loud-voiced, was still unaware that his new Prime Minister was already destined to the peaceful limbo of the Upper House, and that Walpole would very shortly be back in control of the government. During the Queen's lifetime, she and Walpole effectively and successfully ruled the country, while the King was happily convinced that it was he who was making the decisions, and that he was not one of those despicable men who were dominated by their wives.

The alliance between Caroline of Anspach, a woman of forty-three at the time of George II's accession, and the Norfolk squire who concealed an intense political sagacity beneath his bluff, hard-drinking exterior, was a strange one; and one which might well have foundered between their two strong personalities if Lord Hervey had not been at hand to form an essential link, and to soothe the Queen's feelings when they had been particularly wounded by the Prime Minister's rough manner.

Between the Queen and Walpole there was an alliance based on political necessity and not on sympathy, but between the Queen and Lord Hervey there was sincere affection—and this in two people who were in general singularly lacking in both sincerity and affection. Hervey's post of Vice-Chamberlain was not in itself one of much importance, but the close relations he had formed with the Queen, and to some degree with the King, made him too valuable to Walpole to allow of his being promoted to a more responsible office in the government.

For the first decade of George II's reign, until Caroline's death in 1737, the Court was pervaded by the strange character of Lord Hervey. Wherever the Court was in residence, there was the Vice-Chamberlain always within call of the Queen. Whether in the dark rooms of St. James's, or in the more spacious settings of Kensington or Hampton Court, or even in the wooded seclusion of Richmond, Hervey must be at hand to discuss all problems, to interpret the Prime Minister's views, and above all to amuse the Queen. In his youth he had been good-looking in an effeminate way, but later, with his face painted to conceal the pallor caused by constant ill-health, it was in the quickness and subtlety of his intellect that lay his attraction, while the bitterness of his spirit and his genius for intrigue made him feared by all but the boldest members of the Court circle.

His devotion and loyalty to the Queen never wavered, and she in return looked to him for that mental stimulus which the King was unable to provide. It was a curious relationship, almost that of lovers, but with the physical element removed, for the Queen never deviated in her fidelity to the King. Her love for her husband lasted till her death, though it cooled a little during her last years, and to all the courtiers it remained a matter of astonishment that this intelligent and handsome woman should appear to be for ever enamoured of so unattractive and aggressive a man. Her feelings were probably highly complex, and were both con-jugal and maternal, with an infusion of a strong element of sense of duty; while the knowledge that this man, for all his bluster, shouting, and rudeness, was entirely dependent on her, gave her a sense of power which was extremely agreeable to her. Indeed her tactful handling of the King must have been to her almost like a game, a game which she was able to play with brilliant success.

At least the King never deceived her—in the sense that he was com-pletely frank with her about his amours, and the Queen, whatever her true feelings, seldom reproached him. Indeed, in the case of Lady Suffolk she strove to maintain the liaison when the King's interest had long since vanished. The Queen recognised the advantage of having a woman of Lady Suffolk's amiable and ungrasping character in this equivocal position, while in her post as Mistress of the Robes she was obliged to support the Queen's occasional asperities, which no woman in the cir-cumstances could have been expected to resist.

The times had changed since Charles II endowed his mistresses with all the treasures on which he could lay his hands, while they for their part made a handsome income from the sale of titles and preferments. Lady Suffolk on the other hand gained little from her position as a royal mistress. She neither had, nor wished for, any political power, while her material rewards consisted of little more than the gift of the charming Palladian house of Marble Hill near the banks of the Thames at Twicken-ham, which, according to Horace Walpole, had cost the King only ten or twelve thousand pounds to build. The affection of her many friends, amongst whom were Pope, Gay, and Swift, must have been some compensation for the rudeness she received from the King in her latter years at Court. When eventually she received the Queen's reluctant consent to the resignation of her post as Mistress of the Robes and

32 The reception of George I at St. James's Palace on 20 September 1714
*Detail of an engraving by A. Allard*

33  Frederick, Prince of Wales, holding a music party (*c.* 1730)
*From a drawing by J. Farrer after Marcellus Laroon*

34  George II, Queen Caroline and their family
*From an engraving by T. Ryder after the painting by William Hogarth*

retirement from the royal circle, the King was furious—not on account of her leaving, but because the Queen had endeavoured to persuade her to remain. "What the devil did you mean by trying to make an old, dull, deaf, peevish beast stay and plague me when I had so good an opportunity of getting rid of her", were the gracious royal words as reported by Lord Hervey.

It is difficult to discover any virtues in George II's character; but the fact that he was able to keep the affection of the Queen, in spite of the harshness he often showed towards her in public, indicates that there was perhaps a more endearing side to his personality than was seen by his entourage. When he was away from the Queen his affection and admiration for her clearly increased, and the long and frequent letters he wrote to her during his many absences in Hanover must have soothed her feelings which were so often outraged when they were together. "The passion and tenderness of the King's letter to her, which consisted of thirty pages, must be incredible to anyone who did not see it", wrote Lord Hervey, for the Queen showed this somewhat intimate correspondence not only to him but also to Sir Robert Walpole, and there is no doubt she derived much pleasure and comfort from these written words of love which she received so rarely verbally.

In addition to his unexpected epistolary gifts, George had one virtue which was never questioned: he was very courageous. As a young man he had distinguished himself at Oudenarde and Malplaquet, and in 1743 he commanded the British and Hanoverian contingents of the "Pragmatic Army" at the Battle of Dettingen, thus being the last English monarch to command in the field. Furthermore in '45, when the Young Pretender had reached as far south as Derby, he remained perfectly calm when the Court was in considerable panic. Indeed he proposed to take command in person of the troops which were assembling at Finchley. Later, when he was no longer young, he much wished to have an opportunity of again showing his bravery on the battle-fields of Europe like some of his brother monarchs; but, as Walpole prudently resisted this whim, he had to content himself with dressing up at public festivals in the hat and coat he had worn on the famous day of Oudenarde, and thus providing a bizarre spectacle for those who were fortunate enough to see him.

Of intellectual interests he had none. He never read a book, and even disliked to see the Queen doing so, since it showed that she was venturing into some field of the mind where he could not accompany her. In this age when the arts were blossoming to their fullest beauty, the titular head of the nation was as little involved in the intellectual movements which were stirring round him as if he had been the ruler of a race of savages. Music alone was an art for which he had some sympathy, and it was a gesture of unusual generosity, for a man who was naturally parsimonious, to give Handel an annuity of £1,000. It was thus only fitting that Handel in return should have composed the *Dettingen Te Deum* in honour of the King's military prowess.

The coronation, which took place in October, was carried through with considerable splendour, for the new King was determined to show that he did not share his father's dislike of public parade. His graceless figure was given all the dignity that silks and velvets could supply, while the naturally handsome appearance of the Queen was enhanced by a tremendous display of jewels, some being her own and others borrowed "from ladies of quality", while her dress was stitched with diamonds hired from the jewellers of London. Westminster Abbey was filled, as was usual on these occasions, with all the most important people in the country, and the whole ceremony was voted an outstanding success.

There was, however, one figure strangely missing from these decorous revels—the Prince of Wales. As a boy of several years old, Frederick had been left behind in Hanover when his mother and father came to England on the accession of George I in 1714, and there he remained, being brought up by tutors as a German boy, and being allowed, it was said, to consort with indifferent company. His parents felt apparently no wish to have him with them, and even at the coronation, by which time he was a young man of twenty, it did not seem to occur to George and Caroline that the place for their heir to be was in England. Wherever the onus of blame should lie in the hideous quarrels which eventually raged between Frederick and his parents, undoubtedly the latter in their unnatural neglect were initially in the wrong.

Though the people of England were indifferent to the doings of the new King, members of Parliament were scandalised by the continued absence of the Prince, and foresaw the probability of another wearer of the crown who would be as thoroughly German in outlook and speech as the King who had fortunately just been carried to his grave. They were not backward in making their views vocal. Whether the King would have given way to this pressure alone is doubtful, but, as it happened, at this moment it came to light that the Prince, free from parental control, was making a secret attempt to marry Princess Wilhelmina of Prussia. The King was incensed by this show of independence, and ordered the Prince to come at once to England. Thus on a sombre December day in 1728 the heir to the throne landed obscurely at Whitechapel quay, and was driven in a hackney coach to St. James's Palace, where he was received by the Queen. He was already under the cloud of parental disapproval which was to darken horribly during the coming years.

Meanwhile the King and Queen were settling down with tolerable pleasure to the royal round. The King had almost a mania for arranging not only his days but also his weeks with a clockwork regularity, so that it was possible to forecast with considerable accuracy not only where the Court would be in residence on any given date but also, with a fair degree of probability, what the King would be doing at a given moment in the day. As with their predecessors, the winter was spent at St. James's, the spring and summer at Kensington, and the autumn in the lofty panelled rooms of Hampton Court. Windsor played little part in the curriculum, but the royal couple rather unexpectedly made an addition to their residences by building a house on a tree-covered rise in the heart of Richmond Park.

The new house was modelled on Marble Hill, which, as has already been mentioned, was Lady Suffolk's only reward; and the same talented amateur architect, the 9th Earl of Pembroke, with the assistance of the professional Robert Morris, provided the designs. The scale was rather larger than Marble Hill, but it was built on the same clean, Palladian lines, with a fine, large room on the *piano nobile*. The initial intention was not to use the house as a residence but solely as a place in which to pass the night after hunting in the park, while the handsome saloon could be used for the banquets which followed so agreeably after the chase.

In effect, however, it became more than this, for the Queen loved the place prodigiously, and the royal family were able to live more privately there than in the royal palaces. One of the few creative outlets she was allowed was in improving the gardens round White Lodge, as the new house came to be called; and the King, supposing that this work was paid for out of her own revenues, raised no objections. When she died, however, it came to light that Sir Robert Walpole had made loans from the Treasury for this purpose, and the King found himself obliged to repay no less a sum than £20,000.

In whatever residence the royal family were living, the evenings, when there was no Drawing-room or public festivity to disturb them, were given up to card-playing—basset, quadrille, cribbage, or commerce providing a never-failing amusement. The players at the Queen's table were almost invariably her eldest daughter, the Princess Royal, Lady Charlotte Rousey—a submissive and much bullied lady-in-waiting—and one of the lords-in-waiting. At another table would be a larger party headed by the Prince of Wales, before he fell into deep disfavour, and his brother the Duke of Cumberland. The King meanwhile would spend an hour or two in the apartments of the two younger princesses, Emily and Caroline, the attraction being less the presence of his daughters than that of their governess, Lady Deloraine, who became the King's mistress after Lady Suffolk's departure. It was characteristic of the King that he felt no *pudibonderie* about the conjunction of his daughters—or his wife —with his mistresses.

The monotony of these evenings was broken at regular intervals by the holding of a Drawing-room, a reception which those connected with the Court were expected to attend, and to which those who had some good reason to be presented to the King or Queen might receive an invitation. Once a year, on the King's birthday, these rather dull *soirées* were replaced by a positively gala occasion on which the Court temporarily regained some of the magnificence of earlier reigns.

Perhaps as an encouragement to trade, it was a tradition that everyone should appear at these gatherings in new clothes, and this applied not only to hosts and guests, but also to the servants of both, who wore new liveries on these evenings. The clothes of the men were as sumptuous and as richly embroidered as those of the women. The King's stocky figure would be upholstered in scarlet velvet and gold braid, which was a welcome—if not particularly becoming—contrast to his favourite Oudenarde get-up, while the Queen appeared as a magnificent and gracious figure in an elaborate dress of embroidered silk and velvet stitched with jewels. The dresses of the period were low cut, and the Queen could expose a large area of her well-formed bosom, which to the King was one of her principal physical attractions. The young princes and princesses were dressed with equal splendour, so that the royal family, although none except the Queen was handsome, formed as fine a group as the fashions of the day could create.

The proceedings were conducted on these occasions with proper ceremony. The royal party entered the drawing-room in procession led by the Lord High Treasurer, the Master of the Household, and the Lord Chamberlain wearing his gold key of office, all carrying white staffs. Presentations were then made, while the Queen would make those audible, caustic comments to the King or Lord Hervey on the assembly which effectively limited her popularity. In an adjoining room an orchestra played to provide a diversion to gossip and conversation, and later in the evening there would be a ball. The birthday celebrations safely concluded, the Court sank back into the normal quiet ritual for another year.

Beneath this façade, the tension between the Prince of Wales and his parents was increasing, and soon, like a long-smouldering fire, was to break out so openly that no one in the country was unaware of it. The Prince's first serious misdemeanour soon after his arrival in England was a second attempt at a secret marriage. This was engineered by Sarah, Duchess of Marlborough—now old, but scheming to the last—who offered her grand-daughter, Lady Diana Spencer, to the Prince with a dowry of £100,000. It was a well-conceived plan which would have achieved the double purpose of infuriating the King and Queen and aggrandising her own family. The wedding was arranged to take place in her house in Windsor Great Park. The astute Sir Robert, however, got wind of the plot and the Duchess's scheme was foiled.

The Prince was rising twenty-nine, and his parents were at last persuaded that he should marry, and—to avoid any further alarms—that they should choose a suitable bride. The princess selected was Augusta of Saxe-Gotha, a girl of seventeen. The Prince was perfectly amenable to his parents' choice, and on 25th April 1736 Augusta landed at Greenwich to become the wife of a man she had never seen, and eventually—so it was presumed—the queen of a country of whose language she understood not one word.

She was an unsophisticated girl, who had been brought up in great seclusion, and still enjoyed childish amusements. For some time after marriage she spent much time playing with dolls, until her own brood, which eventually numbered nine, began to appear and gave her a more adult occupation. But in spite of her simplicity, the effect she made was good, not only on her future husband but also on the remainder of the highly critical royal family: even the Queen admitted that she seemed a good, sensible girl. This happy impression was never totally lost, even in the darkest days of the Prince's disfavour, and if her behaviour at any time annoyed the King and Queen it was attributed to her husband's influence.

The couple were married at nine o'clock at night in the chapel at St. James's Palace, a supper followed, and finally there was the uncivilised ceremony of seeing them into bed together. Lord Hervey did not fail to record the occasion:

> "The King went after supper to the Princess's apartment whilst the Queen undressed the Princess, and when they were in bed everybody passed through their bed-chamber to see them, where there was nothing remarkable but the Prince's nightcap, which was some inches higher than any grenadier's cap in the whole army."

On the Prince's marriage the King increased his allowance from £24,000 to £50,000 a year; but the Prince was intensely dissatisfied with this sum, contending—quite rightly—that the King on his accession had received in the Civil List £100,000 which was designed for the Prince of Wales—this being the annual sum he had himself received during his father's lifetime. The King, however, no doubt with the support of the Queen, refused to advance another penny, and eventually the Prince arranged for his own supporters to bring the matter up in Parliament.

The King was enraged by what he was pleased to consider the Prince's unfilial behaviour and disloyalty, and, although the motion was defeated, the breach between parents and son, which the appeal to Parliament had caused, was never healed.

In spite of mounting dislike, the two families continued to live under the same roof, the Prince and Princess making the round of the royal residences with the rest of the Court, though the families met only on public occasions. However, the final break was at hand. In the summer of 1737 the Princess was with child; the King and Queen were determined that the birth should take place at Hampton Court, where the Court was in residence for the late summer and early autumn, so that there could be no repetition of the rumours which arose after the birth of James II's son.

On the evening of 31st July, two months before the birth was expected, the Princess's pains began, and the Prince without his parents' knowledge insisted on her being driven to St. James's. Lord Hervey's description of the journey does not bear repetition, but the carriage eventually reached the Palace where, nothing being prepared, the unfortunate Princess was "put to bed between two tablecloths". Shortly after, "she was delivered of a little rat of a girl, about the bigness of a good large tooth-pick case". Incidentally the "little rat" survived to become Duchess of Brunswick and to live till she was upwards of eighty.

The fury of the King and Queen at the Prince's disobedience was unbounded, and they decided on the same drastic step that had been taken by the King's father: to expel him from the royal palaces. "I hope in God I shall never see the monster's face again", said the Queen to Lord Hervey with some lack of maternal feeling. Her wish was granted, for little more than two months later she was dead.

The day following the receipt of the King's letter of expulsion, the Prince and Princess left St. James's Palace for the White House at Kew, of which the Prince had acquired the lease in 1731, as a refuge from parental displeasure. A little later they rented Cliveden, a country house of dignified size, and Norfolk House in St. James's Square for a London residence. In the latter their eldest son, later George III, was born on 4th June 1738.

This unedifying dissension did nothing to increase the popularity of the royal family in the country. Rightly or wrongly, the sympathy of the people was rather on the side of the Prince, and he for his part was never backward in trying to gain the sympathy of the populace at the expense of his father. In any case there was no enthusiasm for the King. His prolonged absences in Hanover, in one case for two years, and his outspoken preference for everything German, which showed a change of heart since he was Prince of Wales, did not endear him to his English subjects. As Hervey wrote: "His Majesty's character with all ranks of people being fallen so low that the disregard with which everybody spoke of him, and the open manner in which they expressed their contempt and dislike, is hardly to be credited."

The King's reluctant returns from Hanover seldom brought much happiness to the Queen, for his temper on these occasions was apt to be even more violent than usual. The journeys were always made at top speed, and the jolting of the carriage exacerbated the piles from which he suffered. Thus there was seldom any sweetness in his mood when he was reunited with his family and English subjects.

On these occasions he could speak of nothing but the superiority of everything Hanoverian—"No English cook could dress a dinner; no English player could act; no English coachman could drive; no Englishman knew how to come into a room, nor any Englishwoman how to dress herself." Whereas in Hanover ... and so the vitriolic comparison would continue. Generally the Queen would listen calmly to these diatribes, but once, losing her usual control, Lord Hervey heard her replying sharply: "I see no reason that made your coming to England necessary, you might have continued there." These were indeed sharp words from his normally dutiful spouse, and the King "in a great huff, trembling with passion, and without a word in reply, went out of the room".

Lampoons and verses of an extreme scurrility about the King were widely broadcast, and referred to his prolonged absences from his kingdom and to his amorous entanglements in the country of his birth. There seemed no limit to the coarseness of the rhymes which were composed and printed on this subject of never-failing interest. It needed all Sir Robert Walpole's acumen and firmness to prevent the general discontent from taking a more dangerous form.

Caroline's interest in the gardens at Richmond has already been mentioned: at Hampton Court, as well, she made alterations to the existing lay-out in order to bring it more into line with the taste of the day. Until that time the great semicircular *parterre*, known as the Great Fountain Garden, which lay in front of Wren's long east façade, had remained as it had been designed during the reign of Queen Anne. Between the paths which stretched away in a *patte d'oie* to the park were complex patterns of scroll work in dwarf box interspersed with many little fountains. None of this conformed to the style that William Kent was advocating, and, possibly under his direction, the whole scheme was simplified. The main lines of the Stuart lay-out remained, but areas of plain lawn took the place of the topiary and beds, and only a single fountain survived to provide a cooling murmur on summer days. The Queen's "improvements" conformed exactly to the sentiment in Pope's Epistle to Lord Burlington:

*Tired of the scene parterres and fountains yield,*
*He finds at last, he better likes a field.*

The Queen's apartments in the Palace looked out over this garden, and in these, too, changes were made to bring them more into the taste of the day. The Queen's Presence Chamber and Great Staircase were altered and embellished to give more interest to Wren's not very imaginative interiors. These works must have been directly instigated by the Queen, for the King showed no pleasure in English royal residences, except for his hunting-lodge. No doubt he considered them all irremediably ugly compared to his beloved Herrenhausen.

In 1739 Kent was appointed to the Court post of Portrait-Painter to the King, but according to Vertue His Majesty declared "that he would never sit to him for his picture". This may have been a mutually agreeable position, and in any case Kent soon came to the prudent conclusion that his talent lay rather in architecture than in painting.

Early in November 1737 Caroline, who normally had excellent health, was suddenly taken seriously ill, and it was discovered by her doctor that the rupture from which she had suffered since the birth of her youngest daughter in 1724 had strangulated. For thirteen years she had kept this infirmity the closest secret, and it was known only to the King, Lady Sundon, her lady-in-waiting, and her German nurse. Her condition became rapidly worse, but she bore the ineffectual efforts of doctors and surgeons to relieve the stoppage with the greatest fortitude. The King, whose bedside manner could hardly have been worse, added to her nervous tension by his alternating moods of excessive solicitation and brutal roughness. The harrowing death-bed scenes, which were prolonged over ten days, were described by Lord Hervey with the utmost sympathy, and it was he who recorded the King's well-known reply to the dying Queen's wish that he should marry again: "*Non, j'aurai des maîtresses.*"

On 20th November Caroline died. The light of her personality, which had given illumination to the Court, was extinguished, and her will, which was "the sole spring on which every movement in the Court turned", was no longer available to give sense and direction to the King's behaviour. His grief was genuine and intense, and was seemingly more enduring than would have been expected of someone of his egotistical and volatile character. The strange story told by Lord Wentworth in a letter to his father a few months after the Queen's death suggests that his grief took a singularly morbid turn:

35    The wedding, in the chapel of St. James's Palace, between Princess Anne, daughter
of George II, and the Prince of Orange, on 14 March 1733
*From an engraving by J. Rigaud after William Kent*

36  "Solomon in his Glory"

George II consoles himself after the death (on 1 December 1737) of his consort Queen Caroline

*From a satirical print published on 19 December 1738*

"A Saturday night between one and two o'clock the King waked out of a dream very uneasy, and ordered the vault where the Queen is to be broke open immediately, and have the coffin also opened; and went in a hackney-chair through the Horse-guards to Westminster Abbey and back again to bed."

However, George was not a man to give way to indefinite mourning, and seven months after the Queen's death Madame Walmoden, who had been his mistress during his Hanoverian visits, arrived in London. "She is at present in a mighty mean, dirty lodging in St. James's Street", wrote the old Duchess of Marlborough; but better accommodation was being prepared for her in the shape of the lodgings at St. James's Palace once inhabited by the Duchess of Kendal, and also a house in Hyde Park. Two years later she was created Countess of Yarmouth and was granted a pension of £4,000 a year. Till the King's death twenty-one years later she remained his constant companion, and although she carried on a fairly profitable trade in patronage—£12,000 from Sir Joseph Bouverie for a viscountcy, for example—she showed none of the intense rapacity which distinguished most royal mistresses of earlier reigns.

Although Caroline had been unable to introduce an intellectual element to the Court as she would have liked, she was at least able to surround herself with a sense of culture. With her death this was replaced by a more frivolous atmosphere in which galas, masquerades, with visits to Ranelagh which had lately opened, played an important part. These worldly amusements were much to the King's taste and provided an opportunity for his senile advances to attractive young women.

The moral tone of the Court was by no means high, but nevertheless there was little of the gaiety which pervaded contemporary society. The Court lay apart from the social amusements of the upper classes, in the same way that it had no share in the intellectual and artistic life of the period. The process which had begun under Queen Anne's lymphatic rule became fully developed under the first two Hanoverians. The Augustan Age received no leadership or encouragement from the choleric old gentleman at St. James's. During his reign Lord Burlington and his school of Palladians were initiating the building of great country-houses in which the arts and literature were fostered, but the unenlightened life in the royal palaces was unruffled by intellectual developments which were preoccupying the more cultivated members of society.

With the Queen's death, too, Lord Hervey's *Memoirs* end, and one senses that he felt that the disappearance of Caroline's active personality left the Court so devoid of interest that nothing remained worth recording. In 1740 he was given the unimportant post of Lord Privy Seal, but two years later Walpole's administration ended, and Hervey's hopes of a political career were extinguished. In 1743 he died.

Although only one-third of George's reign was over when he became a widower, the remaining twenty-three years passed with such immutable regularity that there seems little to mark the passage of years. Occasional references in reminiscences throw a gleam of light on how his days were spent, when no particular diversions were available. Horace Walpole's description, for example, suggests a dull monotony:

"At nine at night he had cards in the apartment of his daughters, the Princesses Amelia and Caroline, with Lady Yarmouth, two or three of the late Queen's ladies, and as many of the most favoured officers of his own Household. Every Saturday in summer he carried that uniform party, but without his daughters, to dine at Richmond: they went in coaches and six, in the middle of the day, with the heavy horseguards kicking up the dust before them—dined, walked an hour in the garden, returned in the same dusty parade; and his Majesty fancied himself the most gallant and lively prince in Europe."

The signing of the Treaty of Aix-la-Chapelle was made the occasion for very special celebrations in which both the Court and the people of London joined. The Treaty was signed in October 1748, but the festivities were delayed until May in the following year. For the enjoyment of the people the town was illuminated, and by order of the King a "jubilee masquerade in the Venetian manner" was given at Ranelagh for the upper strata of society. Except that the visitors wore masks and that "on the canal was a sort of gondola, adorned with flags and streamers and filled with music, rowing about" there was little that was suggestive of a Longhi scene; but none the less Horace Walpole wrote of it as "the prettiest spectacle I ever saw: nothing in a fairy tale ever surpassed it". In London there were fireworks on a grand scale to amuse the crowds, a performance at the Opera House of a serenata called "Peace in Europe", and another masquerade at which the enterprising Miss Chudleigh, on whom the King had cast his ageing but lecherous eye, appeared as Iphigenia, "so naked that you would have taken her for Andromeda".

Revels such as this were a rarity, and, in general, life in the royal palaces was carried on on a constantly shrinking scale of splendour. The King had always had a strong inclination to parsimony; and, once a widower, he saw no reason to maintain his houses in the same way that he had when Caroline was alive. An unnecessary number of rooms was obviously an avoidable expense, so those that were not generally needed were shut up. Horace Walpole wrote to Sir Horace Mann in 1749 on this subject: "Though there are so many vacant chambers, the King hoards all he can and has locked up half the palace (Kensington) since the Queen's death: and so he does at St. James's".

A slight ripple was made on the calm surface of the King's life on 20th March 1751, when he was informed that the Prince of Wales had died suddenly at Leicester House, to which he and his family had moved from Norfolk House. The King's reactions on receiving this news have been variously described, but at least no one suggested that he suffered any sense of personal loss. No money was wasted on an elaborate funeral, and the melancholy ceremony was of the simplest and most austere variety. "There was not one English Lord, not one Bishop, and only one Irish Lord", wrote Bubb Dodington, whose political hopes had crashed with the Prince's death. "The service was performed without either anthem or organ." Very few, indeed, showed any emotion at this unexpected event, except Princess Augusta who was genuinely fond of her husband; but she had at least the compensation of being received more warmly at Court as a widow than she had ever been as a wife.

The first three members of the Hanoverian dynasty were all granted the boon of quick deaths. George I and Prince Frederick had expired after only a day or two's illness: George II was to be equally fortunate. His health as he grew older remained remarkably good, and at seventy-six there was nothing amiss except that his hearing and sight were becoming indifferent. On 24th October 1760 he retired to bed in normal health; but next morning, when his page came to call him, he was found dead on the floor. His family was thus spared those death-bed scenes which, in view of the King's character, might well have been exceedingly painful.

In his will the King left a strange instruction: that his coffin should be laid next to that of Caroline, and that the sides of both should be removed so that their dust should mingle.

# EPILOGUE

With the unlamented death of George II in 1760 this story of three centuries of Court life ends, and there is only space to cast a very cursory glance over the following reigns.

For forty-six years the Hanoverian dynasty had retained its precarious seat on the throne of England, and there had been as little popular enthusiasm for these first two representatives during their lives as there had been sorrow at their deaths. All that can be said, indeed, is that they were less unpopular at some moments than at others. The death of the Prince of Wales in 1751 was regarded as a particularly fortunate event, for it left the way open for his son, who seemed not unpromising.

George III, a young man of twenty-two when he came to the throne, had been kept severely in the background by his formidable grandfather, so that his personality was almost unknown; but his youth and tolerable looks were definite assets in reviving the languishing enthusiasm for the Crown. The populace has always favoured a virtuous ruler, and the fact that the new king had a greater reputation for virtue than for intelligence was on the whole an advantage.

Within a week of his accession he issued a proclamation which made his attitude perfectly clear. It was headed "For the encouragement of Piety and Virtue, and for preventing and punishing Vice, Profaneness, and Immorality". The middle and lower ranks of society saw here a welcome change from the lax morals and free-thinking of the previous king, but in the Court circle, in which piety and virtue had until now been singularly neglected qualities, the proclamation caused great despondency. It was obvious that the palaces were unlikely to provide much amusement for the patrician classes, while the King's marriage in 1761 to the homely little Princess Charlotte of Mecklenburg-Strelitz finally eclipsed any lingering hopes of the Court becoming a centre of fun and fashion.

As the years passed, the Court and the people of the country drifted further and further apart, and the King and Queen became as detached from the aristocracy, with their frivolous pursuits, as they were inevitably from the lives and hardships of the working classes. The royal couple existed like an island of domestic virtue surrounded by a tumultuous sea of loose principles on the one hand and grave poverty on the other. In these circumstances it was not surprising, perhaps, that the King's sons should have rebelled against the isolation and restricted liberty imposed on them, in much the same way that George III himself had revolted against the unedifying example of his predecessor. The decay of the well-intentioned young man who ascended the throne into the miserable old imbecile who shuffled off it sixty years later is a lamentable spectacle, while the havoc which his obstinacy caused to the policy of the country was boundless.

The nineteenth century saw the most extreme contrasts in the tone of Court life. That of George IV at least was not dull. The private life of the King may have been unvirtuous, but he gave to his Court much of the glamour which had effectively vanished from the royal circle since the reign of Charles II. He was a lavish patron of the arts—at great expense to the nation—but none of the exponents, painters, architects, designers of furniture and objects, had any cause to complain of royal indifference to their productions. Unfortunately the more unattractive aspects of a monarch's character are more generally remembered than his amiable qualities—if any; and we are now inclined to see George IV through the eyes of Gillray and Cruikshank, in whose drawings he is portrayed as a self-indulgent and ridiculous dotard, while the magnificent pictures of Lawrence, in which he appears as a noble, almost god-like figure, are largely discounted. No doubt a middle line between these two extremes would be a tolerably accurate assessment.

The feverish atmosphere of George's court was succeeded by the placid, *bourgeois* calm produced by the Sailor King and his pious spouse. In his way of life and interests William was the antithesis of his elder brother. Where the latter adored splendour and display, the former was only happy in the simplest and most modest surroundings, surroundings in fact which reminded him of his early years as a naval officer; while the family life he had enjoyed with Mrs. Jordan and their brood of children was more congenial to him than life in a palace with the childless Queen Adelaide. Thus the Court lapsed back into the condition of social unimportance which it had held during the greater part of George III's reign.

Thus one comes to the long reign of Queen Victoria, and the varying shades of her personal popularity. The gaiety and laughter of the first few years, which seemed to have more in common with the eighteenth century than with the sober years of the century ahead, gave way after marriage to a life governed by the rules of duty imposed by the Prince Consort. The Court thus provided an outstanding example of piety and domestic felicity which Society was expected, however reluctantly, to emulate to the best of its ability. The arts were discreetly fostered, in some directions with perspicacity, in others with a taste which now seems to us unfortunate; but artists were undoubtedly better rewarded during this century than they had ever been in the past.

During the twenty-one years of the Queen's and Prince Albert's marriage the Court, for better or for worse, had a strong influence on public taste. With the Prince's death in 1861 this influence was entirely extinguished, and during the quarter of a century in which the Queen imposed on herself a rigid seclusion the Court was in no way a leader either in the arts or socially. When she was eventually persuaded to show herself again in public, she received a tumultuous welcome, and her popularity reached a pitch it had never before achieved. But from the social angle, from the angle of the world of fashion, Windsor and Balmoral were only places to be frequented as a duty, and out of respect for the ageing head of the State: for amusement the Mecca had long since been Marlborough House with its lavish and somewhat vulgar gaiety.

The sudden revival of the Queen's popularity, and the emotion felt by those who saw her in the course of her public outings, showed how deeply ingrained in the English people was the tradition of monarchy. It had never been fully destroyed even when the wearer of the crown had been unmitigatedly unpopular, but it had needed a strong innate feeling to survive the blunders of some of the unsuitable characters who found themselves as head of the State. But the glamour, which is inseparable from royalty, has always been sweet to the English temperament, and England remains the only country in the world where the traditions of Court life have survived through many centuries until the present day.

# INDEX

The numerals in **heavy type** refer to the *figure numbers* of the illustrations